Historic Churches and Church Life
in Bristol

Bristol & Gloucestershire Archaeological Society

ISBN 0 900197 53 6

Copyright The Several Contributors 2001

Printed by
J.W. Arrowsmith Ltd.
Winterstoke Road
Bristol
BS3 2NT

Contents

Elizabeth Ralph (1911–2000)
(Photograph by G. Kelsey)

List of Illustrations

Notes on Contributors

GERARD LEIGHTON is the third generation of his family to be a member of Bristol & Gloucestershire Archaeological Society. He has been a member since 1951 and has served as Honorary Treasurer of the Society since 1970. He worked closely with Elizabeth Ralph in the Society, and also on conservation matters and during his period as Chairman of the Diocesan Advisory Committee of Bristol Diocese.

REVD CANON DR DAVID WALKER has made a particular study of early medieval Bristol. His edition of the *Cartulary of St Augustine's Abbey, Bristol* was published by the Record Section of *BGAS* as Volume 10, 1998. He was formerly a Senior Lecturer in Medieval History at the University of Wales, Swansea.

FRANCES NEALE is the archivist of Wells Cathedral. She worked in Bristol as assistant archivist to Elizabeth Ralph 1961–3, and her publications include an edition of William Worcestre's detailed description of Bristol in 1480, which was published by Bristol Record Society as Vol. 51 in 2000.

DR JOSEPH BETTEY was formerly Reader in Local History at the University of Bristol. He is a past president and chairman of *BGAS* and worked with Elizabeth Ralph as General Editor of Bristol Record Society.

DR PETER FLEMING is a Senior Lecturer at the University of the West of England and is one of the joint directors of the Regional History Centre. He is also a General Editor of Bristol Record Society and the author of works on late-medieval life in Bristol.

REVD CANON PETER COBB is the vicar of All Saints' church, Clifton, and has published articles on liturgy, church history and the Oxford Movement, including a study with Elizabeth Ralph of *New Anglican Churches in Nineteenth Century Bristol* (1991).

PATRICK BROWN is an architect and part-time lecturer at Bristol University. He has been active in conservation work in Bristol and has published studies of the architecture and furnishings of the medieval churches in the city.

MADGE DRESSER is a principal lecturer in history at the University of the West of England and joint director of the Regional History Centre. She is one of the General Editors of Bristol Record Society and is the author of publications on non-conformity in Bristol and on the history of slavery.

REVD CANON JOHN ROGAN is a former Canon Residentiary at Bristol Cathedral and Secretary of the Bristol Branch of *BGAS*. He is an occasional lecturer in history and religious studies at Bristol University, and has edited *Bristol Cathedral: History & Architecture* (2000)

DR MARTIN CROSSLEY EVANS is Warden of Manor Hall, University of Bristol and has written several studies of churches, personalities and life in Bristol during the nineteenth and twentieth centuries, including *Hannah More* (1999).

DAVID SMITH has been General Secretary of *BGAS* since 1986, and until his recent retirement was County Archivist of Gloucestershire and Gloucester Diocesan Archivist.

I

Elizabeth Ralph MA, FSA, DLitt
1911 – 2000

An Appreciation

GERARD LEIGHTON

I FIRST met Elizabeth Ralph when as a schoolboy I went to a meeting she had organised for the Society at Wells. Petrol rationing was still in force after the 1939–45 war and we travelled by train from Bristol. After visiting the cathedral and other antiquities the day ended with a picnic tea in the garden of the Bishop's palace at the conclusion of which a vote of thanks to Miss Ralph was proposed with the comment that she had organised everything to perfection including the weather, for it was a lovely summer day. These remarks summed up Miss Ralph—she organised things to perfection in an unobtrusive way and set herself and others who worked with her the highest standards which she expected to be met.

Miss Ralph's abilities were many sided and she did not fit easily into a specific mould. She was a local government officer who was also a distinguished scholar. As a scholar she was accepted as an equal in the academic world and was at the same time a professional administrator. She was not university educated but by the end of her life she had received, almost without precedent, two honorary degrees from the University of Bristol. She was a trade union official (NALGO) but equally at ease in the Hall of the Society of Merchant Venturers. She was always known as Miss Ralph. She liked the formality and did not feel happy in the modern world of Christian names. Much of her time was spent in a man's world but she had no need of an Equal Opportunities Commission. David Smith in his notes to the list of officers of the Society included in this volume records the comments made when she was appointed secretary of the Society which she would repeat with disdain.

Miss Ralph's life was spent entirely in the Bristol area. She had grand parents who farmed at Acton Turville near Badminton and for many years she lived with her mother and sister at Henleaze in north Bristol. Her ancestry was Yorkshire professional people particularly the clergy, Anglican and Unitarian. She was proud of her north country roots and what she regarded as no nonsense north country attitudes. Her father was an army officer who served in Palestine in the 1914–18 war and knew Lawrence of Arabia but she did not speak of him often and it would appear that he spent little time with the family. She had an aunt who was an Oxford don who realised her interest in history and arranged for her to go to Fairfield Grammar School in Bristol. Her sister received a less academic education. When she left school she joined the staff of the Bristol Reference Library where her interest in palaeography was noted and led to her appointment as Archives Clerk at the Council House in 1937 at the age of 26. She insisted as a term of her appointment she

Miss Ralph's views which the Council of the Society and the CPAB endorsed were proved right and it was soon demolished.

After her retirement a number of her friends and admirers felt that some recognition of her work as an archivist and scholar would be appropriate. Sir Folliott Sandford a very senior civil servant and member of the Society went to see the Patronage Secretary but discovered such recognition had been barred by the opposition of an influential person whose schemes had been thwarted by Miss Ralph's advocacy of conservation issues. Miss Ralph was not aware of this but she had good friends with a similar background who had been recognised. She would have been proud that it was conservation issues that prevented her being treated similarly.

Over the years the name of Miss Ralph and the Society became synonymous to the membership and many others who had dealings with the Society. Matters were dealt with knowledgeably; chairmen of the Council and its committees were fully briefed so that meetings were meaningful and by regular attendance at the Society's events and field meetings Miss Ralph became well known to the general membership. It was difficult for people to conceive the Society without her in charge. After her retirement the facilities of the Council House were no longer available leaving her with an administrative burden which with increasing age she found exhausting so in 1986 she decided to retire having been Honorary General Secretary for 39 years. She was succeeded by the present secretary David J H Smith FSA who until his recent retirement was County Records Officer for Gloucestershire. He has maintained the standards set by Miss Ralph and the Society is fortunate in having the stability of the long secretaryships of Miss Ralph and Mr Smith.

Miss Ralph with her many contacts from her professional or scholarly work brought into the Society people who could contribute to its affairs and persuaded others that it was an organisation worthy of active support and that the Transactions was an appropriate vehicle for the publication of their research. She regarded the Transactions as the most important of the Society's activities and the reputation of the Society rested upon their quality. The Society was strengthened by the friendship between Mrs Elsie Clifford, Dr (later Dame) Joan Evans and Miss Ralph whose range of interests were complementary and covered most areas of the Society's activities. Dr Joan Evans the art historian and polymath, Miss Ralph the archivist and local historian and Mrs Clifford "the un-crowned queen of Gloucestershire archaeology" as Professor Glyn Daniel called her, made a formidable trio. Dr Joan Evans became editor of the Transactions and was concerned at the financial constraints that limited the ability to publish to the extent she felt appropriate. In consultation with Miss Ralph and others she provided the Society with a handsome "anonymous" endowment to ensure that funds were available for this purpose. To comply with the requirements of The Charities Acts Miss Ralph at a later date made a statutory declaration setting out the position of this endowment and Dame Joan's intentions which for personal reasons she had been reluctant to document at the time of her gift.

In 1968 Miss Ralph was elected to honorary membership of the Society and in 1976, the centenary of its foundation, there was no question but that Miss Ralph be invited to become the President for that year. She took an active part in arranging events, be it the dinner in the Council House in Bristol in April or the centenary meeting in July spread over a number of days during which the principal archaeological and antiquarian sites in Gloucestershire were visited culminating in the annual general meeting held in the Lady Chapel of Gloucester Cathedral. Miss Ralph entertained the Society to tea in the Chapter House prior to a special choral evensong for which the Dean, a member of the Council, chose hymns and music by Gloucestershire composers and Miss Ralph and Canon Gethyn-Jones read the lessons. Miss Ralph was particularly pleased at the support these events received from the membership and was touched that C. Roy Huddleston whom she succeeded as Bristol Secretary travelled down from Cumbria for the occasion. In her Presidential address Miss Ralph spoke on the Society and some of its distinguished or interesting members over the years and she contributed a history of the Society to the special volume of Essays on Bristol and Gloucestershire History published to mark the centenary.

Miss Ralph's reputation as a scholar was based on her work for the Bristol Record Society. It was formed in 1930 with the support of the Corporation and the University "to make available something of the wealth of historical material contained in the city archives and the collections of lay and ecclesiastical corporations". It was thus an ideal vehicle for publication of her work on the medieval and later records under her care at the Council House. She was appointed Assistant General Editor in 1946 working first with Professor David Douglas and later with Professor Patrick McGrath. Amongst its early publications was The Great Red Book of Bristol edited by Dr E W W Veale and Miss Ralph followed in editing other custumals of the city. The appended bibliography of her major publications indicates the extent of her research and knowledge of the history of Bristol and Gloucestershire. It is amazing that she should have had time to produce these works of the highest standard and many more ephemeral articles for the local newspapers, the Canynge Society (Friends of St Mary Redcliffe) Gazette and the Annual Report of the Friends of Bristol Cathedral. She lived most of her life with her sister Jeanette who died in 1993. Jeanette kept house and dealt with all domestic matters. This she enjoyed and was excellent at it for which Elizabeth was much indebted for without Jeanette's support she could not have accomplished what she did. The list is endless and included trustee for the Theatre Royal in Bristol, member of the Council of the Royal West of England Academy, lay chairman of the Friends of Bristol Cathedral, member of the management committee of the National Trust property at Leigh Woods and member of the Council of the University of Bristol and of various of its committees and involvement in academic appointments. She was chairman of the Bristol branch of the Royal Commonwealth Society which has club premises in Clifton where she lunched most days. The Bristol Soroptomist Club (for business women) was another organisation with which she was much involved. She continued her positions as archivist to The Society of Merchant Venturers and to St Mary Redcliffe and put in order the archives of the Bristol Waterworks.

Miss Ralph was a committed member of the Church of England and worshipped at St Peter's, Henleaze from the time when it was built in the late 1920's becoming in due course a churchwarden. After she moved to Clifton in 1970 she went to All Saint's, Pembroke Road where the high church tradition was very acceptable to her. These connections led to her involvement with the church at both national and diocesan level. She was a member of the Church Assembly now replaced by the

Centre: Miss Elizabeth Ralph, President of the Bristol and Gloucestershire Archaeological Society, at the Centenary meeting at Gloucester Cathedral: 14 July 1976.
Left: Mayor and Mayoress of Gloucester, right: Very Rev. Gilbert Thurlow FSA, Dean of Gloucester and Mr Gerard Leighton. *Courtesy* The Citizen, Gloucester.

THE PUBLISHED WRITINGS OF
MISS ELIZABETH RALPH

1939
1. Mayoral sword rests of Bristol (with Professor Edward Fawcett)
   Trans. B&GAS vol 61
2. A Bristol Poll Tax, 1666—transcription from St Peter's Parish
   Trans. B&GAS vol 61

1944
3. Grants of leases of lands in King Street, Bristol
   Trans. B&GAS vol 65

1945
4. English city: the growth and future of Bristol—H. G. Brown (assisted by Elizabeth Ralph)
   J. S. Fry, London; distributed by University of London Press

1947
5. The Deposition Books of Bristol vol 2*: 1650-54 (with H. E. Nott)
   BRS vol 13
   * vol 1: 1643–47 by H. E. Nott BRS vol 6

1952

6. Marriage Books for the diocese of Bristol, excluding the archdeaconry of Dorset, vol 1: 1637–1700
   B & GAS Records Publications OS vol 1

1954

7. Records of coronation celebrations in a provincial town [Bristol]
   Society Local Archivists Bull No 13 1954
   8. Local Archives of Great Britain
   The City of Bristol Record Office (with Betty Masters)
   Archives III No. 18
9. Series of articles on Our City Churches and the Saints
   St Stephen's [Bristol] Review

1963

10. Guide to the parish records of the City of Bristol and County of Gloucester (with Irvine Gray)
    B&GAS Record Publications OS vol 5

1967

11. The church book of St Ewens', Bristol 1454—1584 (with Betty Masters)
    B&GAS Records Publications OS vol 9

1968

12. The Inhabitants of Bristol in 1696—assessments under the Marriage Act 1694 (with Mary Williams)
    BRS vol 28

1971

13. Maps and Plans of Medieval England—P D A Harry and R A Skelton
    contribution on Robert Ricart's Map of Bristol c1480
    Clarendon Press, Oxford. 2nd ed. 1986
14. Guide to the Bristol Archives Office
    Bristol Corporation
15. The Downs 1861—1961
16. St Mark's, the Lord Mayor's Chapel (with H Evans)
    Bristol Corporation

1972

17. A History of Bristol and Gloucestershire (with Brian Smith)
    Darwen Finlayson
18. Government of Bristol 1373—1973
    Bristol Corporation
19. Atlas of Historic Towns vol 2 (M D Lobel and E M Carus Wilson)
    acknowledgements of use of unpublished material by Elizabeth Ralph on medieval Bristol

1976

20. The Society 1876–1976—a history of The Bristol and Gloucestershire Archaeological Society in Essays in Bristol & Gloucestershire History
    B&GAS Centenary Volume

1977

21. History of St Peter's, Henleaze 1927–1977

1979

22. The Great White Book of Bristol
    BRS vol 32

Two ranges of the abbey's accounts have for long been valuable sources for the community's history. Two compotus rolls for 1491–2 and 1511–12 were edited by Gwen Beachcroft and Arthur Sabin in 1938, and a series of manorial accounts for 1491–2 and 1496–7, together with ancillary documents, were published in 1960 by Arthur Sabin, who added perceptive studies of individual manors. A list of *temporalia* drawn up in 1428 provides a detailed, though not always complete, statement of the resources of the abbey's demesne manors.[3] The abbey's cartulary indicates how these resources were acquired and expanded. The accounts present in detail the income available for the canons and the way in which these resources were allocated for the use of the abbey's obedientiaries.

St Augustine's holdings in Somerset reflected the pattern of Robert fitz Harding's scattered acquisitions in that shire. He had purchased the manor of Bedminster from Robert, earl of Gloucester, with the hundreds of Hartcliffe, Bedminster and Portbury. In Bedminster the canons acquired strong interests. The Avon marked the boundary between Bristol and Bedminster, with Bristol bridge providing a direct access to the south through Redcliffe. Under fitz Harding's successors Redcliffe Street developed rapidly and became a distinct suburb, independent from Bristol and, in economic terms, a threat to the borough.

The canons derived great benefits from this expansion and shared in the prosperity of the suburb where they were given a number of houses, lands and rents. Between 1171 and 1190 John of Warminster, the son of a dyer, gave them a tenement with the condition that they paid landgavel to Maurice de Berkeley as lord of the fee. It was a familiar condition to be repeated in later deeds. In the decades which followed they received some fourteen grants in Redcliffe Street, sometimes described as lands, sometimes as rents, and occasionally as gardens. Peter la Warre, Isabella of Kenfig, David Long and John Germund, all familiar Bristol names, gave rents to the canons to maintain the anniversary of the death of close relatives.

Profitable use of a tenement depended upon maintaining sound buildings on the site. In 1255, Abbot William Long and Robert Pumfreit laid down the terms on which Robert was required to rebuild a house on one particular plot.[4]

The later rentals do not allow a precise figure of the abbey's holding in Redcliffe. They record the names of those holding eight tenements; a ninth tenant is named and is said to hold more than one tenement, and it was also recorded that six rents were not being paid.

A major interest in Redcliffe was the mill which the abbey held on the Trivel stream. Henry II already had a mill on that stretch of water, but he gave permission for the canons to build their mill on condition that it did not prove detrimental to his own mill. In later accounts the clerks referred to the Trivel Mills for which the standard render was £20 10s., a figure which is confirmed by the 20s. paid regularly

---

[3] *The Cartulary of St Augustine's Abbey, Bristol*, ed. David Walker, Bristol and Gloucestershire Archaeological Society, Record Series, vol. 10 (1998), cited hereafter as *Cart. St Aug.*; *Two Compotus Rolls of Saint Augustine's Abbey, Bristol*, Bristol Record Society, vol. ix, cited hereafter as *Comp. Rolls*; *Some Manorial Accounts of Saint Augustine's Abbey, Bristol*, Bristol Record Society, vol. xxiii (1960), cited hereafter as *Man. Accts*. A list of the *temporalia* is printed in *Comp. Rolls*, p. 38; entries are provided in full in each of Sabin's studies of individual manors in *Man. Accts*.

[4] *Cart. St Aug.*, nos. 481, 496–9, 500, 502, 550, 559, 561, 589, 590.

as rectorial tithes. In 1428 Trivel mill was said to be "ruinous, vacant and worth-less".[5] It was obviously restored, for in 1491–2 the full payment of £20 10s. was made. Twenty years later payments had once again fallen into arrears.

Once the urban development in Redcliffe had been absorbed into the borough of Bristol all these holdings were regarded as tenures within the borough. Redcliffe was a small part of the whole manor of Bedminster but the Berkeley tenure was often described as Bedminster and Redcliffe Street. Its development was an interest-ing example of how, in a rural manor, the combination of river moorings, trade and easy access could create a small but very profitable urban development. The abbey built up a share of that urban growth. There is one slight hint that further expan-sion might have occurred and that the abbey's interest might have been extended. One donor, Elias Norreys, who gave the canons a house in Redcliffe Street also gave them three messuages on the road from Redcliffe to Bedminster, but that appears to be an isolated incident.[6]

To the west of the Avon, Bedminster extended to the boundary of Portbury. Here Robert fitz Harding gave the canons Leigh, identified in King Stephen's charter of confirmation as *Legam scilicet juxta Bristou*.[7] A small manor, identified as part of Bedminster, was held in 1086 by one of the king's clerics, Thurstan, whose father held it in the reign of Edward the Confessor.[8] He had one plough team, and two cattle and six pigs, which points to a mixture of woodland and arable farming. The rich resources of the woodland were much valued by the canons. It has, for example, been estimated that sixteen boatloads of kindling, taken to Bristol across Rownham ferry, were necessary each year for their use. In the thirteenth century there was conflict between the abbot and Alexander de Auno, of Ashton, over their rights in the neighbouring woodlands of Abbots Leigh and Stoke Leigh. Each gave up the claim to have common in each other's woodland and each agreed to enclose their own woods securely. If the fencing proved weak and stray animals broke through, they were to be returned without dispute.[9]

At an earlier date (c. 1179 × 1222), a more complex matter of jurisdiction was settled. Hugh de Gurney and his wife Lucy have "heard and understood" the char-ters of Robert fitz Harding and William, earl of Gloucester, which established that in Leigh the canons should not be answerable to anyone except in an issue of murder. They agreed that in future their men of Leigh were to come to two legal hundred courts on the understanding that if they were amerced they should give satisfaction, not to Hugh and his wife, but to the abbey.[10]

There can be little doubt that much of the woodland had been transformed into arable land. In 1428 the manor had 200 acres of arable land, 12 acres of meadow and 30 acres of woodland.[11] In his study of Leigh, Arthur Sabin emphasized the critical importance of the manor in three respects. It was developed as a well-

---

[5] ibid, no. 9; *Comp. Rolls*, pp. 6, 174, 256.
[6] *Cart. St Aug.*, no. 559.
[7] ibid, no. 1.
[8] Domesday Book, I, ff. 86, 91.
[9] *Cart. St Aug.*, no. 288; this agreement was reached between 1234 and 1264.
[10] ibid, no. 105.
[11] *Comp. Rolls*, p. 38; *Man. Accts.*, p. 179.

lords of Berkeley, but the canons' tenure does not seem to have left any mark in their financial records.

Further along the coast at Clevedon the church was given to the abbey by William of Clevedon. He and his successors held one knight's fee there of the earls of Gloucester,[20] and he may have been drawn to contribute to the foundation of St Augustine's through the influence of William, earl of Gloucester, or through direct contact with his close neighbour in north Somerset, Robert fitz Harding. His manor was comfortably rather than richly endowed; already by 1086 it could sustain a variety of stock. Exeter Domesday Book recorded that there were six plough teams (48 oxen), 7 mares, 1 cob, 22 cattle, 25 pigs and 115 sheep.[21] The rectorial tithes were a valuable asset, and by the fifteenth century the canons were drawing rents from tenures in the manor. In 1540–41 they had revenues from $46\frac{1}{2}$ acres.[22]

To use one manor as a centre for financial and administrative purposes was a normal feature of the pattern adopted at St Augustine's. Such a centre was Rowberrow. It was a manor held by Robert son of Robert of St Denis of Axbridge, a sub-tenant of the Maureward family. In the last years of the twelfth century Robert conveyed it to David la Warre of Bristol, who was seeking to invest the wealth generated in trade in a country estate. He leased it to John la Warre. Between 1199 and 1216 John conveyed it to St Augustine's. It does not appear to have been simply a pious donation. The canons were prepared to invest heavily in this manor. To secure their tenure they paid out large sums of money: 53 marks to John la Warre, 3 gold coins to Robert son of Robert of St Denis, and 16 marks to Geoffrey Maureward, who could certainly drive a hard bargain. At later stages the canons paid 1 mark and returned to him the land in Draycott which was part of their original arrangement to secure an amelioration of the annual payments which they had promised to make. They followed that with a payment of 15 marks to be quit altogether of their annual render.[23] The surrender of the outlying territory of Draycott may have been a temporary measure. In 1428 the abbey had 4 acres of arable and 12 acres of meadow there and drew an annual income of 13s. 4d.[24]

In 1428 small tenements in Somerset were linked with Rowberrow. There was a house in Shepton Mallet worth 4s. a year. In Weston-super-Mare William son of Azo gave them a virgate between 1189 and 1191, which was assessed as 6 acres of arable and 1 acre of meadow, and which was still valued at 4s. a year in 1428. The canons' interest in West Harptree was of a different order. Early in the thirteenth century Michael of Stourton gave them a virgate of mixed tenures—a half-virgate in Gorwell, two separate quarter-virgates, 30 acres of demesne in Gorwell, a meadow and a parcel of enclosed land. For all this they were to pay a rent of 8s. a

---

[20] *Red Book of the Exchequer*, ed. H. Hall, Rolls Series (1896), I, p. 290. He also held two fees of Henry Lupello in Somerset (p. 234). His grant is recorded in a number of confirmations (*Cart. St Aug.*, nos. 6, 23, 34, 51, 52).

[21] For his fee, *Domesday Book*, I, f. 198b; for the stock in 1086, Exeter Domesday, *Domesday Book*, III, f. 450.

[22] *Man. Accts.*, pp. 39, 180.

[23] *Cart. St Aug.*, nos. 299–313. Geoffrey Maureward and Maurice of Barrington held a fee of half a knight of the bishop of Lincoln in 1219 (*Book of Fees*, p. 263).

[24] *Man. Accts.*, pp. 193, 194.

year. In 1428 their holding was assessed at 122 acres.[25] A major grant, and in economic terms a more important grant, was made by William son of William son of John of Harptree, who gave the canons pasturage for one thousand sheep and sixty draught animals, together with pannage for twenty pigs in East and West Harptree.[26]

By far the most curious tenure linked with Rowberrow lay in Baggridge. In 1219 or early in 1220 Robert II de Berkeley gave the abbey a small estate there which he had purchased from William de le Fremonte. He defined it as land which the canons should hold as a virgate. William, it appeared, had borrowed money from Jacob of Hereford and other Jews living in Bristol and had pledged his land for 30 marks. He was also in debt to Christian merchants there. When William could not repay his debts, Robert paid a substantial price to have his lands and hold them at fee-farm, and undertook to settle his debts. He paid 23 marks, a palfrey worth 20s., and a robe worth 20s. Unfortunately William had alienated some, if not all, of his land which Robert had then to recover. Some had gone to relatives. William's son, Ralph, had 16 acres with woodland and meadow; his sister, Emma, and her husband had 1 virgate. A lesser tenant had 1 furlong and rights of common pasture. William had also sold 26 acres to Henry de Montfort, with woodlands and meadows. Robert de Berkeley had to buy out their interests. Emma and her husband surrendered their claims in return for an annual rent of half a mark; their son, Reginald, gave up his claim for a similar sum. Henry de Montfort was paid $12\frac{1}{2}$ marks and received small parcels of land in Baggridge. It would seem that William de le Fremonte's son was not penalised. Robert's generosity cost him something in excess of £46.[27]

For the canons this proved to be an isolated collection of land and rights lacking the cohesion of an identifiable manor. In 1428 it consisted of 2 messuages, each with 1 acre of land and 8 acres of meadow. At that stage its value was rather low, but by the end of the century it was producing £4 a year.[28]

The rectories of two churches, Weare and Pawlett, provided a stable income. Robert fitz Harding's son, Robert, was closely associated with Weare and held Pawlett. His successors gave their patronage to St Mark's hospital and were generous in the grants which they made to the hospital. The manor of Pawlett was given to St Augustine's to maintain its charitable work, and the abbey's title was clear. Hence the appearance of the rectory and manor of Pawlett in later accounts. The practical work passed to St Mark's and the hospital and abbey worked out a *modus vivendi* in 1251. The standard pension from the rectory of Weare was £9 6s. 8d. (with a slight decline in 1511–12). Pawlett as a rectory and manor produced £19 18s. 0d. in 1491–2 and £18 2s. 2d. in 1511–12.[29]

Beyond the boundaries of Somerset the abbey had the rectory of Halberton (Devon) and the manor and rectory of Fifehead Magdalen (Dorset). Halberton was given to the abbey by William de Bosco and Gregory de Turri, who shared the lordship of the manor. Both men were prominent in the entourage of William, earl

---

[25] *Cart. St Aug.*, nos. 319–23; *Man. Accts.*, p. 193.
[26] *Cart. St Aug.*, no. 323.
[27] ibid., nos. 133, 158, 328–36.
[28] *Comp. Rolls*, pp. 248–9; *Man. Accts.*, p. 193.
[29] *Cart. St Aug.*, no. 591; *Comp. Rolls*, pp. 285–6.

Improvement and development are the keynotes of the canons' management of this manor. Middleshaw was uncultivated and the canons secured a series of quit-claims which left them free to make assarts and to bring it and neighbouring land into production. They could enclose and fence off their land, and they could make ditches. Even on that upland area of the manor, drainage was essential to bring the land into cultivation. They had to acknowledge that, once that had been achieved, some tenants would have access when the land was fallow and after harvest.[40]

By far the major exercise in land reclamation lay in the marshes below the ridge-way and especially in Kingsmarsh—part of the line of salt marshes which, in terms of the modern shoreline of the Severn, lie well inland. Here the canons made a sustained attempt to improve the drainage of the marsh. They had to secure quit-claims to make major changes possible. In particular, they had to secure the agree-ment of Nicholas Poyntz, with a clear definition of their mutual responsibility for maintaining the main dike which divided their lands. One quitclaim included the plain statement that the canons could level or close other dikes on the marsh and build new dikes at will, provided that they did not damage the grantor's free tene-ment.[41] Although they do not appear to have been involved in building or main-taining sea-defences, without which a drainage system could not be sustained, the canons were contributing by their management of the marshland to the series of independent attempts to check inundation along the coast. Sabin considered that the draining of the marsh in Almondsbury was an accomplished fact by the end of the fifteenth century, but constant repair and maintenance were essential. In 1491–2 payments were made for scouring and deepening rhines and for repairing a sluice. In 1496–7 payments were recorded for scouring and deepening the rhines and dikes in Newland and the Great Rhine, and for digging 124 perches (682 yards) of the dike from Tockington to a field called Hudmede. This routine work was associated with repairs to the Middlewall and the Severn walls and the link between sea defences and marshland management is clearly established.[42]

For any community or large household the tenure of a fishery was a major asset. Fish was an essential element of diet in times of abstinence. Writing about Thomas II Lord Berkeley (1245–1321), John Smyth noted that in his progress from one house to another he usually spent Lent at Wick, in Arlingham, "for his better and nearer provision of Fish".[43] Arlingham was renowned for the number of fish weirs with which it could harvest the rich resources of the Severn. Robert fitz Harding gave St Augustine's half of his fishery there, together with the tithe of the other half.[44] This went far towards supplying the fish which was the canons' staple food in the penitential seasons and on fast days. His grandson, Robert de Berkeley, added $10\frac{1}{2}$ putchers in his fish weir and a free fish trap in the fishery of Ruddle. The claim to tithes was challenged by the monks of St Peter's, Gloucester, and before 1189 the canons had come to terms, retaining the tithes but paying the monks one mark

---

[40] *Cart. St Aug.*, nos. 433–48; for the right to dig drainage ditches, no. 436; to make assarts, no. 439; for the intention to bring land into cultivation, nos. 439, 447.

[41] ibid, no. 444.

[42] *Man. Accts.*, pp. 90 and n. 66, 91.

[43] Smyth, *Lives*, I, p. 164.

[44] *Cart. St Aug.*, no. 73.

a year. In 1237 Thomas de Berkeley also contested their claim, but he eventually reached accord with Abbot William of Breadstone and agreed that the canons were entitled to them.[45]

A more complex issue had been raised slightly earlier in the thirteenth century. Under the patronage of Robert de Berkeley and the family of Peter of Wick, Robert Knivet had built up a holding in Arlingham, part of which was associated with the fisheries. Between 1211 and 1220 he gave himself and his land to the monks of Dore abbey. The connection did not last, for on second thoughts, Robert gave himself and his land to St Augustine's. Over a period of not more than nine years Robert de Berkeley confirmed these grants to Dore and to St Augustine's. However short the interval between these transactions may have been, the monks of Dore acquired a claim to both land and fisheries.[46] In the event, the canons established their claims, but it was an expensive business. They paid 50 marks and an annual rent of 2s. to the monks, who were still claiming their rent in 1511. In the charter in which he confirmed this settlement Adam, abbot of Dore, claimed that Robert de Berkeley had granted these fisheries to Dore and that Robert Knivet held them of the abbey. He also describes in detail the small community of fisherman who operate the weirs.

By comparison with their fishery, the parcels of land which the canons acquired in Arlingham were of much less importance. They secured 4 virgates from Robert de Berkeley and 2 virgates, with other less clearly defined land, from Robert Knivet. Two daughters of Peter of Wick made small donations; Joyce and her husband, Robert de Caple, gave 4 selions with a house, messuage and garden, and her sister Margaret, wife of Ralph the Welshman, gave half an acre.[47] Much more significant was the property which Elias of Bristol, a canon of Hereford cathedral, gave the canons. Between 1221 and 1230 he gave them all the land he held of Robert de Berkeley to provide a corrody in St Augustine's for his brother, John. To secure this endowment of $2\frac{1}{2}$ virgates he paid Robert de Berkeley 32s. and 2 palfreys and 2 separate rents.[48]

The comparative value of fisheries and landed property can best be seen from the valuation in 1428: £1 16s. for land, and £10 for the fisheries. The income from Arlingham in 1491–2 was £8 1s. 6d., and in 1511–12 £8 17s. 0d; and there may have been a further decline if Henry VIII's instructions to demolish the weirs had been carried out in whole or in part. In the early seventeenth century, the old valuation of £10 was restated.[49]

Higher up the Severn lay Ashleworth, with a fishery called Ashleworth weir. The canons' tenure of this fishery was threatened in the thirteenth century by William of the Park who claimed in the shire court in Gloucestershire that its use was detrimental to his free tenement of Brawn, in Sandhurst. In what may have been an uncomfortably vague assurance the canons undertook to ensure that he should not in future suffer excessive damage.[50] At the end of the fifteenth century two local

[45] ibid, no. 159 and Additional Document no. 15.
[46] ibid, nos. 138, 139.
[47] ibid, nos. 257, 271.
[48] ibid, no. 142.
[49] *Comp. Rolls*, p. 280; *Man. Accts.*, pp. 165–7.
[50] *Cart. St Aug.*, no. 372.

sive transactions. Walter secured Robert's manumission for which he paid half a mark. He also secured from the lord of Hill a grant of the virgate farmed by Alfred. It was to be held by Walter for his lifetime and thereafter by Robert and the children produced by his marriage to Helen. For that grant Walter paid 10 marks to Roger son of Nicholas and half a mark to his wife. An investment of £7 was no light undertaking.

In fact Robert proved to be an astute and successful farmer and he bought up more land in Hill. He had three daughters who eventually inherited his virgate. In a series of charters to St Augustine's he gave the canons $20\frac{1}{2}$ acres of arable land and 2 acres of meadow. In the next generation the canons also acquired the virgate on which the family's prosperity was founded. A further $15\frac{1}{2}$ acres were given to them by other virgate holders, and 11 acres which were gradually purchased by David Long a burgess of Bristol.[63] The value of the manor in 1428 is not clear but by the end of the century it was producing corn and barley estimated to be worth £10 and £5 8s., and food supplies were being sent to the abbey.[64]

In 1428 St Augustine's held 28 acres of arable and 2 acres of meadow in Stone. Two donations in the mid-thirteenth century were recorded, but they do not appear to cover the whole of that holding. William of Stone gave his land called Hitching next to 'Horethurum', which was possibly Hagthorn. He was at one time in financial straits and the abbot loaned him $4\frac{1}{2}$ marks for his urgent needs. In doing so he took the precaution of stating that if the canons' tenure of this land should be challenged, William must repay the $4\frac{1}{2}$ marks and pay any expenses which they might incur. Reginald of Uley married his daughter and William gave her 2 acres of land which he and his wife subsequently gave to the abbey. The small marriage settlement suggests that William was a very minor tenant.[65]

The measure of the small tenements which the canons held in Wanswell and Saniger is to be found in 1428 when they consisted of 3 messuages, 28 acres of arable land and 2 acres of meadow.[66] In 1219–20 Robert de Berkeley gave the abbey the virgate held by Reginald Luffinc, together with Reginald himself. That would match the 28 acres of arable. Later in the century Philip of Leicester gave the canons 2 acres in Wanswell in the croft called Shortland. They also received from John Sewake $1\frac{1}{2}$ acres in Wanswell and a rent, part of which was paid by Robert of Saniger and his wife.[67] A gradual extension of the abbey's interests in Berkeley is reflected in the grants of land in Ham, near Berkeley mill, by Robert de Berkeley, and of land in Berkeley by William Coby, and in grants of the woodland of Lorridge and the chapel which had been built there.[68]

Robert fitz Harding gave Cromhall to St Augustine's when he became a canon. The measure of its potential lies in the assessment of this manor as 2 hides in 1086.

[63] *Cart. St Aug.*, nos. 174–212.

[64] *Comp. Rolls*, pp. 38, 120, 122, 125; *Man. Accts.*, p. 148. The list of *temporalia* printed by Sabin gives a total of 30 acres. The summary published in 1938 gives a total of 40 acres.

[65] *Cart. St Aug.*, nos. 213–6.

[66] *Man. Accts.*, pp. 148–9; the meadow was not included in the list in *Comp. Rolls*, p. 38.

[67] *Cart. St Aug.*, nos. 131, 158–60, 258, 262.

[68] ibid, nos. 126, 145, 149, 152, 153; *Man. Accts.*, pp. 93–4, 103, 153.

Only small additions were made in the thirteenth century when the canons were given a number of holdings which included 7 acres.[69]

The land which the canons acquired in Codrington was defined in a complex fashion. Roger de Cantilupe gave them a quarter of all his land in this manor. Part of that was made up of a quarter of 7 fields, each separately identified, and a quarter of his meadow. The rest consisted of $16\frac{1}{2}$ acres, each separately identified, and there is no indication that the grant is limited to a quarter of those acres. In a confirmation by his son, Roger, the donation is described as 6 acres; the canons had their barns in one acre, and the other 5 adjoined it. The donor's grandson, Richard, identified two grants, one of 6 acres and the other of a quarter of the donor's land. There was an added complication. Before 1248 Richard de Cantilupe arranged with the canons to exchange all his land in Codrington for a variety of holdings in Arlingham.[70] In June 1485, the abbot leased the manor to John Poule, with its two barns and its byres and other buildings. The lessee was also given the rectorial tithes of corn from Wapley. Two rooms in the manor house, one on the ground floor and one on the upper floor, on the south side of the building, were reserved for the use of the abbot and any other obedientiary when they paid a formal visit to the manor. The abbot of Stanley was entitled to a pension in place of the tithes of Wapley, the church of which had been given to that abbey in the twelfth century by a royal chamberlain, Ralph fitz Stephen.[71]

In the sixteenth century Codrington was linked for administrative purposes with Arlingham and the two nearby villages, Wapley and Hinton, and with another small tenure near Wotton under Edge. Here Juliana de Pontdelarch, wife of Robert de Berkeley, bought a cotset at Coombe and a half-virgate next to the parson's court in Bradley. These she gave to Reginald of Cam who gave them to St Augustine's.[72] A full understanding of the value of these estates is limited by the fact that the farmer was answerable to the master of new works at the abbey, who was not required to account to the treasurer. John Martin's account for 1491–2 and John Newland's account for 1511–12 both recorded the lease by which Codrington was placed in John Poule's care, but the financial details of his administration are not recorded.[73]

To an almost overwhelming extent this record of the possessions of St Augustine's is dominated by the family of Robert fitz Harding and their many gifts to the abbey. To a lesser extent the generosity of donors from a very different level of the social scale increased the abbey's lands and income. There remains a third element. During the critical years of conflict between Stephen and the Empress Matilda, Bristol was a major centre. Robert, earl of Gloucester, Matilda's half-brother, was a strong and unwavering supporter of her claims, and the castle at Bristol was a focal point for those who had rallied to her cause. That her son, the future Henry II, should be brought by his uncle to Bristol was doubly significant. He would, like other boys of his age, learn the skills of fighting and the pattern of life in the

[69] *Domesday Book*, I, f. 163; *Cart. St Aug.*, nos. 467, 470.
[70] *Cart. St Aug.*, nos. 386–9.
[71] ibid, no. 394; *Comp. Rolls*, p. 206.
[73] *Cart. St Aug.*, nos. 268–71. For a rent due from Hinton, see *Comp. Rolls*, p. 150.
[73] *Comp. Rolls*, pp. 206–13.

Jerusalem"(**403**). He describes the steep ascent to **St Brandon's Chapel and Hermitage** *[Map: 40]*, "as far as the chapel of St Brandon on the summit" (**323**) which "is said, as the hermit there told me that sailors and knowledgeable men say, to be higher than any pinnacle, whether of Redcliffe Church or of other churches, by the space of 18 fathoms" (**325**). St Brendan's chapel itself was 8½ yards long and 5 yards wide, while the circumference of its walled enclosure measured 180 steps (**324**). It is interesting that the hermit passes on sailors' techniques for estimating height, as St Brendan's was a sailors' chapel. Worcestre's Bristol notes include two prayers to St Brendan, perhaps acquired from the hermit (**78**).

Last of the hermitages was the deserted **St Vincent's Chapel** *[Map: 41]*, at Ghyston Cliff in Avon Gorge, which Worcestre visited several times. Its dramatic situation "on a certain most high rock or grim crag, plunging down to the river flowing from Bristol" (**65**), appealed to him. "The hermitage with a church, in honour of St Vincent" was "sited on a most dangerous rock called Ghyston Cliff, in a deep place of the rock, at a depth of twenty fathoms down the said rock, above the river Avon" (**405**). Worcestre made several versions of his calculations, "climbing up to the high ground ... walking and counting, on Sunday 2[4]th September ... 1480" (**66**), measuring 20 fathoms from the ground down the cliff to the chapel, and a further 40 fathoms to the low water mark in the river below (**55, 63, 66, 437**), the latter "proved to me by a young man, working as a smith in Redcliffe Street, who told it me, he having descended right from the very top of the rock down to the waterside" (**63**). The hermitage itself had a hall 9 yards long and 7 (or 3) yards wide, a passage from the hall to the church, "dug into the aforesaid rock", 16 yards long; the chapel itself was 8 yards long and 3 yards wide, and the kitchen 6 yards long and 3 yards wide—a 'suite' of caves in the limestone cliff (**63, 65**).

CONCLUSION

William Worcestre's catalogue of churches and chapels, from the ancient parish church of Holy Trinity to the half-rebuilt St Augustine the Less, from cathedral-like St Mary Redcliffe to deserted St Vincent's hermitage, is certainly comprehensive. His observations and notes, all collected over a few weeks in the late summer of 1480, give an instant impression of the wealth and variety of church building in prosperous late medieval Bristol, just before the religious upheavals of the next century. His obsession with sizes and shapes serves to place all these churches firmly on the ground in and around the town, providing the physical context into which can be set the wealth of detail contained in surviving pre-Reformation church books, accounts, wills and other archives—a strong framework for the social and religious functions of the churches which are studied elsewhere in this volume.

At the same time, his repetitive measurements and his lack of interest in appearances can make dry and exasperating reading, and are a salutary reminder that, remarkable early topographer though he was, Worcestre is a medieval and not a modern 'church tourist'. His interests in church buildings are mechanical, numerical and practical, and not aesthetic. Yet, while preoccupied with recording present shapes, Worcestre shows a clear sense of the past: All Saints founded before the

Norman Conquest, the suggestion that St Augustine the Less might be the original site of St Augustine's Abbey, and the contrast between "the old church" and the 14th century quire at St Augustine's Abbey itself. His antiquarian and historical interests are also seen in his enthusiasm for copying old chronicles and other documents. He found ample material in Bristol churches. It is clear from his comment on the Fraternity of Kalendars, "founded in most ancient times, before the time of William the Conqueror of England, about the year of Christ 700, as I have seen and read in confirmatory documents in an ancient hand, of the time of St Wulstan, bishop of Worcester" (**387**), that he enjoyed studying original documents. He made extensive copies "from a paper book, a great volume of chronicles" belonging to John Burton, priest at St Thomas's (**339, 416**). He considered asking the Prior of the Kalendars "if there remain among their documents any documents of their fellow Sir Thomas Botoner", his uncle (**33**). He certainly used the Kalendars' library at All Saints, as he made "Brief notes from the chronicles of Marianus Scotus found at the Library of All Saints"(**266**), while the table of measures he "found in a certain little book kept in St Stephen's church, Bristol, in the south aisle" was copied out twice (**224, 452**). He copied out Saints' days and a table of years from a "chronicle I found in a portable breviary in the church of St John", the Hospital at Redcliffe (**114**). He was given access to "the obit book of the calendar of the Friars Preachers" and copied out entries including members of the Berkeley and Gurney families and other notables, and "Brother William Botoner", presumably a relation, who died 15th December 1429 (**286**). He made a list of founders and benefactors of St Katherine's Hospital, presumably from a similar book kept in the church (**470**), and laboriously wrote out the history of the Knights of St John of Jerusalem "copied down from a board hanging in Temple Church" (**195**).

Underpinning Worcestre's dryly repetitive notes on churches is another theme, which has two aspects: Worcestre's interest in people, and other people's interest in Worcestre. Both are revealing about the attitude of Bristolians to their many churches at the end of the 15th century. For his part, Worcestre clearly had a facility for making acquaintances who were interested in aiding his quest for information about churches: master masons at important churches, the young blacksmith climbing in the Avon Gorge, the obliging plumber at Redcliffe, the knowledgeable parishioner of St Augustine the Less and the "many people" who told him the story of the Jewish synagogue under St Giles. He is interested in Bristol citizens such as John Barstaple and Thomas Knapp who founded chapels, and in Elias Spelly and his fellows in the only stained glass window in Bristol which he felt moved to describe. They are a varied selection, not academics, antiquarians or churchmen. At the same time, he was given remarkable freedom of access to Bristol churches, both of parishes and of religious houses, which implies that parish priests, monks and friars must have sanctioned his pacing around their quires and chapels, as well as producing books for him to examine and copy. There are very few churches which, for some reason, he does not seem to have entered. The churches were flourishing on the patronage of wealthy laity, whether guilds or individuals. Surviving pre-Reformation church books and accounts show how citizens were closely involved in their churches, just as the churches with their festivals and guild services were an

written by E. G. Cuthbert F. Atchley and published in 1905 and 1906. Atchley was
a Bristol physician and surgeon who lived in Whiteladies Road. He became fascinated by medieval church history and liturgy, and published numerous general articles on medieval services, ritual, vestments, the use of incense, votive offerings and
other liturgical matters. He also published specific accounts of the medieval records
and service books of several Bristol churches including St Nicholas. Some of his
work was published in the *Transactions of the Bristol and Gloucestershire Archaeological
Society*.[6] Other work, including that on St Nicholas, was published in the *Transactions
of the St Paul's Ecclesiological Society* in London. Atchley read several papers to this
Society and these were subsequently published in the Society's *Transactions*. His connection with the *St Paul's Ecclesiological Society* may have come about through the
influence of the bishop of Bristol, George Forrest Browne, who was a vice-president.
Atchley's research on the records of St Nicholas resulted in two major articles, one
on medieval parish clerks in Bristol, the other a general survey of the medieval
records of the church.[7]

The existence of these various accounts, and in particular Atchley's work, makes
it possible to attempt some description of the late-medieval records of St Nicholas
and of the evidence they provide for the religious life of this important Bristol
church. Unless otherwise stated in the references, this essay is based upon the
above-mentioned sources.

THE CHURCH BUILDING

The earliest references to St Nicholas Church occur in the twelfth century when it
became one of the possessions of the Augustinian abbey in Bristol. There is a reference to St Nicholas in a charter of St Augustine's abbey dated 1154, and possession
was confirmed to the abbey by Henry II in 1170.[8] St Augustine's abbey remained
its patron throughout the Middle Ages. There were sixteen well-preserved charters
dating from the twelfth to the fourteenth century, whereby pious Bristolians made
bequests of land, valuables and money to the church in return for prayers and
intercessions. Six of these charters were made during the time of Walter Filomena,
the first vicar of St Nicholas whose name is known. He was vicar from 1240 to
1286.[9]

It is probable that St Nicholas was enlarged during the late fourteenth or early
fifteenth centuries when several testators left sums of money towards the building
costs.[10]

The church consisted of an upper church of two aisles, and beneath was a crypt

[6] E. G. Cuthbert F. Atchley, "The Halleway Chantry at the Parish Church of All Saints",
Bristol, *B.&G.A.S. Transactions*, XXIV, 1901, 74–125. See also *Archaeological Journal*, LVIII,
1901, 147–81.
[7] E. G. Cuthbert F. Atchley, "Medieval Parish Clerks in Bristol", *St Paul's Ecclesiological
Society Transactions*, V, 1905, 107–116; "Medieval Parish Records of the Church of St Nicholas, Bristol", *St Paul's Ecclesiological Society Transactions*, VI, 1906–10, 35–67.
[8] David Walker, ed., "The Cartulary of St Augustine's Abbey, Bristol", *B.&G.A.S. Transactions: Record Series*, 10, 1993, Nos. 15, 19, 23.
[9] Lewis J. Upton Way, *op.cit.*, 121–44.
[10] David Walker, *op.cit.*, No. 475; T. P. Wadley, *op.cit.*, 9, 68–9, 138.

or "crowde" as it was known in Bristol. The building formed part of the town wall, so that the south wall of the crypt was 15 feet thick. The chancel extended over the south gate of the town, at the entrance to High Street from Bristol Bridge. The narrow gateway surmounted by the chancel is shown on Millerd's map of 1673. In order to accommodate the traffic passing below it, the chancel was much higher than the nave of the upper church, and was approached by a flight of twelve steps. During the 1760s Bristol Bridge was rebuilt and widened, and the medieval gateway beneath the chancel of St Nicholas was removed. This work necessitated the demolition of the chancel and the whole of the upper church, and a new shorter building was erected above the medieval crypt. It was this eighteenth-century Gothic-style building with a spectacular plasterwork ceiling which was destroyed by the bombing in 1940.[11]

William Worcestre's notes on St Nicholas's church have been discussed elsewhere in this volume by Frances Neale. The medieval crypt of four bays with two aisles survives, and the quality of the architecture no doubt reflects a similar high standard in the upper church. The structure of the crypt dates from the mid fourteenth century. The vaulted roof is supported on huge pillars, and the vaulting is enriched with sixty-six carved bosses. Among the subjects portrayed are the Crucifixion, the Virgin and Child and crowned heads said to represent Edward II, Queen Isabella and Edward III. Like the similar crypt or crowde of St John's church which also forms part of the town wall and where the medieval gateway remains, the crowde of St Nicholas was used for services and as a meeting place of the guild or fraternity of the Holy Cross. The crowde had its own procurators or churchwardens whose accounts were kept separate from those of the upper church. It was much used by wealthier parishioners as a place of burial, although the church also possessed a small cemetery on Welsh Back for those who could not afford burial in the crowde. In 1383 John Wilkyns the elder of Bristol gave to the vicar of St Nicholas, John Crome, a vacant plot of land 156 feet long by 38 feet wide, to make *de novo* a cemetery for the parishioners.[12]

As will be shown in more detail later, St Nicholas played an important part in the life of the busy medieval town and port of Bristol. Its structure incorporated a principal entrance to the town, and its parish stretched south along the river Avon, including within it the "Welsh Back" with its important harbour, and half of the area of the Marsh on which Queen's Square was later to be built. St Nicholas provided a water supply for that part of the town, the curfew for the whole town was rung each night from its tower, and its bells provided the standard time for the town and established the time at which services were to be conducted in chantries, as well as in the other parish churches of Bristol.[12] The clock is mentioned in various late-medieval documents. For example, in 1481 a proclamation of the Mayor, Sheriff and Corporation of Bristol ordered that no traders in the market were to sell any products, corn, fish, poultry, cheese, fruit or vegetables "before the houre of XII

[11] Andor Gomme et al., eds., *Bristol: An Architectural History*, 1979, 54–6, 172–3.

[12] T. P. Wadley, *op.cit.*, 104, 188, 189; R. Leech, "The Topography of Medieval & Early Modern Bristol", *Bristol Record Society*, XLVIII, 1997, xxviii; *Calendar of Patent Rolls*, Richard II (1381–85), 222, 26 January 1383.

THE EVIDENCE OF WILLS

The collection of late medieval wills preserved among the records of Bristol Corporation in the Great Orphan Book includes several wills made by parishioners of St Nicholas, and legacies made to the church by others. Abstracts of many of these wills were printed by T. P. Wadley in 1880, and they are informative about the church, crypt, chantries and the furnishings. They reveal details of altars, statues, lights and tombs, and provide indications of the clergy, chaplains, chantry priests, deacons and clerks. Above all, they show the continuing desire of testators to be buried in the crypt, to be remembered at the altar, and to benefit from the regular round of masses, prayers and intercessions. Tightly hemmed in on all sides, St Nicholas lacked an adjacent churchyard, and richer parishioners were buried in the crypt. The number of those who wished to be buried there must have caused great difficulties, but there is no evidence that their wishes were denied.

A typical example was Walter Glover who died in 1383. He requested that his body be buried in the crypt of St Nicholas, and ordered legacies to be given to the vicar, chaplain, the clerk and to the building work in progress on the church. He also left money to the Fraternity of the Holy Cross, to the diocesan cathedral at Worcester, and to the four orders of friars in Bristol, who were requested to celebrate masses for the repose of his soul. Several testators during the late fourteenth century mention building work which was being carried out at the church. Few were as generous as Thomas Knappe, merchant and former mayor, whose will is dated 1404. He left £20 to the fabric of St Nicholas. Thomas Knappe or Knapp was a wealthy merchant and burgess of Bristol. He had already founded a chapel of St John the Evangelist, close to the harbour on the river Avon at Welsh Back. This was within the parish of St Nicholas and some of the accounts of Knappe's chapel were included with the parish records. Thomas Knappe's intention was that there should be daily masses in his chapel at 5.00 am, so that mariners, servants and workers in and around the harbour should be able to attend before starting work. In his will Knappe also left £20 to provide two chaplains to celebrate masses in his chapel, and it was there that he wished to be buried. The chapel measured 39 feet by 18 feet. When John Droys, burgess, made his will in 1417, he also asked to be buried in the chapel "on the Back of Avon". Some wealthy families had their own vaults and tombs in the crypt. In his will of 1385 Adam Pountfreyt desired to be buried in the new tomb he had built ("in nova tumba quam ibidem construxi"). William Coder, burgess and cloth merchant, in his will of 1473 wished for burial in the crypt of St Nicholas, under his marble stone beside the bodies of his two wives. In return he left the church 100 marks (£66 13s 4d) to purchase a set of vestments, and money to pay twenty poor people to hold torches about his body on the day of his burial; each was to be given a gown with a hood of Welsh cloth.

Perhaps mindful of the damage successive burials would inflict on the fabric, Thomas Beell, burgess, in 1493 left money for the repair and restoration of the crypt after his burial. Another cloth merchant, John Fuyster, burgess, evidently had a family vault in the crypt and wished to be buried "by my Moder and under the same stone".[16]

---

[16] T. P. Wadley, *op.cit.*, 9,11, 68–9, 99–100, 149–50, 180.

Wills also provide evidence concerning the origin of many of the valuable items possessed by the church and for the altars which existed within it. Thomas Gilemyn, burgess, left a silver girdle to the image of St Nicholas, together with a mazer or wooden drinking cup bound with silver and six silver spoons. Reference has already been made to gifts of vestments. Henry Gildeney's will of 1430 refers to "the chancel of the crypt"; and David Ap Pollangham in 1495 mentions the altar of St Citha there. Joanne Thorne's will of 1523 mentions St Michael's altar "in the crowde", while a century earlier, in 1423 John Hethe desired to be buried before the image of the Cross ("coram ymagine scilicet Crucis ibidem"), by which he presumably meant a crucifix. Several early wills refer to the Fraternity of the Holy Cross which was based in the crypt. It was no doubt the existence of this Fraternity which explains the large roof boss depicting the Crucifixion at the east end of the crowde. There are also numerous references to lights, candles, lamps and candelabra. Lights were kept burning before the statues of the Blessed Virgin and St Katherine, and there was a candelabrum before the Rood in the upper church.

CHANTRIES

Many testators left money for a priest or chaplain to say masses for their souls for limited periods, and in addition there were four permanent chantries established at St Nicholas. The number of clergy employed in the church beside the vicar would therefore have fluctuated but was always considerable.

Few details survived in the records of St Nicholas concerning the earliest chantry foundation. This was founded by Eborard le Frenche or Franceys in 1350. It was a large and elaborate chantry, employing four priests, two at St Nicholas and two at St Mary Redcliffe. The foundation deed of Eborard le Franceys' chantry was enrolled in the *Little Red Book of Bristol*, providing a detailed account of the complex provisions. The goods provided for the two chaplains at St Nicholas were to be kept in a coffer, the translation of the Latin list is as follows:

> One missal worth four marks; one chalice with a silver spoon gilded worth 26s 8d; one corporal or linen cloth for the altar, with a *burse* or cloth case, together worth 5s od; three sets of vestments worth five marks; three towels for the altar worth 6s od; one *manutergium* (cloth for hand washing?) for washing worth 12d; two cruets of pewter for wine and water worth 12d; with an honest custodian to keep them safely.[17]

The chantry was endowed with numerous houses and other property in Bristol. At the time of the suppression of the chantries in 1547 there was one priest, William Smythman, at St Nicholas, the other position being vacant. Smythman was 42 years of age and was paid £6 per annum. The plate, jewels and ornaments belonging to the chantry in St Nicholas were said to be worth £3 6s 2d. Smythman was granted a pension of £5 per annum.[18]

---

[17] Francis Bickley, *op.cit.*, 195–8. For a comprehensive discussion of the chantries in Bristol see the numerous publications by Clive Burgess, especially " 'For the Increase in Divine Service': Chantries in the Parish in Late Medieval Bristol", *Journal of Ecclesiastical History*, XXXVI, 1985, 46–65.

[18] J. Maclean, "Chantry Certificates", *B.&G.A.S. Transactions*, VIII, 1883–4, 237–40.

A second chantry was founded in 1481 by William Spencer, a Bristol merchant who had been mayor in 1466, 1474 and 1479. According to the terms of the foundation which were included in the vestry book, the chaplain of Spencer's chantry was to celebrate mass each day at the altar in the Lady Chapel of St Nicholas, to take part in all the other services in the church and to assist in "the mynystratian of the sacraments to the grete multitude of people in the said parish". He was not to be absent without the consent of the vicar. Because it was conducted in the Lady Chapel in the upper church, this chantry came to be known as "Our Lady Service". At the time of the suppression the chantry priest was Thomas Gwynne aged 50 years, who received £6 per annum. The property belonging to the chantry was valued at £7 3s od per annum. There was no plate or jewels, and the ornaments were said to be worth 18s od. Gwynne received a pension of £4 per annum.

The third permanent chantry foundation was Spicer's Chantry. This was established by Richard Spicer, a Bristol merchant and burgess, in 1377, and endowed with tenements and property in the streets surrounding St Nicholas. The foundation deed is also enrolled in the *Little Red Book of Bristol*. Richard Spicer made detailed arrangements for the conduct of his chantry. The chantry priest was to be present at mattins, mass and vespers, and not to sleep outside the town of Bristol without reasonable cause and only with the permission of the vicar of St Nicholas. The chantry foundation was placed under the supervision of successive mayors of Bristol, and the chantry priest had to take an annual oath of obedience to the Mayor.

Each year the anniversary of Richard Spicer and his wife was to be celebrated with an obit consisting of vespers, mattins of the Dead, and a Requiem Mass, at which money was to be given to the poor and to the clerks, bedesmen and church-wardens of St Nicholas in return for their attendance. Two torches were to be provided at a cost of 6s 8d, and after the obit they were to be used at the daily chantry mass throughout the year. A lamp was to be provided to burn before St Mary's altar at a cost of 10s od. In 1547 the chantry priest was William Hunte, aged 40, whose salary was £7 1s 5½d per annum. The income of the chantry from rents was £12 4s od per annum, and the ornaments were valued at 15s od.[19]

Particularly interesting was the chantry belonging to the Guild or Fraternity of the Holy Cross which met in the crypt or "crowde". This was a lively association with its own priest and altar, and its own "procurators" or churchwardens whose accounts were separate from those of the upper church. The Guild chapel had its own rood screen with the figure of the crucified Christ on the large cross. The accounts mention screens, pews, lights and organs in the crowde. This Fraternity and its chantry evidently remaind popular throughout the later Middle Ages, and is frequently mentioned by testators in their wills. Walter Glovere and Nigel Chepstowe both made legacies to "the fraternity of the holy Cross" in 1383, John Inhyne of St Leonard's parish, left money in 1390 for masses "in le crowde" of St Nicholas, as did John Bentley, burgess, in 1416, and John Hethe, burgess and merchant, in 1423. William Coder, in his will of 1473 left 13s 4d to the procurators of the crypt and 6s 8d "to the chaplains of the fraternity, celebrating therein", in

[19] Francis Bickley, *op.cit.*, 202, 215.

return for prayers to be said for his soul.[20] Some indication of the continuing popularity of the Fraternity can be gained from the fact that its members continued to raise large sums of money each year. For example, the surviving account for 1523 includes the entry "Received during the year of the brodyrs and systers of the crowde x li xis iiiid".

In 1547 the Chantry of the Holy Cross was described as "A Chantrie called Crowde Service, founded by divers well disposed persons, for a priest to Synge in the said parish church, within the Crowde there for ever". The office of chantry priest had been vacant for the previous few months. The income was said to be £6 12s 8d per annum, and the ornaments were valued at 15s 10d.

The purpose of such fraternities was to provide the benefits of a chantry, with perpetual masses, for the members. Since it was dedicated to the Holy Cross, elaborate services and ceremonies took place each year at the Feast of the Holy Cross or Holy Rood day.[21] At St Nicholas this was celebrated in May, and some indication of the ritual and festivities can be gathered from the procurators' accounts for 1531. Former members of the fraternity were commemorated with a Requiem Mass conducted by ten priests, with clerks, sexton, bell-ringers and expenditure on wax for the candles. The mass for the departed was followed by a feast for current members. Bread, butter, cheese, saffron cakes and 14 dozen of ale were consumed at a total cost of £1 12s 11d. The income of the chantry came from the rent of two houses in Baldwin Street, five in Broadmead and one in Tucker Street.

Also within the parish of St Nicholas were two other chantries. The chantry of St John the Evangelist on Welsh Back, founded by Thomas Knappe has already been discussed. The other was the Chapel of the Assumption of Our Lady on Bristol Bridge. This was consecrated in 1361. The chapel was situated above and across the roadway of Bristol Bridge. It was of ornate and high-quality architecture, with a vaulted roof, a tower over 100 feet high, and delicate four-light windows filled with painted glass. The chapel was managed by the Fraternity of the Assumption of Our Lady, and the objects of the Master and Brethren of the Fraternity are set out in the chantry certificate of 1548. Their primary purpose was to maintain a priest "to Synge Divine Service in the said Chappell for ever'. They were also charged with the duty of distributing alms to the poor and prisoners, but the rest of the income from their lands and endowments was to be "bestowed toward the maynteynance and reparyng of the Bridge of Bristowe aforesaid, piers, arches and walls there for the defence thereof agaynste the Rages of Sea, ebbynge and flowing daylie under the same". At the time of the suppression the annual income of the chapel was £27 6s 0d, of which 10s 0d was distributed to the poor each year. The chantry priest was Thomas King, aged 44, who received £6 per annum. Ornaments and goods of the chapel were valued at £7 11s 0d. There were 20 ounces of plate and 3 fodders (58 cwts.) of lead covering the roof.[22]

---

[20] T. P. Wadley, *op.cit.*, 149–50.

[21] At St Nicholas the celebrations took place on the Feast of the Invention of the Holy Cross (*Inventio Sancte Crucis*) on 3 May.

[22] S. Seyer, *Memoirs Historical & Topographical of Bristol*, Bristol, 1823, II, 38–42.

THE PARISH CLERKS

An agreement recorded in the vestry book of St Nicholas in 1481 throws much light on the often shadowy figures of the parish clerks and specifies their duties precisely. Incidentally, the clauses provide a remarkable picture of the active life of the church, the regular daily round of services, the festivals and special occasions, the number of clergy and other staff employed in the church, the amount of bell-ringing, and, above all, the care with which the church was kept. The details contained in this rare and informative agreement would have been totally destroyed with the rest of the records of St Nicholas in 1940 if their importance had not earlier been recognised by E. G. Cuthbert F. Atchley. In 1905 he read a paper entitled "Medieval Parish Clerks in Bristol" to the St Paul's Ecclesiological Society, and this was subsequently printed in the Society's *Transactions*.[23] It includes a transcript of the St Nicholas agreement of 1481. Parish clerks were important minor officials in medieval parish churches. They were in minor orders, but were permitted to marry. At St Nicholas during the later Middle Ages the church was served by a clerk, an assistant who was known as a suffragan, and there are occasional references to an under-suffragan and a sexton. The original duties of the parish clerk and his assistants included reading the psalms with the priest, answering the responses and reading the epistle, and teaching the children. At St Nicholas, the clerks performed these duties, but also had other tasks. These are precisely specified in the agreement of 1481 which was drawn up by a notary public, Richard Blewet. It is headed

> "Howe the Clerke and the Suffrigan of St Nicholas Churche Aught to do In the sayde Church after the use laudable of years paste and the Agreement nowe of all the worshypfull of the paryshe the yere of Our Lord MCCCCLXXXI".

Why the agreement was drawn up at this time and carefully copied into the vestry book is unknown, and there is no reference to any dispute over the Clerk's duties. It lists the functions and duties to be performed by the clerk and his suffragan in detail with financial penalties specified for any failures. In a few of the quotations the spelling of the original has been modernised and the contractions extended.

Each evening the suffragan was to fasten the church doors and search the church "for fear of sleepers". Next morning he was carefully to set open the doors, check and put fresh oil in the two lamps, and clean water in the holy water stoup. The suffragan was to ring the first bell both for mattins and "evensonges", and the clerk was to ring the second bell, "and bothe at the Ryngyng of the last pele".

> "The Saturday the Clerke and the suffragann to ring None with ii belles, a pele of leyneth (length) convenient with-owte any fayle excepte dowbyll (double) Festes under payne of iiii d to each that fayles in this same'.

Every Saturday the suffragan was to sprinkle the church with water and make it clean, under pain of 6d for every failure. He was also to prepare the crowde, the stairway leading to the upper church and the church doors. Both clerk and suffragan were to "leye forthe the bokes in the quire", before Mattins and Evensong, and to

---

[23] E. G. C. F. Atchley, *St Paul's Ecclesiological Society Transactions*, V, 1905, 107–116.

put them away securely clasped after the services were ended. At the principal feasts when incense was used in the services, the clerk and suffragan were to ensure that the copes worn by the priests at the censing of the altars were laid out, and were put away, neatly folded, afterwards. Also at the principal feasts they were to see that the altar frontals and curtains were in place, and that the altars and statues were clean "to see Copppeweste (cobwebs) avoyded and duste from altars and imagery under payne of vi d". The suffragan was to assist the priest with putting on his cope and with the incense.

Every quarter the clerk and suffragan were to sweep the windows, walls and pillars "under payne of iiii d to eche of them as ofte as they fayle". At nine o'clock each evening the suffragan was to ring the curfew with one bell for a full quarter of an hour. This was the curfew for the whole town. At the feast of St Nicholas the clerk and suffragan were to prepare the throne for the boy-bishop. This important feature of church life at St Nicholas will be described later in this account.

For the important drama of the Easter Sepulchre, when the Sacred Host and a crucifix were ceremonially buried on Good Friday evening and watched over until they were restored to the altar on Easter Sunday morning, the clerk and suffragan were to prepare the Sepulchre and receive vi d for their supper. They were also to tend the light which hung over the Easter Sepulchre and receive iiii d for their dinner. For mass each day the suffragan was to ensure that the wine and water were ready and the book (missal) and chalice were placed on the altar "under the payne of ii d".

The clerk and suffragan, wearing their surplices at the altar, were to receive the vicar's chasuble and other ornaments, and were to ensure that they were folded and put away "when Mass ys donn". At the elevation of the Host during mass the clerk was to ensure that the sacring bell was rung. The suffragan was responsible for ringing the bell at "Our lady mass in lent". In an interesting entry, the suffragan was also given the task of "Ryngyng for Dundore under payne of vi d", that is to ring the church bells during a thunderstorm in the widespread belief that this would avert God's anger and drive away the storm.

The clerk was to provide "springals" for sprinkling holy water, and to carry the holy water for sprinkling the church "to every house, abydyng soo convenient a space that every man may receyve hys Holywater". During visitation of the sick, the suffragan was to accompany the priest and carry the surplice, book, holy oil and stole. During his absence the clerk was to safeguard the church.

Each day the clerk was to sing or read the Epistle during mass, "to synge in Redynge the Epistele Dayly". During Lent, when Evensong was conducted earlier, a separate peal on the bells was required before Compline, and this was part of the clerk's responsibilites. The suffragan was responsible for preparing the burning coal or charcoal for the censors, and for replenishing the oil in the lamps within the church "as often-times as needith". He was to ensure that albs, amices, towels and altar cloths were washed and ready for each festival. The costs of washing to be borne by the churchwardens. The clerk was to ring the bells for the service of None "with a solempne and a convenient pele in length" at 3.00pm, and to ring the curfew at the principal feasts when it was rung at 8.00pm instead of 9.00pm.

The suffragan was to warn the churchwardens when the censors, candlesticks and "ship" or vessels to hold the incense were required, presumably so that these valuas "laudable customs . . . to the honour and comen wele of this worshipful towne and all the inhabitants of the same'. Various later sources have preserved some of the entries in the records of St Nicholas which relate to the boy bishop. The inventory of church goods made in 1432 lists a mitre and "a crowch" or crozier for the boy bishop. The churchwardens' accounts included payments for putting up hangings in the church, to "dressing the bishop's gate" and to decorating the bishop's stall. Sadly, no record survives of any of the sermons preached by the boy bishops at St Nicholas.

The ceremony of the boy bishop did not survive the early stages of the Reformation. In July 1541 Henry VIII's government issued a Royal Proclamation which ordered that the ancient and colourful ceremony which was enacted in several parish churches and cathedrals, should be discontinued immediately. The Proclamation alleged that

"... children be strangelie decked and apparayled to counterfeit priestes, bishoppes, and women, and so be led with songs and daunces from house to house, blessing the people and gathering of money; and boyes do singe masse and preache in the pulpitt, with such other unfittinge and inconvenient usages, rather to the derision than any true glory of God, or honour of his saintes."

THE CHURCHWARDENS' ACCOUNTS

Included in the medieval records of St Nicholas which were destroyed in November 1940 were churchwardens' accounts beginning in 1520; separate accounts kept by the proctors for the crowde or crypt for the years 1523, 1531 and 1548; and some accounts of the Chapel of St John the Evangelist on Welsh Back for 1548. The notes made on these various accounts by E.G. Cuthbert F. Atchley and by J.F. Nicholls and John Taylor provide a good indication of the layout, services and colourful appearance of St Nicholas, and of the lively church life in which revolved around it.

Income was derived from shops, houses and other property in Bristol and from occasional collections or "gatherings". There were, for example, gatherings for lights before various statues, for Our Lady mass, and on Good Friday. Rents for seats or pews in the nave or in one of the galleries provided a source of income, as did payments for burials within the crowde and charges for the use of the processional cross at funerals. Regular payments were made for decorating the church with holly, yew or rosemary at Christmas and Easter, for "palms" or sprigs of willow, flowers and other greenery on Palm Sunday and for wine given to the priests and clerks that sang the Passion in the rood loft. Other recurring charges included payments to men who watched the Easter Sepulchre during the liturgical drama of Good Friday, Holy Saturday and Easter Sunday.

Money was also spent on the elaborate structure of the Easter Sepulchre and on coals to warm those who watched over it, enacting the role of the soldiers ordered by Pilate to guard the tomb of Christ. As with other Bristol churches, the expense of the elaborate annual Corpus Christi procession was considerable. Large sums each year had to be spent on wax for the numerous candles and other votive lights. For example, the accounts for Easter 1524 record the purchase of eight altar candles weighing between 2 lbs and 3 lbs, two large candles weighing 10 lbs for the high altar, the paschal candle weighing $22\frac{1}{2}$ lbs, two font tapers weighing 8 lbs, two "tapers for the angels", weighing 3 lbs, and the light kept burning before the Easter Sepulchre. The large paschal candle which was kept alight between Easter and the Ascension was part of an elaborate construction, and as late as 1542–43 there are references to

"a yard and di, of tafeta for to make stremers for the pascall .... iiii s
for iiii yards of blekyd clothe for the pascall tre .... xv d".

There were regular expenses for the processions at Corpus Christi and on St George's Day and Michaelmas.

Finally there were annual payments to priests for celebrating the "obits" or memorial masses which had been endowed by past benefactors. There were more than ten of these, including a mass for "All Good Doers" on St Martin's Eve (10 November).

The altar dedicated to the Virgin Mary in the upper church was an important focus of popular devotion, and is constantly referred to in the churchwardens's accounts. For example, in 1520 there are references to the employment of a priest (Sir Robert) at £6 13s 4d a year, and to extra payments to him for conducting additional services. Some revenue was also received from offerings.

"In primis, recevyd for our lady lyght .... vii s vi d
Gatheryd for our lady masse .... v s vi d
Paid Syr Robert for singing our lady masse in lente .... vi s iii d
For mending the whyt vestments of our lady awter .... ii d ob".

There are references to four altars in the upper church, including the high altar, and three altars in the crypt, as well as two organs. In 1541, the organs in the church were repaired. Surplices had to be provided for the parish clerks and for the boys in the choir. For example, in 1522 the second clerk's surplice cost 4s 4d, and in 1522 the wardens paid "for mendyng a childes surplis belonyng to the choir 1d." Evidently the surplices and other church linen were washed by the sexton's wife, for the 1530 accounts include the following:

"Item to the sexton for his yere wages .... xxii s iiii d
Item to his wyffe for washing of the churche gere .... viiii s
Item more to his wyffe for skoring .... iii s iiii d".

The last item relates to the annual task of scouring or thoroughly cleaning the wax-encrusted candlesticks.

Remarkably, the church possessed a public toilet just outside the north door, and the accounts for 1524 included payments for repairing "the pissinge place with-oute the churche Durre".

On May Day there were parish revels which involved Robin Hood and Little John. The costs in 1520 included payments to the minstrels "for mete and drink for the Kyng and the qweyn and all theire company". In 1526 the churchwardens paid for "two pair of hosyn for Robin Hood and Lytyll John, vi s and for lyning of the same viii d".

It would be unwise to take this as a typical celebration of the feast. The participation of both the king and the bishop of the diocese made it extremely unusual. It was probably the only time the monarch was in the city for Corpus Christi and, as Bristol was on the very edge of the diocese, the bishop visited it very infrequently. It could be argued that the mayor and chief citizens were there only because of the presence of the king. All the parish processions may not have come together usually and St Augustine may not always have been the destination of the procession.

Medieval Bristol was such a compact city and its eighteen parish churches within and just outside the walls were so close together that it is difficult to imagine that each parish could have had a separate outdoor procession on the same day within its own boundaries. The presumption must be that there was one procession for the whole city especially if the mayor and city council and the city guilds took part. There are in fact payments in the churchwardens' accounts of All Saints in 1468–69 for the "berynge up of the beste cros on Corpus Christi days at the procesione abowte the towne" and in 1515–16 under the costs for Corpus Christi day "for beyring of the Shryne to ij fryers abowte the paryshes",[6] which seem to confirm it. The only fact that suggests otherwise is that at least three parishes had vessels in which to carry the Blessed Sacrament on that day. All Saints had a monstrance given by Thomas Halleway, who died in 1454, and his wife Joan, a "worschypfull Jewell with ij Angelys y-callyd a monstrande to ber the precyouse Sacrament with dyverys Relykys [relics] closyd yn the same of lvij unces and Quarter", to which description a later version of the bede-roll adds "on Corpus Christi day".[7]

St John's, according to an inventory of 1471, had a silver gilt cup weighing $38\frac{1}{2}$ ounzes "for the sacrement on Corpus [Christi] Daye"[8] and St Stephen's listed in its 1494 inventory "an emayge off our lady that the Sacramentte is boryne ynn onn Corpus-day christi wythe a Tabarnakle [and] angels, off Sylvyre, y-ameld [enamelled] and alle gyld, weying j^{c}l honces [150 ozs]". The Host was apparently borne as it were in our Lady's womb.

Strangely none of the inventories of these parishes lists in its inventories a canopy to carry over the shrine or monstrance during the procession, as was widely the custom in the fifteenth century. Only Christchurch lists in its 1555 inventory "a grete canopy of saten of Brygges [Bruges] to bere over the sacrament." When Queen Mary came to the throne and Catholic practices were restored, the churchwardens either bought back a canopy which had been sold in Edward VI's time or had a new one made. There is a reference in the 1554 accounts "Pd to Mr Watley ffor the canabe xxxviijd" and three years later, a payment "for iiij staves to beare the canabye"[9]

It could be that the parishes took it in turn year by year to be responsible for carrying the Host.

    [6] Bristol Record Office, hereafter BRO, P/AS/Ch W 3.
    [7] BRO P/AS/ChW/1 fols 137, 164. E.G.Cuthbert F. Atchley "Some more Bristol Inventories" in *Transactions of St Paul's Ecclesiological Society* 9 (1922) hereafter Atchley (1922) 19 *The Pre-Reformation Records of All Saints, Bristol Part I* ed. Clive Burgess, Bristol Record Society's Publications Vol. XLVI (1995), hereafter Burgess, 14, 28.
    [8] BRO P/StS/ChW/1 fol 4; Atchley (1992) 40.
    [9] Rubin 252–55.

Martha Skeeters, however, in a recent book has argued that All Saints was always responsible, at least for the period from 1498 to 1538. The evidence she adduces is that "In 1498 the parish of All Saints began paying two friars to bear the shrine holding the sacrament in their contingent of the Corpus Christi Day procession . . . This practice continued until the surrender of the friaries in 1538 . . . It is conceivable that a reference to "shrine" rather than "tabernacle" year after year indicated the parish's relics rather than the sacrament. However the entry for 1499 specifically refers to bearing the sacrament in the Corpus Christi Day procession and the entry for Palm Sunday in 1512 refers to the sacrament in the shrine." She says that "None of the other parishes record payment for carriage of the sacrament [and] this is an important fact, for it indicates that the parishes did not have separate processions". Unfortunately this is not quite true. In the accounts of St Mary Redcliffe which cannot be dated precisely but are said to be "about 1520" there is a payment to "ij friars for bearing of the shrine xvjd" but this may have been very exceptional.[10]

All Saints indeed had "a shrine in the which to bear the blessed sacrament in and holy relics on certain days of the year" one of them being Corpus Christi day. The shrine does not appear in any of the inventories but is referred to in the list of do-gooders. John Jenkins alias Stainer, who was churchwarden in 1480-81 and again in 1483, paid 33s 4d to have it gilded.[11] All parishes, however, must have had a shrine or some such for the procession of the Blessed Sacrament and relics on Palm Sunday and they rarely appear in inventories, unless they were of precious metal.[12]

It is not clear why All Saints paid the friars to carry the shrine for forty years, as Skeeters admits. She suggests that "All Saints probably was given the honoured position among the parish contingents because of the communal quality of its dedication, all saints and all souls suggesting the unity and continuity of the Christian community".[13] If St Augustine's Abbey were the destination of the procession, the fact that All Saints was in the gift of the Abbey might be relevant, although so were St Nicholas, St Leonard and St Augustine the Less.[14]

The reason may be that All Saints was the base of the Guild of Kalenders. Its chantry priests used All Saints' altars and one was clerk of the parish for twenty eight years.[15] There is no surviving evidence that it was connected with the Corpus Christi celebrations in any significant way. Its records were destroyed "by mischance", possibly in a fire in 1463–64 and on four occasions between 1501 and 1506 All Saints paid the prior or "ij prists of the calendars" for taking part in the procession.[16] However William Worcestre in 1497 surprisingly says of the college or

[10] BRO P/StS/ChW/1 E. G. Cuthbert F. Atchley "Some Inventories of the Parish Church of St Stephen, Bristol" in *Transactions of St Paul's Ecclesiological Society* 6, 163, 167.

[11] BRO P/Xch/CW/1(a)

[12] Martha C. Skeeters *Community and Clergy : Bristol and the Reformation c 1530–c 1570* (1993), hereafter Skeeters, pp 18f, and n.44 on 212; BRO P/StMR/C/5b *Bristol and its Environs* (1875), 122–23.

[13] Burgess 22,30.

[14] Such as the elaborate shrine given to the Corpus Christi Guild in York in 1449 *Archaeologia* 10 (1792), 469–71.

[15] Skeeters 213, 218.

[16] Skeeters 70; C.S. Taylor "The Chronological Sequence of the Bristol Parish Churches" in *Trans BGS* 32 (1909), 211.

Fraternity of Kalendars that it was "vocate et fundate in honore festi Corporis christi".[17] This could not possibly be so as the Guild goes back to the Anglo-Saxon period on his own evidence, centuries before the feast was instituted, but in his own time it must have honoured the feast in some significant way for him to have described it in these words. Many towns and cities had a Corpus Christi guild which assisted in the celebrations, as at Beverley where the Corpus Christi fraternity was charged with the procession's organisation and led it through the town.[18] Perhaps the Guild of Kalendars was the equivalent. It was originally Bristol's chief religious guild and doubtless for a long time its only one. Its membership included both laity and clergy and the mayor was its patron and protector. It has been said that "crafts [ie guilds] were assisted by the friars in organising the Corpus Christi celebrations" elsewhere although little evidence is given[19] Certainly the friars received payments in Exeter but it was probably for wine.[20]

St Augustine's in some ways seems an unlikely goal for the Corpus Christi procession as it was outside the city walls, although not far outside. The only other large church was St Mary Redcliffe which was also outside the city and indeed in another diocese. St Augustine's never won much respect from Bristolians. They made generous bequests to their parish churches, to the four Bristol friaries and the local hospitals and almshouses, and even token gifts to the Cathedral in Worcester but few left anything to the abbey.[21]

There are references in churchwardens' accounts from various parishes of payments for the expenses involved in celebrating Corpus Christi. In some cases they are listed under a separate heading, which indicates the importance and expense of its celebration[22] It is not easy to interpret the accounts because many which survive are only copies. Very few of the original paper drafts, which probably contained more detail, survive.[23] The surviving copy of the accounts of St John's for 1541–42 has a note to the costs for Corpus Christi and Easter "as hyt aperyth more playner by particular summes In the paper boke . . ."[24]

There are many references of payments for bearing cross and banner on Corpus Christi day in parish accounts but in the accounts of St Ewen there are references to "bearing the banner to St Austins" in 1477–78, 1481–86 and 1488–89. In the last case the entry reads : "Item for berying of the baner in the rogacyon weke and to seynt Auston when the hoffer the baners iiijd". As none of the other entries are specifically connected with Corpus Christi one might assume they all refer to the Rogationtide procession. In the 1485–86 accounts, however, there are two entries "Item for berynge of Baneres in the Rogacion weke iijd" and "Item for berynge of the baner to seynt Augustyn jd". The other entries may, then, refer to the total

[17] N. Orme "The Guild of Kalendars" in *Trans BGAS* 96 (1978), 38.

[18] BRO P/AS/ChW/3 1501–2, 1502–3, 1504–5, 1505–6.

[19] *William Worcestre : The Topography of Medieval Bristol* ed. Frances Neale. Bristol Records Society Publication Vol 51 (2000), hereafter William Worcestre, 387.

[20] Rubin 232–43.

[21] Rubin 260.

[22] A.G. Little and R.C. Easterling *The Franciscans and Dominicans of Exeter* (1927), 26.

[23] Joseph Bettey "St Augustine's Abbey" in *Bristol Cathedral. History and Architecture* ed. John Rogan (2000), 330.

[24] eg BRO P/AS/ChW/3; P/Xch/ChW/1(a); P/StJB/ChW/1(a).

annual payments to the banner bearers, one being for the Corpus Christi procession which ended at St Augustine's. The following year's accounts, covering the visit of Henry VII, seem to confirm this for they also have two entries : "Item for berynge of the baner to seynt Austyn jd". "Item for berynge of the Baners for Rogacion weke iijd" (the words "to Seynt" after "Baners" having been struck through as if the scribe had realised the banners did not go to St Augustine's during the Rogationtide procession).[25]

Some places had a traditional processional way which was used for royal or episcopal entries and also for the Corpus Christi procession. Some others, the more common, followed the boundaries or linked the periphery to the centre, the parishes to the cathedral, the suburbs to the market place.[26] There are a few medieval Bristol deeds which could refer to one in Bristol. A Christchurch deed refers to "a way called the Procession Way" and a St Ewen's deed to "a processional way" but they are more likely to refer to routes for processions round the church building or the parish boundary. The latter explicitly refers to a right reserved to St Ewen's.[27]

Earlier local historians have assumed the High Cross in the centre of the city was the focus of the Corpus Christi procession. John Taylor spoke of it as "the rallying standard on occasions of public ceremony and on the celebrations of religious festivals" of which he thought Corpus Christi was the greatest. Alderman Francis Fox actually said in a passage, which Taylor later quoted without qualification, "it was customary for the company to go in procession to the High Cross". The judicious Latimer in his description of the feast avoided all mention of the route of the procession.[28] There is no mention of the High Cross in connection with Corpus Christi in any churchwardens' accounts but it could well have been the meeting point for the various components of the procession if its destination were St Augustine's.

It is interesting that if the Corpus Christi procession did normally end at St Augustine's, it must have left the city through St John's Gate, gone over the river Frome and along the street now called very appropriately Host Street. "Before the making of the drawbridge [c 1714], this street was the unavoidable line of route from St John's Gate to the Great House or St Augustine's Abbey"[29] Unfortunately it does not seem to have been so called before the nineteenth century. It appears as Horse Street on Benjamin Donne junior's New and Correct Plan of Bristol, dated 1800. William Worcestre knew it as Hore Street, possibly after William Hore Mayor

---

[25] See Introduction to *The Church Book of St Ewen's Bristol 1454–1584*. Transcribed and edited by Betty R. Masters and Elizabeth Ralph. Records Section of the Bristol and Gloucestershire Archaeological Society. (1967) hereafter Masters and Ralph, xvii f.

[26] BRO P/StJB/ChW/1 (b) i, 87 transcription of St John's Church Book by Revd Potto Hicks.

[27] Masters and Ralph, 102, 110, 118, 120, 124. I have presumed to read "baner" instead of "barer" in the penultimate reference in spite of the transcribers' opinion. For the importance of the Rogationtide processions see [Eamon Duffy *The Stripping of the Altars* (1992), hereafter Duffy, 279.

[28] Rubin 267f.

[29] Roger H. Leech *The Topography of Medieval and Early Modern Bristol* Bristol Record Society's Publications Vol XLVIII, 49, 58, Masters and Ralph, 256. Another instance is a court case in 1489 relating to St John's procession path Atchley (1922), 37 n. 3. Roger Leech kindly pointed out to me that a plan drawn by William Halfpenny dated 4 June 1742 (BRO 04479 (2) fol. 64a) marks a Procession Way in two places.

in 1312[30] and it is so called, in the two surviving compotus rolls of the Abbey in 1491–92 and 1511–12[31] J. Dallaway, in his 1834 edition of William Worcestre's account of medieval Bristol, records a tradition, though only to dismiss it, that the Host was carried in procession along the street. "Hore-street was at first corrupted into Horse-street, now, by a pretended correction, it is written and called Host-street, because, it is said, that the Host was carried in procession through it. This was not done exclusively, for whenever the ceremony was required for any person 'in articulo mortis', it was taken to him through any street in the town." Dallaway and John Taylor, who uses the same argument, were quite right. The viaticum could be taken anywhere, wherever there was someone in extremis.[32] What neither seems to have realised, however, is that the tradition could relate to the Corpus Christi procession rather than the last rites. This, together with the fact that the tradition predates both Catholic Emancipation and the influence of the Oxford Movement in the Church of England when such a tradition would have been appreciated or might even have been invented, make it more likely that it could be an authentic memory.

There seems, then, to be at least a possibility that the Corpus Christi procession went to St Augustine's Abbey. It is odd that only the St Ewen's churchwardens' accounts actually refer to St Augustine's but the detail is totally irrelevant to the costs of the celebrations. From a tantalising brief summary of the accounts of St Nicholas, which were destroyed in the second World War, it appears that processions on other feasts went to the abbey, in 1545 on St George's day "to the trynyte colege," and in 1547 on Michaelmas day, "pd ffor berying of Copes on myghellmas daye to the Colege iiijd". These entries date from after the dissolution of the monastries, when the abbey had become a cathedral in 1542. It could be argued that they had always gone there, although in 1542 the St George's day procession in fact went to Christchurch, but of course it could also be argued that they went there only after 1542 when the abbey had become the cathedral of the new diocese.[33]

The participants in the Corpus Christi day procession in Bristol are the subject of some disagreement. The only group for which there is plentiful evidence is the parish parties. The surviving churchwardens accounts, almost invariably include payments for the carrying of a cross and banner. There are payments for the attendance of priests (in one case as many as eight),[34] of deacons and subdeacons in their copes, dalmatics and tunicles, and of clerks or sextons. There are less frequent references to children carrying candlesticks, thuribles and ships (incense boats), sometimes to them singing. In one instance we are told they were singing "Salve

[30] F. Fox "The History of the Guilds of Bristol" in *Trans BGAS*, 3 (1878–9), 95; John Taylor *A Book about Bristol* (1872), hereafter Taylor, 272; J.F. Nicholls and John Taylor *Bristol Past and Present* hereafter Nicholls and Taylor Vol II   (1881), 257; John Latimer *Sixteenth Century Bristol* 1908, hereafter Latimer I, 5f.

[31] Taylor, 353.

[32] William Worcestre, 18, 42, 46, 176, 180, 186, 206]. Robert Ricart refers to it in 1491 as Horsstrete [Robert Ricart *The Maire of Bristowe Is Kalendar* ed. Lucy Toulmin Smith. Camden Society (1892), hereafter Ricart's Kalendar, 47.

[33] *Two Compotus Rolls of Saint Augustine's Abbey, Bristol* ed. Gwen Beachcroft and Arthur Sabin. Bristol Record Society's Publications Vol IX, (1938), 96, 97, 158, 161, 175.

[34] J. Dallaway *Antiquities of Bristol in the Middle Centuries including the topography by William Wycestre and the Life of William Canynges* (1834), 55n; John Taylor, 354.

festa dies", a hymn known to have been sung in other places.[35] There are references to the carrying of torches from time to time. At St Mary Redcliffe in about 1520 four "flowered" torches and four "unflowered" torches were carried.[36] St Nicholas actually had a bequest from Robert de Otry, for the annual purchase of two torches weighing 16 lbs of wax for Corpus Christi day.[37]

In most places the trade guilds participated in the Corpus Christi procession and indeed in some cases organised it.[38] Fox, Taylor and Latimer all accept that the guilds took part in Bristol but Martha Skeeters concluded that "the procession in Bristol appears to have been primarily ecclesiastical" although she qualifies this elsewhere by saying "apparently ... only the Bakers' Guild participated probably because of the obvious connection between the host and baking bread".[39] The Bakers Company Book does indeed have entries in 1538 "For beryng of the pagentt [pageant] on Corpus Christi day iiijd ... Item for the beryng of the torches xijd".[40] She has, however, overlooked important evidence in the Little Red Book of Bristol in which the ordinances of the trade guilds were entered and subsequent amendments recorded. There is clear proof that at least five other guilds, including some of the most important, processed and carried a light, namely the Weavers, the Shoemakers (Cordwainers), the Coopers (Hoopers), the Barbers and the Mariners.

The earliest reference concerns the Weavers. According to their 1419 ordinances "toutz les meistres et servants de dit art" were to take part in the "generalx processions" and contribute "a toutz maners, coustages et despences queux serront faitz en après sur lour lumier et torches encontre les festes de Corpus Christi, Nativitee Seint John le Baptistre, dez Appostles Petre et Powle." The Shoemakers complained to the Mayor and Common Council on two occasions, in 1425 and 1429, of their difficulty in maintaining their "ancient" practice "davoir lour lumier en le fest de Corpus Christi ardant en la procession generalle en lonour de sacrement". Eventually, in 1453, it was agreed that it was the responsibility of the journeymen cobblers to find the money for it, and for a light to our Lady in St Mary Redcliffe. The Barbers and the Coopers made similar complaints in 1439 about the problem with their lights "brennyng in the fest of Corporis Christi in the generall processione in honoure of the blessed sacrament." In 1445, ordinances were registered with the Mayor and Council establishing the Hospital of St Bartholomew and a Fraternity of Mariners which supported it. They include a general rule "that every Mayster and Mariner that longeth to the seyd porte at every ffeste of corpus christi be redy in

[35] E.G.Cuthbert F. Atchley "On the Mediaeval Parish Records of the Church of St Nicholas Bristol" in *Transactions of St Paul's Ecclesiological Society* hereafter Atchley (1906), 56.

[36] Nicholls and Taylor II, 163

[37] BRO P/AS/Ch W/3 1514–15; Rubin 246.

[38] BRO P/St MR/ Ch W/5b cf D. Rock *The Church of our Fathers* ed. G. W. Hart and W. H. Frere (1905), Vol II, 342 and J. C. Cox *Churchwardens' Accounts* (1913), 238–41.

[39] Atchley (1906), 45.

[40] Rubin 258, 261.

[41] Skeeters 28, 217.

[42] BRO 08155 (1) fol 77.

[43] *The Little Red Book of Bristol* ed. F. B. Bickley (1900) Vol 1 xxi-xxii, Vol II 121f, 145, 148f, 151, 155, 165, 188. cf W. Hunt *Historic Towns : Bristol* (2nd edition 1887), hereafter Hunt, 82f.

[44] *op.cit.* Vol II, 84f, 173, 115.

hys beste araye to go in procession with the lyth of the seyd crafte during the seyd procession in the worschup of God, of the Holy Sacramen, oure lady Seint Mary, and alle the holy compayne of Hevyn".[45] To this list of five guilds which took part in the procession with the Bakers, should probably be added two more, the Dyers and Tanners. The ordinances relating to them in the Little Red Book do not specifically refer to Corpus Christi or indeed any procession but they lay down that part of the money paid in fines should be used for the maintenance of their lights. This regulation was made for the dyers in 1407 and re-enacted in 1439, and for the Tanners in 1415, in the last instance "de lour lumier a diverses temps del an".[46]

It seems highly likely, then, that all the guilds took part in the Corpus Christi procession, dressed like the Mariners in their best clothes, and carrying their lights (which seem to have been quite distinct from the more numerous torches). There is no surviving evidence in some cases but, except for the chance survival of the Bakers Company Book, we should not have known that they took part as the Little Red Book is silent where they are concerned.

Latimer and even the more expansive Alderman Fox were silent about the participation of the Mayor and town officials in the Corpus Christi procession, presumably because they could find no reference to it in the records. Skeeters thought that "it is difficult to believe that the municipal authorities participated when the procession is not mentioned in the Mayor's Kalendar and no payment for it is made in the city's audits which are extant from 1532", and concluded that "the secular leadership ... avoided the Corpus Christi procession." She even speculated that "participation risked a reading or reception of the procession by observers that was not to the corporate elite's advantage".[47] Ricart's Kalendar, however, lists the Mayor's commitments for only a quarter of the year, from September to December, and, as Latimer pointed out in 1908, "the chief financial business was in the hands of the Sheriffs, whose accounts have not been preserved".[48] There is a list of the sheriff's expenses submitted to Star Chamber in 1518, recorded in the Great White Book of Bristol, but it does not include any expenses specifically for Corpus Christi.[49] However, a 1516 ordinance of the town council decrees that any member of the council who is a former mayor or sheriff and absents himself from "any common assembly for the worshipp of the town" shall be fined 40d or 20d respectively. The "sundry tymes" on which failure "to accumpany the Mayor" (as a note in the margin puts it) incurs a fine, specifically include the "Corpus Christi procession".[50] There can be little doubt then, that the Mayor and town officials if not the whole council processed with the parish parties and the trade guilds in the Corpus Christi procession. There is no surviving evidence that the council regulated the procession, laying down the order in which the guilds were to process as happened in some towns such

---

[45] Skeeters, 28–30,218.

[46] Latimer I, 11.

[47] *The Great White Book of Bristol* ed. Elizabeth Ralph Bristol Record Society Publications XXXII (1979), 72–74, 77–78.

[48] *The Ordinances of Bristol 1506–1598* ed. Maureen Stanford Bristol Record Society Publications Vol XLI (1990), 11.

[49] Rubin, 261, 263.

[50] Duffy, 44.

as York[51] or decreeing that the streets should be decorated.[52] There is evidence in churchwardens' accounts, however, that church bells were rung during the procession, as happened elsewhere.[53] Most of the evidence is for the reign of Queen Mary when the feast was restored after its suppression under Edward VI, but sixteen ringers were paid 5s 4d in about 1520 at St Mary Redcliffe and the Churchwardens at St John's in 1540 "payd for Rengen ijd".[54]

Very little is known about the order of the procession. One hint that the Mayor and council processed behind the guilds as on other holy days comes in the address of the Shoemakers in 1425 to the mayor, sheriff, bailiffs and members of the Common Council claiming their right to have their light on the feast of Corpus Christi burning in the general procession in honour of the Sacrament "et auxi daler devant les Mair et Viscont en les veilles del Natwitke de seint John Baptiste et des Appostles Petre et Paule en lonour de mesmes lez Seints, et all reverence de vous et de toute la ville . . ."[55]

Latimer boldly states that, after the procession, "the afternoon was spent in the performance in the open air of miracle plays, in which every craft claimed its special part, to the enjoyment of the whole community".[56] Historians of drama have been fascinated by the Corpus Christi plays which began to appear in the fourteenth century, but none of them has been able to find any clear evidence of them in Bristol. Only four cycles survive, the York, Coventry and Chester plays and the Townley cycle, perhaps to be associated with Wakefield. Some have tried to find a link between the plays of Coventry and Bristol and suggested that as Bristol and Coventry were both cloth towns and some members of the Coventry guilds were Bristolians, the Coventry plays may have been performed in Bristol by the Weavers and other companies.[57] Dublin, too, had Corpus Christi plays, and as it has been suggested that the Easter play at Dublin came from Bristol, from St Augustine's Abbey, the Corpus Christi plays may have come from Bristol.[58] These cycles, however, are probably not typical. The Corpus Christi play had many and varied manifestations. As one scholar put it, "Our detailed knowledge is slight though references, in church account books, for example, are many. There were plays inside church, and in the market place, plays organised by churchwardens and parish clergy, by the Corporations of towns or by religious guilds, and even some performed, in later years, by professional companies".[58] Churchwardens' accounts in other places show expenses for hospitality for players and payments for costumes on Corpus Christi day[59] but none have come to light in Bristol. There is however,

[51] Rubin, 248; BRO P/StJB/ChW/1(b) 1540; P/StMR/ChW/1(A); P/StT/ChW1 1554 FOL 66 1554; Gloucester Public Library, Hockaday Transcripts St Mary le Port, Churchwardens' Accounts 1558.

[52] BRO P/StMR/C/5(B); P/StJ/ChW/1b,79.

[53] *The Little Red Book* Vol II, 145.

[54] Latimer I, 5–6.

[55] Hunt, 109. The idea was taken up by G. T. Watts *Theatrical Bristol* (1915), 6.

[56] W. S. Clark *Early Irish Stage* (1955), 10–13; Diane Dolan *Le Drame liturgique de Pâques en Normandie et en Angleterre au moyen age* (1975), 168–70.

[57] R. T. Davies *The Corpus Christi Play of the English Middle Ages* (1972), 18.

[58] Rubin 279; Cox *Churchwardens Accounts* (1913), 280–84.

[59] Hutton 31–33, 60, 67.

some evidence of plays at other times of the year. The Robin Hood play, perhaps the most popular in England,[60] took place, probably as part of the May revels, at St Nicholas. In several years "hosyn for Robyn hoode and lytyll John" were provided.[61] Then there were the St Katherine players. They are mentioned only once, in Ricart's Kalendar. On St Katherine's eve (24 November) the Mayor and council were to go to evensong in St Katherine's chapel in Temple Church then to a feast in "Kateryn halle" (the Weaver's Hall near Temple Church) after which they were to return home "redy to recceyve at theire dores Seynt Kateryns Players making them to drynk at their dores and rewardyng them for theire playes".[62]

Apart from this there is nothing known of the players or their plays. The only link between players and the Corpus Christi celebrations which has so far come to light is a payment in the City Chamberlain's account for 1557 "to my lord Backleyes [Berkeley's] players for playinge before Mr Mayre and his bretherne vs." It was made on 18th June which in that year, was the day after the feast of Corpus Christi. The play, however, seems to have been in private, perhaps in the Guildhall. It was not part of the public celebrations.[63]

Pageants were also performed in Bristol. When Henry VII visited Bristol in 1486, pageants of various kinds were organised to greet him. At the Town Gate there was one "with great melodie and singing", and at the High Cross and at St John's Gate there were pageants which seem to have consisted only of lavishly dressed little girls, "many mayden children richely besene with girdells, beds and onches [beads and brooches]" and speeches by Prudence and Justice. Along what must have been Host Street, there was a pageant staged by one of the guilds, the Shipwrights, "with praty conceyts playing in the same without any speche" and another of a completely different kind, a mechanical model, a "pageante of an olifante with a castell on his bakk curiously wrought, the Resurrection of our lorde in the highest Tower of the same, with certeyne imagerye smyting of bellis, and al went by weights marveolously wele done".[64]

"Pageant" can also mean a wagon on which a play was performed[65] and this meaning has been given to the references to pageants in some Bristol records. One scholar says that "according to the minute books of several guilds . . . a number of crafts owned pageants which may have been used for performances on Corpus Christi or other feast days", a suggestion attributed by him to Elizabeth Ralph.[66] Fox, too interpreted "pageant", as a "stage on which the plays or mysteries of the Guilds were performed . . . and for this purpose was borne from place to place. The Bakers Company definitely had a pageant which was part of the Corpus Christi procession. In its book there are references in 1538 for "beryng of the pageant on Corpus Christy day iiijd."; and for "beryng of the torches   xijd; in 1544 to "a pageant with

---

[60] Atchley (1906) 67; Nicholls and Taylor II 162.

[61] Ricart's Kalendar 80.

[62] *City Chamberlains' Accounts in the Sixteenth and Seventeenth Centuries* ed. D. M. Livock Bristol Record Society's Publications Vol XXIV (1966), 39.

[63] *A Bristol Miscellany*, 4–5.

[64] Fox, 97.

[65] E. K. Chambers *The Mediaeval Stage* (1903) Vol II 136–38.

[66] D. H. Sacks "The demise of the Martyrs : the feasts of St Clement and St Katherine in Bristol, 1400–1600" in *Social History* 11 (1986), 142n.

iiij vanes of silk"; and in 1554 "for dressyng of the pagent and the staffe"vs; "for a torch to the same" xiiijd; for the berying of the same iiijd,[67] There is sufficient detail in this case for it to be clear that the Bakers' pageant was not a wagon—it cost less to carry than torches—but some kind of standard, occasionally dressed with small flags. It had nothing to do with Corpus Christi plays.

There were also minstrels in medieval Bristol which have sometimes been linked to the Corpus Christi celebrations. "The four minstrels of the town" are included in a list of those who were to have liveries provided at the expense of the town in an ordinance of 1391 in the Little Red Book, and in a fifteenth century list of the bailiff's payments the mayor is given five marks "for his minstrels".[68] Presumably they played at civic functions when the mayor was feasting and perhaps accompanied him when he was entertained in the halls of the guilds. The Bakers accounts for 1538 included a payment of 15s to "iiij mynstrelles", which comes very near to a reference to Corpus Christi day but that is the only indication that minstrels were in any way involved in the Corpus Christi celebrations.[69] It can hardly be used as evidence of Corpus Christi plays in Bristol.

A celebration would not be complete without a meal. The surviving churchwardens' accounts in Bristol contain many references to a dinner or breakfast amongst the costs of Corpus Christi day, the earliest being in the All Saints' accounts for 1456–57 "a dinner for the priests . . ." On occasion it is made clear that the parish paid for more than just the priests. All Saints in 1472–73 paid for the "priests and the clerks", St Ewen's in 1494–95 supplied "breakfast for the choir" and "wine for the parson's dinner" and in about 1520, St Mary Redcliffe bought bread, ale and "all manner of victuals" for the "priests, friars, clerks, deacons and children of the choir".[70]

Details of the food are not often given. St Ewen's accounts do so in three years, 1486–87, 1489–90 and 1490/91. In 1486–87, when Henry VII took part in the procession, there was bread, beef, mutton, lamb and chicken seasoned with spices, mustard and vinegar. In 1490–91 there was a goose as well. One of the few surviving medieval sets of accounts for St Mary Redcliffe, for 1554, lists beef, two cows "hengis" a calf's head and bacon.[71]

Not surprisingly costs for the dinner began to spiral. At All Saints in 1456–57 it cost 2s 4d and rose on one occasion, in 1478–79 to 8s 6d. At St Ewen's in 1457–58, the first time a dinner is mentioned, it cost 9½d; in 1483–84 it was 4s 4d.[72] St John's had the same problem and in 1471 it was agreed that "the procutors and wardens shall dispende over corpus Christi day in a diner to the parson prestis and clerkis that were att the procession with the pareshe and attended to the worship of the same iijs and no more and yf they do hitt shall be att ther owne coste".[73] St Ewen's made a similar decision in 1536 "by consent of the whole parishioners that

[67] BRO 08155(1), fols 77, 90, 111; BRO 08155(1), fols]

[68] *The Little Red Book* Vol I, 10; Vol II, 65.

[69] BRO 08155(1), fol 77.

[70] Burgess, BRS . . . 97; Masters and Ralph, . . .139; BRO P/St MR/C/5(b).

[71] Masters and Ralph, 120, 127, 130; BRO P/StMR/ChW/1(a), fol 66.

[72] Burgess, 97, 126, Masters and Ralph, 36, 115.

[73] BRO P/St JB/ChW/1(b)i, 19.

the proctor [warden] for the time being shall be allowed for the breakfast upon Corpus Christi day, 2s od for the parson, priests and clerks and the proctors and no more".[74] All Saints was even more drastic. Probably in the late fifteenth century, an ordinance was recorded "Item where it has been yearly used before this time that on Corpus Christi day on the church cost the proctors gave a dinner unto the vicar and the priests and the clerks, it is now agreed and ordained that from henceforward the dinner to be left and the vicar, the priests and the clerk for the time being to come on that day shall have of the proctors money, that is to say the vicar to have 8d, every priest of the church 4d and to the clerk 2d".[75]

The question may be asked when and where the dinner took place. The obvious time would seem to be after the procession and indeed in a few rare instances churchwardens' accounts do refer to "the dinner to the priests and clerks on Corpus Christi day after the procession", as in the All Saints' accounts for 1472–73 and the following year[76] In the three detailed accounts of the dinner for St Ewen's there is an item "for fewell and servauntes labour" which could indicate that the food was hot and therefore eaten indoors. In the sixteenth century in the accounts of All Saints after the abolition of the dinner there are payments for "wyne given in the Marshe".[77] There are similar entries in the accounts of St John's, "a potell of wyne in to the mersh" in 1537, and again in 1542 and 1543, and in those of St Thomas in 1544.[78] Could it be the case then that the dinner was a meal eaten outdoors after the procession in the Marsh in the same place where the wine was later drunk? It is an attractive theory as it might help to decide whether the procession did go to St Augustine's. The Marsh, however, had been divided since the diversion of the river Frome in the thirteenth century between the area now occupied by Queen Square and what until recently was known as Canons Marsh, and there was no bridge between them until a drawbridge was built in the eighteenth century.[79] If the eating and drinking after the procession was in Canons Marsh that would suggest the procession ended on College Green, but "the Marsh" would more probably mean the area on the town side of the Frome where archery practice and wrestling matches took place.[80] A payment in the St Mary Redcliffe churchwardens accounts for 1554 "for a pottell of secke [sack] for the quiar at the crose in the Marsh"[81] might provide a clue but crosses were erected in any open space. The drinking in the Marsh might have been something quite separate from the eating. It has been suggested, on the evidence of the All Saints' accounts, that "During the Corpus Christi procession there was a station or halt for wine, in the Marsh, during the sixteenth century, and after it was over, a dinner or breakfast (it is called both) was provided".[82] An entry in the Christchurch accounts for 1557 "Item for a pottell of

[74] Masters and Ralph, 169.

[75] Burgess 3.

[76] Burgess 112, 115.

[77] BRO P/AS/ChW/3. The first is actually 1498.

[78] BRO P.St JB/ChW/1(b)i 69, 92, 96; P/St T/ChW/1.

[79] Nicholls and Taylor I 122–23; Latimer *The Annals of Bristol in the Eighteenth Century* (1893) 99.

[80] Latimer I, 7.

[81] BRO P/StMR/ChW/5(b).

[82] E. G. Cuthbert F. Atchley "On the Parish Records of the Church of All Saints, Bristol" in *Trans BGAS* (1904), 271.

wyne upon Corpus christi day in pcession vjd" is most naturally interpreted so and the St Mary Redcliffe accounts in about 1520 could also be understood like this. The costs for Corpus Christi begin with the costs of breakfast including ale, and go on to payments to those taking part in the procession, ending with "for a pottle of wine in the Marsh". The 1554 costs, however, begin with payments to those taking part in the procession then comes the reference to the bottle of sack for the choir in the Marsh and then the costs of the breakfast ending with a cryptic entry "for too make the quiar and synyng men of All Hallow [All Saints] for the bryngyng some of the proessechyng [procession] for too drink vjd".[83] It seems impossible to draw any firm conclusion.

Indeed one has to admit that the attempts to interpret the snippets of information about the Corpus Christi procession in Bristol are both speculative and inconclusive. This is largely due to the nature of the evidence. Most of it is contained in the surviving churchwardens' accounts, which, by their very nature, record only what the churchwardens had to pay for. Some things must have paid for by others. Many things which we should like to know about the procession did not involve payments at all. Much evidence has probably been lost. Our knowledge of the participation of the Mayor depends on one ordinance but it must have been mentioned in other records. However, one can say there is a possibility that the procession went to St Augustine's abbey. Some, if not all, of the guilds took place in it as well as the parish parties, and so did the Mayor and Sheriff and probably the other members of the council. Of the Corpus Christi plays in Bristol there is no trace and there is no evidence of how the procession was organised or ordered. The role of the parish of All Saints in it is rather a mystery.

---

[83] BRO P/StMR/C/5(b); P/StMR/ChW/1(a), fol 66.

VII

St Augustine's Abbey and The Manor of Abbots Leigh

JOSEPH BETTEY

ABBOTS LEIGH was part of the original endowment of St Augustine's abbey which was founded just outside the medieval town of Bristol in 1140. Throughout the Middle Ages the manor remained one of the valuable possessions of the Augustinian canons. It was not the richest or most extensive of the abbey's widespread properties, but it was conveniently situated just down the Avon from Bristol, and was within easy walking or riding distance, crossing the river via the Rownham ferry, which was itself one of the abbey's possessions. Leigh woods along the banks of the Avon provided timber and fuel, and the open downland south-west of the manor gave pasture for hundreds of sheep. There was arable land towards Chapel Pill and Crockern or Crockarn Pill, and the Merecombe brook provided power for a water-mill at Radford. Rents of livestock, corn, wool and eggs were brought up the river to the abbey; barges also brought timber and stone for building work, and loads of firewood for the abbey kitchen and malt-house. The manor house provided an ideal retreat for successive abbots, and the demesne sheep flock produced an income which helped to maintain the abbot's household.

A remarkable amount of late-medieval documentary evidence survives concerning the monastic economy at Abbots Leigh, including court rolls, leases, rentals and *computa* or manorial account rolls. Several years ago these sources were carefully studied and a few were published by the late Arthur Sabin. The early part of this account is based on his work.[1]

Throughout the Middle Ages the manor was known simply as Leigh. In the Domesday Survey it is recorded as *Lega*, a form which was to persist during the early Middle Ages. In 1086 it was part of the royal manor of Bedminster, and the church at Abbots Leigh remained a chapelry of Bedminster until the Reformation. By the early twelfth century Bedminster with Leigh had come into the hands of Robert Fitzharding, and in 1140 he gave the manor of Leigh to the Augustinian abbey which he founded on his land at Billeswick, across the Frome from the town of Bristol.[2] Later, grants made by members of the Berkeley family brought land at Long Ashton, Ham Green, Portbury, Tickenham and Clevedon into the possession

---

[1] G. Beachcroft & A. Sabin, eds., "Two Compotus Rolls of St Augustine's Abbey, Bristol", *Bristol Record Society*, IX, 1938; A. Sabin, ed., "Some Manorial Accounts of St Augustine's Abbey, Bristol", *Bristol Record Society*, XVII, 1960; A. Sabin, "Compotus Rolls of St Augustine's Abbey, Bristol", *Bristol & Gloucestershire Archaeological Society*, LXXIII, 1954, 192–207. I am grateful to Miss Elizabeth Sabin for allowing me to make use of her father's notes.

[2] Walker, ed., "The Cartulary of St Augustine's Abbey, Bristol", *Bristol & Gloucestershire Archaeological Society, Record Series*, 10, 1998, xxvii, 1.

of the Augustinian canons, and the income from these lands was included in the manorial accounts for Leigh.[3] The manorial court met twice a year, in spring and autumn and was presided over by the Chamberlain who was a canon from the abbey. The court dealt with the tenure and condition of properties, regulated the manorial farming, punished those who had transgressed manorial regulations and elected manorial officials including the reeve, constable, hayward and shepherd. From the 1308–18 court rolls it seems probable that there were about seventy households in Leigh at that time, although the number was to be reduced considerably by the Black Death of 1348–49. The number of tenants in 1386 was about 50. As well as the manor house and its grounds, there were some 200 acres of arable land, 12 acres of meadow land, extensive woodland along the river Avon and grazing land on the downs.[4]

The manor house stood close to, but not on, the same site as the present Leigh Court. The medieval house appears to have provided a comfortable country resid-ence for the abbots, away from the pressures they faced as head of a rich, busy monastery close to a major town and port. The records are careful to describe the house as "Mansio cum cooperatura tegulorum" (manor house with a tiled roof). No doubt the tiled roof distinguished it from the thatch-roofed cottages of the tenants. The abbots clearly enjoyed spending time there. A visitation of the abbey by the bishop of Worcester in 1284 found that the abbot, Godfrey Giffard, who was an old man, lived at Leigh with one of the canons. Abbot Walter Newbury (abbot 1428– 63), who was responsible for a great deal of building work on the abbey itself and on its estates, was said to have "built diverse houses of office at the Maner of Lygh in Somersetshire." Likewise the forceful Abbot John Newland (abbot 1481–1515), who supervised so much building work on the abbey church and on its properties, also spent much time at Leigh and was said to have "rebuilt" the manor house. During the late fourteenth century considerable building work was done on the manor house at Leigh and on the barns and other buildings. There is mention of a walled garden, an oxhouse, a dovecote or "columbarium", and a barn. This work was supervised by the abbey's master mason, Nicholas Waleys, who was paid 2s od for his visit to Leigh in 1386 and the account roll records that he and his men consumed three fowls while they were there. Nicholas Waleys was a prominent architect or master mason, who was responsible for the early work on the central tower of the church at St Augustine's abbey. As well as his work at St Augustine's abbey he had earlier designed the elegant spire of Bridgwater parish church. When he died in 1403 he was buried in the abbey church.[5]

The Leigh manor house was situated conveniently close to the manor of Portbury where the Berkeleys, the wealthy patrons of St Augustine's abbey spent so much time. It was no doubt convenient for the abbot to meet the abbey benefactors in the neighbouring manor. The fourteenth century accounts show that the manor was being carefully managed and farmed under the direct control of the abbey, through

[3] A Sabin, 1960, 4.
[4] *Ibid.*, 179.
[5] I. H. Jeayes, "Abbot Newland's Roll", *B & GAS*, XIV, 1889–90, 129–30; Somerset Record Office, Abbots Leigh *Compota Rolls* 1386–7, 1387–8; John Harvey, *English Medieval Architects*, 1984, 311–2.

a reeve who was appointed at the manorial court and was answerable to the Chamberlain, one of the Augustinian canons. Wheat, barley, oats and beans were supplied to the abbey by barge, or were consumed by the abbot and his household at the manor house. Even more important were the livestock sent to the kitchen of the abbey. They included cattle, pigs, fowls, ducks and geese. The important sheep flock produced a lucrative annual wool crop, as well as dung to fertilise the arable fields. Timber was supplied for building work at the abbey, and firewood for the abbey kitchens. Also important as a source of food was the dovecote or pigeon house; in 1386, for example, it produced 208 doves. Abbey servants on the demesne farm at Leigh included four ploughmen, a shepherd, pigman, dairyman and three woodmen. The account rolls for 1387–8 show that the demesne farm produced more than 30 quarters of wheat, barley, and oats, and $5\frac{1}{2}$ quarters of beans. The stock on the farm consisted of 1 bull, 20 oxen, 7 cows, 3 bullocks, 2 yearlings, 52 wethers, 63 ewes, 22 hogasters, 37 pigs, 11 young pigs, 27 piglets, 8 geese, 30 ducks, 44 capons, and 109 cocks and hens.

By the early fifteenth century the abbey, like the owners of most great estates, had leased the demesne lands at Leigh, and was beginning to receive rents from its tenants in money rather than in kind or in labour service. For example, in 1429 the demesne lands were leased to William Baker of Leigh. His lease included the land, a bull and 17 other cattle, a corn-wain with iron-bound wheels, another cart and wheels, two ploughs, harrows, a dung-cart, an iron-bound bushell measure and an eight-gallon brass pot. No doubt Baker himself also provided some cattle and equipment. There is no mention of the sheep flock which apparently the abbot retained in his own possession. In 1429 William Baker was still paying rent in kind. As well as loads of wheat, barley and oats which had to be delivered to the abbey, his rent consisted of 12 geese, 24 fowls and two loads of hay which had to be provided for the horses of the abbot, the chamberlain and various abbey servants when they visited the manor house.[6] The lands at Abbots Leigh continued to be leased by the abbey throughout the fifteenth century.

By the 1490s all the forty or more tenants at Leigh paid a money rent for their tenements. The rent collected in 1491–92 amounted to nearly £54, while expenses for tithes and servants in the manor house came to less than £5. Grain, eggs and poultry continued to be supplied to the abbey, and it seems likely that the abbot still received the considerable income from the sheep flock, since this does not appear in the account roll of the abbey. Another source of income for the abbey came from the fines and other "perquisites" imposed by the manorial court, and from the "heriots" or death duties paid by the tenants. The account rolls also show that each year during the early sixteenth century barge-loads of firewood were sent up-river to the abbey from Leigh woods.

The court rolls of the late fifteenth century show the close supervision which the abbey continued to exercise over its tenants at Abbots Leigh. The Chamberlain still presided over the manorial courts at Easter and Michaelmas, accompanied by the Steward or Seneschall. By the late Middle Ages this latter office was occupied by a member of one of the local gentry families who, throughout the country, were

[6] Public Record Office, SC 6/1107/12–13.

increasingly involved in the economic affairs of the monastic houses. At St Augustine's the Poyntz family, who held estates in Bristol and around Iron Acton in south Gloucestershire, held the office of steward for many year's. During the early years of the sixteenth century, the position of steward was held by Sir Robert Poyntz (d1520) who founded the impressive chantry chapel in the Gaunt's hospital church (St Mark's) in Bristol. At the courts the tithing men from the abbey's lands at Portbury, Ham, Clevedon and Tickenham made their reports, generally assuring the Chamberlain that all was well. Twelve jurors representing the tenants of Abbots Leigh were sworn in and reported on tenancies, defaulters, offences against manorial regulations or customs and made orders for the management of the common fields. There are references to the common shepherd, to ale-tasters, the manorial mill at Radford, to the Messor or hayward, and to the woodmen. The court also dealt with minor offences committed within the manor, such as damage caused by pigs, failure to maintain hedges and ditches and disputes between neighbours. Such offences brought profit to the abbey from the fines which were imposed. The water-mill at Radford was also a profitable perquisite for the abbey, and tenants were obliged to have their corn ground there. In 1308 the miller was fined for leaving the mill and going to Bristol for the day, thereby depriving the abbey of a day's toll. During the 1380s there are references to a windmill ("unius molendini ventritici"), but this does not appear to have lasted for long.[7]

From the evidence of these accounts, it is clear that although during the later Middle Ages the abbey was no longer directly involved in farming the demesne land at Abbots Leigh, and that the abbot and canons now depended upon money rents instead of the labour services which the tenants had rendered in previous centuries, nonetheless the manor continued to be a profitable and valuable source of income and produce for the abbey. In 1491–2 the abbey's total income from Leigh and its associated lands amounted to £62 5s 6¾ d. By the time of the dissolution in 1539 this had risen to £89 3s 0¾ d. The manor house continued to be used as a retreat by the abbot as it had been since the foundation of the abbey in the twelfth century. It should not be supposed that the abbey tenants living at Leigh were necessarily remote from contemporary affairs or totally confined within a rural backwater. The busy town and port of Bristol was close at hand, and news of political upheavals, religious controversies and contemporary events would soon have reached Leigh. Moreover, ships passing to and from Bristol had to negotiate the treacherous tidal river past Leigh around the Horseshoe Bend in the river Avon, and many vessels no doubt waited for the tide at Hung Road. It is clear from later evidence that many men from Leigh worked as shipwrights and carpenters. The late-medieval court rolls contain evidence that some men from Leigh spent part of their time at sea. In November 1473 for example three men failed to attend the manorial court and were said to be "in partibus transmarinis". Since there were only two courts a year, it is probable that many other tenants took part in voyages during the summer months but returned in time for the court. When Abbot Newland admitted John Roche and Thomas Colyns as tenants in 1498, he stipulated that "non erit

[7] Bristol University Library, Special Collections, DM 177, Court Rolls of Abbots Leigh 1461–83, 1488–94, 1496–1589; Somerset Record Office AID 79/1-9 Court Rolls of Abbots Leigh 1306–18, 1386–8, 1428–9;A. Sabin, 1960, 46–53; 179–181.

marinarius neque ibit trans mare sub pena forisfacture tenementum (not to be mariners nor go across the sea, under penalty of forfeiting the tenement)".[8]

The survival of so much documentary evidence for Leigh enables a picture of the late-medieval village to be reconstructed. The main road ran from Rownham ferry, along its modern course to Portbury and Crockern Pill. Branching off from this major road, to the north east, the village street led to the church, with many of the farms, cottages and tenements on either side of this street. Beyond the church the former road continued as Horsewell Lane, going down into the valley, skirting the manor house to the left, and leading eventually to St Katherine's Pill. Here there was another ferry across the Avon, which was used by the Berkeleys to reach their manor house at Portbury. Here also was St Katherine's chapel, a chantry foundation on the wooded banks of the Avon.

North east of the thatched farmhouses, cottages and crofts along the village street was the manor house with its tiled roof, and around it the farm buildings including the well-built barn, sheep-house and dovecote. The late medieval topography of Abbots Leigh was to survive with few changes until the early nineteenth century, and can still be traced on a detailed, large-scale estate map drawn in 1800 by Richard Richardson of Bath. The triangle of roads around the church still runs along the eastern side of the manor house and down to St Katherine's Pill on the river Avon, where the field-name Chapel Leaze indicates the position of the former chantry. The manor house is surrounded by farm buildings, yards, courts, orchards and a walled kitchen garden, while the field called Culvers Close shows where the dove-cote once stood. The large warren, containing 654 acres, occupies the south and west parts of the manor, and another 318 acres is occupied by Leigh Woods. This surviving medieval landscape was to be swept away following the building of an elegant new manor house by the Miles family in 1814, and the transformation of its surroundings in accordance with the proposals made by Humphry Repton in 1814.[9]

Occasionally the abbots of St Augustine's were obliged to take strong measures to protect their rights. An example occurred in 1528 when there was a dispute over Rownham ferry. The ferry provided an important means of crossing the Avon downstream from Bristol, and was a link between south-west Gloucestershire and the adjacent part of north Somerset including Abbots Leigh. It was owned by the abbey. In 1528 Thomas Alye, who was a tenant of John Kekewyche, lord of the manor of Ashton Theynes on the Somerset side of the river, claimed the right to establish a ferry across the river. He also appears to have under-cut the prices of St Augustine's ferrymen. St Augustine's prices are unknown, but Thomas Alye charged "of every fote man a farthing and for every man and a hors a halfpenny for the passage over the said water".

The abbot of St Augustine's, William Burton, took decisive action to frustrate the rival ferry. He sent his servants to Thomas Alye's house and seized his boat. Thereupon Alye brought a suit against the Abbot in the Court of Star Chamber, and the evidence given by the numerous witnesses reveals the whole story. According to the

[8] Bristol University Library, Special Collections, Leigh Court Rolls.
[9] Bristol Record Office, 25015 Map & Survey of Abbots Leigh 1800; Bristol University, Special Collections, Repton's Report on Abbots Leigh 1814.

witnesses, there was a long history of disputes between successive abbots and the lords of the manor of Ashton Theynes over rights to provide a ferry at Rownham. Numerous documents and various aged men were produced to testify to the sole rights of the abbey to the ferry. Thomas Alye's allegation that his boat had been seized in a violent and riotous manner by the abbey servants was countered by Thomas Colyns aged 60, one of the abbey tenants from Abbots Leigh, who had witnessed the incident. Alye claimed that the abbey servants had so beaten him with their staves that he was sore for more than a week thereafter. Colyns in his evidence stated that the incident was remarkably and unbelievably free of violence. He deposed that he had crossed in Alye's ferry from the Abbots Leigh side of the river to the Gloucestershire side

> "which landed this deponente upon the soile of the frehold of the said abbate, and then this deponente saw the seyd Hugh, John and Walter, servantes to the seyd abbate, take the seyd bote peasably and in esy manner, withowte gevyng any threttenyng wordes, for that they fowned the sayd bote doing hurte and damage upon the freholde of the seid abbate, and from thens they in peasable wyse conveyed the seyd bote by water to a place callyd Lymottes in the seyd countye of Gloucester".

As often with Star Chamber cases, the judgement of the court has not survived, but clearly the abbot emerged victorious, since the ferry remained as a valued possession of the abbey, and later passed to the Dean and Chapter of Bristol cathedral. The episode illustrates the readiness of the abbot and canons to fight for their rights, and the importance of this convenient route for reaching their lands and manor house at Abbots Leigh.[10]

The long-standing relationship between the abbey and the manor was soon to be rudely shattered. The coming change was heralded in 1534 when Parliament declared that the King was now Supreme Head of the Church, and that the Pope no longer had any power in England. The abbot, William Burton, and his 18 canons were obliged to swear individually that they accepted this revolutionary change. They duly did so in their Chapter House at Bristol on 9 September 1534. Immediately thereafter, the King's chief minister, Thomas Cromwell, set in train a series of enquiries into the state of the monastic houses, examining their finances and searching for any scandal or evidence of neglect and slackness which might be used in support of moves to suppress some of the monasteries. The financial inquiry, known as the *Valor Ecclesiasticus* was compiled during 1535, but the results for Bristol have not survived. The evidence of the royal commissioner who came to St Augustine's still exists. His name was Richard Layton, a young priest, anxious to rise in the service of Thomas Cromwell and not above manufacturing evidence of scandalous conduct by the monks in order to please his master. He came to St Augustine's abbey on 24 August 1535, but apparently found nothing wrong nor any failings of the canons which he could report. When he left, however, he ordered the abbot and canons that they should not go outside the precincts of the abbey, but remain confined so that they might strictly observe their monastic rule.[11]

---

[10] P.R.O. STAC 2/19 Henry VIII, 1/132; Somerset Record Society, XXVII, 94–108.

[11] J. H. Bettey, *The Suppression of the Religious Houses in Bristol*, Bristol Historical Association, 1990, 10–11.

It is an indication of the attachment which the abbot, William Burton, felt towards his manor house at Leigh that he wrote a servile letter to Thomas Cromwell protesting at this restriction, and asking among other things that

> "I heartily pray you to give me licence and liberty to walk to my manor places nigh to Bristol for the comfortable health of my body and for the saving of expenses".[12]

No reply appears to have been received to this letter. In the following year, 1536, Cromwell was able to persuade Parliament to pass an Act for the Dissolution of the Lesser Monasteries, whereby all religious houses with a net annual income of less than £200 were suppressed and all their lands, property and wealth given to the King. With an annual income of almost £700, St Augustine's abbey was well outside the provisions of this Act, but it was a strong indication of the way things were going. In common with many other monasteries, the abbot of St Augustine's had already begun the attempt to safeguard his own position and that of his canons, and had begun to grant long leases of the abbey properties to laymen.

At Leigh the manor house and the demesne lands were leased to the bailiff, John Colyns, in July 1535. The lease was granted for the lives of John Colyns himself, his wife, Alice, and his daughter, Elena at £10 per annum. In October 1537 a further lease was granted to John Colyns for 60 years of the Shepehouse, Shepehouseclose and the common pasture for 500 sheep for £1 per annum. In 1538 John Colyns was granted for life the office of bailiff. Other leases of abbey lands at Leigh were granted to Robert Philippes.[13] Presumably some rooms in the manor house were reserved for the abbot, but clearly at Leigh, as at many other monastic properties throughout the country, the major concern was to tie up the properties in an attempt to prevent royal confiscation. Such plans were to prove futile.

Although the years 1537 and 1538 saw the "voluntary" surrender to the Crown of many monastic houses, at St Augustine's it still seemed possible that the abbey would be allowed to continue. When Abbot William Burton died in the summer of 1539, royal licence was granted to elect a successor, in spite of the fact that all over the country monasteries were surrendering to the Crown and the monks and nuns were being granted pensions. At St Augustine's the canons met in the Chapter House and elected Morgan Gwilliam, who had been the prior, as their abbot. He survived in his office for only a few months, for on 9 December 1539 the abbot and eleven canons surrendered the monastery into the King's hands. They were granted pensions and departed; forty-six officers of the household and monastic servants were also paid their wages and dismissed. All the estates and property of the abbey, including Abbots Leigh, now passed into the King's hands. The former abbot, Morgan Gwilliam, was granted a generous pension of £80 per annum, together with the use of the manor house at Abbots Leigh during his lifetime with the garden, orchard and dovehouse, and the right to 20 loads of firewood each year for his house.[14]

Having been a monastic possession since 1140 Abbots Leigh now became a royal manor. The change produced a further source of information about the manor, since

---

[12] *Ibid.*
[13] Sabin, 1960, 16.
[14] J. H. Bettey, *op.cit.*, 20–22.

the royal commissioner, Sir Richard Poulet, who was the King's Receiver dealing with the recently-acquired monastic properties in the west country, instituted an enquiry into the finances of the former estates of St Augustine's during 1540–41. This lists the sources of income from Abbots Leigh, including the adjacent lands belonging to the manor at Long Ashton, Portbury, Clevedon, Tickenham and Ham Green (Hampegrene). It also includes the income (17s 0d) from the water-mill at Radford, and the rent (10s 0d) for a stone quarry at "le Cleves" beneath "Lygh-wood". It includes the income from the demesne and specifies the leases granted to John Colyns and Robert Philippes. John Colyns is now described as "bailiff to the lord king". The net receipts from the manor including the additional properties are given as £60 7s 4½d. Richard Poulet's accounts for 1540–1 list John Colyns as bailiff and Richard Ewence as reeve. They also refer to a rental of 35 hens and 145 eggs, which are to be provided for the landlord.[15] No evidence survives concerning the reaction of the tenants at Leigh to these upheavals, but the change from monastic to royal ownership can have made little difference to them. John Colyns continued as bailiff, and the royal commissioners were just as determined to collect all the rents and other dues to which they were entitled as the Augustinian canons had been. For the tenants, the annual round of seasonal labour and the traditional concerns of seed-time and harvest continued as before.

The change to royal ownership was to be short-lived. On 4 June 1542 Henry VIII's government ordered the creation of the diocese of Bristol, and the manor of Abbots Leigh, together with its manor house, was to be one of the endowments of the newly-created bishopric. Throughout the Middle Ages the medieval town of Bristol, lying to the north of the river Avon, was at the extreme southern tip of the large diocese of Worcester. Churches and communities south of the Avon, St Thomas, Temple, St Mary Redcliffe and Bedminster, were part of the Somerset diocese of Bath and Wells, as was Abbots Leigh. In 1541 the Henrician government, as some recompense for the vast wealth which had been confiscated from the suppressed monasteries, established five new dioceses. One of these was the diocese of Gloucester which included Bristol north of the Avon, and was to have the former Benedictine abbey church of St Peter in Gloucester as its cathedral. A year later, in 1542, apparently as an afterthought, or possibly because of pressure from prominent Bristolians, a new diocese of Bristol was created, and Bristol was for the first time declared to be a city. The new diocese was to consist of all the parishes within Bristol, together with some others from south Gloucestershire and Abbots Leigh from Somerset; in addition the county of Dorset was to be taken from Salisbury diocese to become part of the diocese of Bristol. This curiously-constituted and administratively-impossible diocese was to remain in existence until 1836. For the cathedral of the new Bristol diocese, the former Augustinian abbey church was chosen, while the bishop's palace and houses for the cathedral canons and staff were situated in the former monastic buildings. Since the nave of the abbey church had recently been demolished as part of an incomplete scheme of re-building, the new cathedral church consisted only of the chancel, transepts and side chapels.[16] The result of these new arrangements was that the tenants of Abbots Leigh now found

---

[15] Sabin, 1960, 179.
[16] J. Rogan, ed., *Bristol Cathedral: History & Architecture*, 2000, 36.

themselves once more under ecclesiastical ownership, this time episcopal instead of monastic. The first bishop of Bristol was Paul Bush, a former monk, who had been rector or head of the Bonshommes' monastery at Edington in Wiltshire. Although he was a considerable scholar and theologian, he seems to have been ill-equipped to cope with all the pressures of his new and unwieldly diocese. Certainly he spent much time in the peaceful seclusion of his manor house at Abbots Leigh rather than at his episcopal palace in Bristol, and several of his surviving documents and letters were written from Abbots Leigh and conclude with phrases such as "Gevon at my house at my maner of Lyghe" or "In manerio nostris de Lighe".[17] Although the manor house had been granted to the last abbot, Morgan Gwilliam, for his lifetime, he does not appear to have lived there, and it is not clear whether he was recompensed for the loss of his house. In any case, Gwilliam's will was made in London in 1543, and he died quite soon afterwards.[18]

There was to be another, final twist in the story of the ecclesiastical ownership of Abbots Leigh. Paul Bush remained as bishop throughout the remaining years of Henry VIII's reign, and when the nine-year-old Edward VI came to the throne in 1547 the bishop accepted the religious changes which swiftly followed. It is clear from his writings that Paul Bush was conservative in his religious views, although he supported the introduction of the Bible in English and did not oppose the new English services in the Prayer Books of 1549 and 1552. In the House of Lords he voted unsuccessfully against allowing clerical marriage, but when in 1549 it became permissible for the clergy to marry, Paul Bush soon found a wife. She was Edith Ashley, daughter of Henry Ashley, gentleman, of Monkton Up Wimborne in Dorset. Paul Bush's sister, Margaret, was married to one of Edith Ashley's brothers. To occupy the hitherto unheard of position of wife of a former priest, a former monk vowed to celibacy, and indeed now the bishop of a diocese must have presented innumerable difficulties for Edith Bush. She was no doubt glad of the opportunities to escape the public life in the bishop's palace at Bristol and occasionally to retreat to the rural seclusion of the manor house at Abbots Leigh.[19] But soon Paul Bush found himself under pressure to surrender Abbots Leigh to the government. John Dudley, Earl of Warwick and later Duke of Northumberland, had triumphed over Edward Seymour, Duke of Somerset, for control of the young King, Edward VI. Now he needed to reward his supporters, and among them was Sir George Norton who coveted the episcopal manor of Abbots Leigh. In the face of this threat to the endowments of his bishopric, Paul Bush began to grant long leases of the episcopal manors. In this he was following the precedent set by late-medieval abbots in their unsuccessful attempts to avoid royal confiscation of their properties. In January 1548 Bush granted a lease of his valuable manor of Ashleworth in Gloucestershire to Thomas Seymour, Lord Sudeley for seventy years. The manor of Minsterworth was leased to Sir John Thynne and Cromhall manor was granted to Thomas Throckmorton. The bishop's manors and lands in the lower Severn valley including the rich manor of Almondsbury were also leased to laymen for long terms. Other leases were granted to members of his own or his wife's family. In June 1550 he leased the Dorset manor

[17] J. H. Bettey, "Paul Bush, the first bishop of Bristol", *B&GAS*, 106, 1988, 169–172.
[18] P.R.O., PCC Wills, Pyning 8.
[19] J. H. Bettey, *B&GAS*, 106, 1988, 170.

of Fifehead Magdalen to Henry Ashley of Wimborne St Giles for eighty years, and later in 1550 he leased the manor of Horfield to another of his wife's relatives, John Hawles of Monkton Up Wimborne, Dorset. Earlier while Paul Bush was head of the Bonshommes' house at Edington he had appointed his elder brother, John Bush, to the post of steward of the monastery's estates in Wiltshire. As bishop of Bristol he granted a lease of the manor of Abbots Leigh to his brother in 1550.[20]

Such leases, however, counted for little with the Duke of Northumberland, a ruthless Tudor nobleman with his supporters clamouring to be rewarded for their loyalty, and the pressure upon Paul Bush to surrender the manor of Abbots Leigh continued unabated. With the support of the Dean and Chapter of his cathedral, Bush delayed matters for as long as he could. Finally, in February 1551, Paul Bush was summoned before the Privy Council, yet still he refused to yield up the property of his bishopric. The record of the Privy Council meeting gives an account of this dramatic encounter, and of the remarkable bravery with which Bush faced all the majesty of the Privy Council in the splendid palace at Greenwich.

"This daie the Busshop of Bristoll was before the counsaill tooching his aunswere to be made to the Kinges Majesties request for Sir George Norton, knight, who desired upon reasonable recompence to have of the Busshop the manour of Lie, in Somerset, which manour the same Bishop affirmed that he had graunted in lease unto his brother [John] Bushe. Marie, he saied he had don it upon this condicion, that if his successour, the Busshop that hereafter shall be, woll dwell upon yt him self, that than Busshe shulde suffer him to have it, taking of him recompence for the chardges alreadie bestowed upon it, which he thought had cost him cc [li] above the rent lymited in his lease. And albeit that the Counsaill perswaded the Busshop as muche as was possible to tender the Kinges Majesties request in this case, yet wolde he in no wise yelde therunto, but departed, refusing to commune of the matter."[21]

The Tudor government was not deterred by Bush's adamant refusal to discuss the matter, and soon after the bishop, together with the Dean and Chapter of the cathedral received a sharp reminder of the Privy Council's power. The Council wrote to remind the recalcitrant clerics that it was the King's own wish that they should relinquish ownership of Abbots Leigh, with a strong hint that harsh penalties could follow any further refusal, leaving them in no doubt as to what they must do,

" . . . Nothing doubting of your good conformitie in that behalf hath willed us on his Majesties behalf to make request unto you for possession. Wee doe therefore desire and pray you with convenient diligence to procede thereunto, and advertisinge us of your doinges, wee shall not fayle to make report to his highness of your redy mynde and good disposcion to the satisfaction of his Majesties requests accordingly

Your loving Frendes."[22]

[20] Bristol Record Office, DC/E/1/1 Bristol Cathedral Leases 1542–1585, fols 35v, 46, 47, 51v–52.
[21] Acts of the Privy Council, NS, 3, 1550–2, 210.
[22] B.R.O., DC/E/1/1.

On 2 May 1551 Paul Bush surrendered ownership of Abbots Leigh to the Crown, reserving some rights in the manor during his lifetime, but with the reversion to Sir George Norton.[23] Shortly the grant was ratified by the Dean and Chapter in the cathedral Chapter House in the presence of Edmund Gorges and Hugh Denys, the local commissioners or agents for the Duke of Northumberland.[24] The power and ruthless determination of those who rose to the top positions in Tudor governments is well illustrated by this ceremony. The long history of the Bristol Chapter House can have witnessed few scenes more humiliating to the Church dignitaries than this, as the Duke of Northumberland's men compelled them to sign away one of the endowments of the diocese.[25]

Paul Bush's problems were not ended by the surrender of Abbots Leigh. With the death of Edward VI and the accession of Queen Mary in 1553, Bush found himself in an impossible situation as a married bishop. The situation was not altered by the death of his wife, Edith, in October 1553, and Bush was forced to resign his bishopric. With the departure of Paul Bush, Sir George Norton came into full possession of the Abbots Leigh estate, and it was to remain in the Norton family's possession for the next two centuries. Abbots Leigh thus became a fully secular manor. It is ironic that following the departure of the abbots and the bishop, the place began regularly to be known as Abbots Leigh, instead of by the earlier name of Leigh. A century later, in 1651, it was to have its brief moment of national significance. Charles II, fleeing from defeat by Cromwell's army at the battle of Worcester, found shelter at the manor house, before successfully escaping to France.[26]

[23] Calendar Patent Rolls, Edward VI, 4, 1550–3, 152.
[24] B.R.O., DC/E/1/16 Chapter Act Book 1, f 51v.
[25] Somerset Record Office, APD 90 Grant and confirmation, 25 May 1551; APD 95 Grant to Sir George Norton 23 September 1551. These documents survive among the Norton MSS.
[26] J. Collinson, *History of Somerset*, 3, 17, 153.

VIII

Centuries of Change: Bristol Churches since the Reformation

PATRICK BROWN

WHEN Worcestre recorded his perambulation (see "William Worcestre: Bristol Churches in 1480", pp. 29–54, and Map p. 28) there were eighteen parish churches in the city; by the year 2000 there remained twelve, five had disappeared completely, and one had been dismantled and re-erected elsewhere in Bristol. Of those no longer existing, the last—St Augustine—was pulled down as recently as 1970. Of the remainder two only were still parish churches, and one of these, St Mary Redcliffe, will not be considered here: St Mary is nationally famous, and has been fully documented, the latest treatise by Michael Q Smith[1]—published in 1995— being specially relevant.

Of the twelve remaining, some would be recognisable to Worcestre, but he would be amazed by substantial changes in their surroundings, and some fabrics would seem strange to his eyes attuned to late mediaeval design: four were rebuilt in the eighteenth century. The one church which, apart from the larger scale and new style of the neighbouring buildings, would seem both externally and within familiar to fifteenth century eyes, would be St Stephen.

The first major upheaval, begun under Henry VIII, would entail substantial losses of images in glass, stone and painting, and removal of roods and many screens, but with minimal consequential damage to the building fabric. Through to the middle of the seventeenth century, such losses were compounded by the activities of Puritans and the zealots of the Commonwealth. With the Restoration matters improved, but significant changes would occur in fittings and furnishings: in the early eighteenth century, for instance, remarkable baroque reredoses were installed in some chancels, several of them surviving to the twentieth century. Altars, pulpits and seating were replaced in new forms, completely new churches were put up on four existing sites, and in the nineteenth century a substantial return to mediaeval liturgical forms once again transformed interiors. Add to these many variations the wilful destruction of war-time bombing, a post-war liturgical revival, and demographic and other changes leading to church redundancy, and it is perhaps surprising that so much still survives for us to see.

Over some five hundred years, therefore, a number of factors have been conducive to changes in church buildings, but more especially in their interior arrangements. Worcestre provides us with a sort of "snapshot" of the situation in the late fifteenth century, but for long thereafter individual church records—sometimes reinforced by visual evidence within the buildings—must be used to trace what has happened.

---

[1] Smith, M Q, *St Mary Redcliffe—an architectural history:* 1995.

For the early nineteenth century, however, Bristol has a particularly valuable record in the Braikenridge Collection of drawings in the City Art Gallery. This is a substantial assembly of accurate drawings—mostly watercolours—of views and buildings in the city, undertaken in the decade from 1820 to 1830. This is a particularly felicitous timing, since the interiors are recorded only two or three decades before almost all of them would be recast in the Gothic Revival. During the nineteenth century a number of illustrated volumes[2] continues coverage, by which time more precise records were becoming available through photography; here, again, Bristol is fortunate in its significant collection of photographs from the earliest days of the new medium through to the late twentieth century in Reece Winstone's systematic assembly and publication of this material.[3] These resources have been drawn on generously in what follows, but it is the church buildings themselves which are the architect's primary sources, and experience over some thirty years plus revisits to examine the current state of these fabrics has been invaluable in making the assessments which follow.

TWO CENTURIES OF ADJUSTMENT; 1550 to 1750

The upheavals created from Henry's reign through to the Elizabethan Settlement have been well documented by Eamonn Duffy and Joe Bettey[4] and need not be detailed here. Suffice to recall that the chief impact on our churches was the destruction and loss of much mediaeval work—stained glass, statues, paintings, screens, roods, vestments and church plate were destroyed or sequestered. Under Mary was a brief respite, but then the despoliation returned. Through all this, however, the buildings remained relatively unscathed, as this was all a protest against Rome, not a destruction of the Church itself. From this period we can but lament the loss of so much of value and beauty, whilst nurturing what remains.

In the early seventeenth century, under Laud's edicts, the orgies of damage were stemmed, and seemliness restored to the area of the "stripped altars". A major loss had been removal of the stone altars from chancels. In their place the Canons Ecclesiastical of 1604 had ordained that ". . . Tables are provided, and placed for the celebration of Holy Communion . . . in so good sort within the church or Chancell, as thereby the Minister may be more conveniently heard . . .";[5] this brought various responses, with the table regarded as a movable element in the furnishings, and dissent between those who sought "altar-wise" placing, and the proponents of "table-wise" but in any case with varied locations within the chancel or sometimes beyond. Laud insisted on reversion to pre-Reformation practice, the table to be replaced at the east end, and contained within a decent railing to protect this special area both from parishioners and from dogs. In this period a considerable amount of

---

[2] Barrett; N & T—especially Vol II; Stone.
[3] The Winstone archive is now held by John Winstone, his son, at Wookey. Many volumes were published covering various decades of photographs of Bristol, frequently including views of the churches. See esp. "Bristol in the Blitz", and volumes dealing with early decades in photography.
[4] Duffy: Bettey (1) and (2);
[5] Canon LXXXVII

splendid new joinery in pews, pulpits and other fittings was produced, some of which survived later transformations. No Bristol interior remains intact from this phase, but St John the Baptist is very nearly complete. A late mediaeval structure, over a crypt and on the city wall, it has a narrow nave, with chancel of the same width through a broad moulded arch; beyond the sanctuary, behind the altar, is a vestry. The church, now vested in the Churches Conservation Trust,[6] has a complete set of early seventeenth century pews (reputedly of 1621)—not yet the high-sided box pew soon to become a standard for seating—an unusual cruciform stone font of 1624, with cover, a set of Laudian rails, for long consigned to the crypt, sanctuary with communion table of 1635, and two Jacobean chairs. At the west end the full-width organ gallery also retains much joinery in panels of the same date.

This is the nearest realisation of an interior from this era. Other churches have some elements; St Philip and Jacob has an octagonal pulpit with Jacobean carved embellishment, a font cover of similar date, and even a wrought iron sword rest of 1610, the earliest extant in the city. From Braikenridge's drawings we know that other churches were furnished similarly, before the great restorations of the late nineteenth century swept so much away.

The middle decades of the seventeenth century naturally saw very limited action in church building or furnishing, but after the Restoration churchmen could again take heart and look to their buildings and fittings. In particular, in Bristol, in the early years of the new century a series of very splendid reredoses was installed, in the briefly popular baroque style; five of these survived to this century, but one only remained after the 1940s Blitz. It is remarkable that they had lasted even this long, as the style was much scorned, especially during the Gothic Revival period, and is even now little understood by many, being associated with Romanism. Fortunately they were recorded and described by Dening.[7] The only extant reredos from the group is that in St Thomas, having been removed from the earlier church at the late eighteenth century rebuilding (see below). It is in fine carved hardwood, in the normal two-storey triple-panel form. The large central painted panel is flanked by bold fluted Corinthian columns on quarter-pilaster responds, beyond which are narrow outer panels, terminated by full pilasters; this lower level is crowned by a full moulded entablature, broken forward over the columns and pilasters, and with a triangular pediment similarly articulated. Above is a smaller panel—cut down by some 1.3m from the original design—having a characteristic scrolled pediment with open centre, the whole crowned by seven candlestick's, and two carved figures (these not part of the original). The reredos is of high quality in design and workmanship, the panel paintings being the weakest parts. The work was commissioned by the parish in 1716, the cost ". . . not to exceed £170 . . .",[8] a figure which perhaps helps to explain why this, with others of a similar richness, was not replaced when so much disappeared later. There were similar altar-pieces at St Mary-le-Port, St Nicholas, St

---

[6] The Churches Conservation Trust replaces the original Redundant Churches Fund established in 1968 to take in care those buildings becoming redundant which are deemed vital to retain, but cannot be found an appropriate alternative use. Well over 200 churches are now vested in the CCT.

[7] Dening, pp 120–137, with plates.

[8] Dening, p. 129.

Fig 1. City churches seen from Castle Green, November 2000. Behind St Peter (from left): St Nicholas, St Mary-le-Port, All Saints and Christ Church. (Photograph – Leon Collard)

Peter, and St Stephen, the first three in-situ until destroyed in the bombings. Writing of that in St Peter, Nicholls and Taylor note that ". . . the huge Corinthian altar-piece which now blocks the east window of the chancel was the result of the order given to one Mr John Mitchell of London, who appears to have been paid £140 for this laborious but incongruous addition to the furniture of the church . . .".[9]

The other major transformation in the churches in the period from 1660 through the next century was in seating. Almost universally mediaeval pews, often no doubt with rich and entertainingly carved ends, such as can still be seen in many Somerset churches, were taken out to permit the installation of high-sided box pews, sometimes with linings of silk and velvet, and even with their own heating-stoves for families of sufficient wealth. These groups of boxes were not aligned in parallel rows facing the altar, for by now the churches had become preaching halls, or 'auditories' as Wren called them, where the spoken word from the pulpit took precedence over the Communion table. In addition to filling the space with these blocks of pews, it became customary to add galleries on two or three sides, to take even more parishioners. It is recorded of St Peter that ". . . in March 1698 the sacred building was pewed by . . . J Mitchell from London, (who was) paid £105 for the upper stack, and

[9] N & T Vol II, p. 128.

Fig 2. Interior of St Peter's Church 1828.

£61-10-0 for the lower ..."[10], Johnson's view of 1828 (Fig 2) shows this interior, with pews, high-set pulpit with tester or sounding-board, and the baroque reredos backed by a diffuse painting covering the whole east wall.

By the mid eighteenth century it seems likely that most, if not all of the city's parish churches would have been re-ordered in line with the current liturgical usage and fashion. Pews, two or three-decker pulpits, richly carved and moulded, with perilous-looking suspended sounding-boards, fine twisted baluster Communion rails, Communion table with plain white cloth covering, reredos, decalogue boards, and sometimes a font looking more like a garden ornament than the traditional form from the middle ages: in fact the font more often was retained from the earliest foundations of the church, regarded perhaps as a vital link in the continuity of Christendom. Thus St James, having seen the same variations in furnishings as its sister churches, still has and uses its Norman font in the context of Victorian furnishing generally.

FOUR GEORGIAN CHURCHES

Despite the destruction of fittings and furnishings of the sixteenth century, compounded by the harassments and alterations of the seventeenth, the English Church

[10] Ibid.

Fig 3. St Nicholas' Church and Bristol Bridge 1824.

set high on a mound at the head of flights of stairs, including Christmas Steps, climbing north from the old Frome valley, past the chapel of the Three Kings of Cologne, and interrupted now by the later Perry Road with its busy traffic stream. The church stands at the foot of the hill which was then the main route northward to Gloucester—now St Michael's Hill—with many seventeenth century timber-framed houses and the splendid U-shaped range of Colston's Almshouses nearby; whilst much war-time damage occurred all round, this enclave was spared to provide an adequate historical setting for the church.

The mediaeval St Michael had a nave with a single aisle to the south, all above a crypt, and a west tower. By the beginning of the eighteenth century growth in population in the parish led to serious consideration to building an aisle on the north side, but eventually it was decided to demolish all save the tower, which had been expensively restored only thirty years earlier, and to start again. The architect would again be Thomas Paty, although a scheme had earlier been proposed by his father, James, in 1766; this was not taken up, but Thomas' design was realised in just two years, between May 1775 and June 1777, a remarkably short period. Superficially the new St Michael looks similar to the recently completed St Nicholas, with its box-like exterior, straight parapets, and west tower, but here constructed in soft grey sandstone with cream stone dressings. In fact it is very different, comprising nave with both north and south aisles, set against the original tower, with a completely new crypt under the whole: this crypt looks now exactly as built, with a series of large square piers (about 1.5m by 0.75m on plan) carrying flat groined vaults set very low, all over a stone flagged floor. It is an impressive space, almost Piranesian in impact, but if it is to be employed in the context of a re-used main space, its floor level would need to be lowered. At the time of writing the church is going through the processes of redundancy, a new user being sought.

The exterior again presents a version of early gothic revival style. The nave with aisles is without clerestorey, and the large two-light aisle windows are widely spaced; they have a central mullion dividing to Y-tracery, commonly used at this time, without cusping. The overall impression is still of a mediaeval church. Inside, however, this is rapidly dispelled, and the design has puzzled commentators ever since its completion. The wide nave has a plastered barrel-vault, terminating in a shallow chancel through a broad pointed arch, to a three-light east window. To each side, instead of the expected arcade of round or pointed arches is a deep moulded classical horizontal entablature, carried on four sturdy columns on high octagonal plinths, which would have corresponded more closely with the height of the box pews than they do now with the Victorian replacements. The columns are normally referred to as Tuscan, but with their square capitals on fluted neckings and moulded bases they are nearer Roman Doric in character. The wide aisles have flat plastered ceilings, the panels separated by plat-bands with soffite panels as to the main entablature. The church suffered damage during the war; and Ison's photograph of the interior shows the nave open to the timber roof trusses[17]: at that time it looked very barn-like, reminding us that in fact the parishioners were working to a tight budget in Paty's scheme: whereas at St Nicholas a handsome subsidy towards the cost had come from the Bridge Commissioners, at St Michael it is recorded on a foundation plate that voluntary contributions were a main source of funding.

The interior is somewhat hybrid in character, and critics have been less than enthusiastic. Ison thinks that St Michael "... cannot be accounted one of Paty's best works ...", and Barrett contents himself with a mere description, noting the crypt "... with a vault ... for a place of burial; this was 20ft broader on the north

[17] Ison, Pl 12a.

and 5ft on the south side than the former church . . ."; Nicholls and Taylor, stating that much of the structure is "modern", then regret that the ". . . style (is) neither Christian nor Pagan, but an indescribable combination of both."[18] In keeping with the practice of its times, a large preaching space was provided, and, whatever our estimation of its architectural qualities, the church's prominent location must predispose us to seek its retention in an appropriate new life: at the time of the Bishop's Commission[19]; in 1968, it was hoped that it could be taken by another Christian community, possibly as the University chaplaincy, which would have been very suitable, or be declared redundant.

Finally, in the light of the ways in which churches are now often used, it is intriguing to know that at St Michael, as early as 1794, a musical entertainment was held, presumably to raise funds. Tickets were five shillings each, a substantial sum for the times, with books of words at three pence, tickets available from ". . . Jack's Coffee House etc . . .". The performance would begin at 6.45 in the evening with ". . . a grand selection of Sacred Musick . . ." and ". . . Servants are desired to keep the places at half past four . . .".[20]

Located at the very heart of the city, at the intersection occupied by the Bristol Cross in Worcestre's time, is the third and certainly the most sophisticated in design of this Georgian group. This is Christ Church, sometime known as Holy Trinity, and easily identified by its elegant spire diagonally across from the domed tower to All Saints. Here there is no hint of the gothic, which, in view of the two earlier rebuilds, might seem surprising, since it is yet another creation from the Paty dynasty, this time William. Thomas had already undertaken a survey of the old church three years before the beginning of new work. Barrett notes that the mediaeval church was '. . . a low building of the model of a quarter cathedral . . .", a sufficiently ambiguous, if intriguing description to convey little, but his rather crude engraved view suggests a church with little claim to grandeur. He goes on to say that in the new building the ". . . style is nominally Grecian . . ."[21], which is wide of the mark, but excusable in the state of understanding of historical styles at that time. In fact the new Christ Church, especially its main interior space—and allowing for unhelpful later modifications—can stand comparison with the best of national classical design at the end of the century, although the constrained site presented the architect with a considerable problem. Once again, although as late as 1751 the church was ". . . greatly repaired and beautiful . . . (and) new pewed . . . (at a) cost of £1500 . . ."[22] only thirty years later it was declared by Paty—hoping perhaps for a new commission?—to be ruinous and decayed: what had the vestry been doing in the

[18] N & T Vol II, p. 167.

[19] The Bishop of Bristol's Commission on "Bristol Historic Churches" was convened in 1967, and the Report issued in mid-1968. Eight churches were considered: St George, Brandon Hill; Christ Church, City; St James, City; St John the Baptist, City; St Michael the Archangel; St Philip and Jacob; St Stephen, City; All Saints, City. Elizabeth Ralph was one of the Commission's members, as was the author, who produced a complementary booklet, "Eight Bristol Churches", looking specifically at the architecture and the setting of the buildings.

[20] N & T Vol II, p. 170.

[21] Barrett, p. 465.

[22] Ibid., p. 466.

meantime? Demolition in preparation for the new building began in 1786, and a few years later the church of St Ewen, on the other side of Broad Street, was demolished to make way for the new Council House building: at that time the two parishes were combined.

The exterior is mainly concealed by enclosing buildings, except on the south side, to Wine Street. Here it looks bleak, with high-set small windows above plain walling. Until 1941 there were small single-storey structures attached—explaining the high fenestration—and the setting would be much improved if something could again be established here. The poet Southey—"I was christened in that church"—in a letter of 1806 refers to the row of shops below the windows, on the roofs of which crowds(?) used to stand on civic occasions.[23] The main exterior interest at Christ Church is the tower with spire; assessed and criticised many times, it is not entirely as built, having been modified in 1883, but the distant relationship to St Martin in the Fields is still evident. The octagonal spire still plays an important part in city views, despite the continual encroachment of twentieth century buildings, and in closer inspection it is obvious that Paty had a proper understanding of the rules underlying classic architecture, which could be assimilated through the many handbooks and books of plates then available for study.

The interior is specially compelling, but it is necessary to recall that a great "restoration" of 1883 made substantial modifications which did nothing to enhance its visual attraction; the box pews were—of course—replaced, but the delicate painted pine reredos was also taken out and replaced by a rather dour stone tribune. Part of the reredos was later returned, but brought forward and used as a kind of choir screen, where it looks out of place. What Paty created was a delightful, simple volume, in which the short four-bay nave with its aisles is approximately square, covered by a noble plastered ceiling in a series of saucer domes, supported on six slender Corinthian columns, forming a sort of "hall church", in which the central vault rises only slightly higher than those to the aisles. The columns with their crowning impost blocks are reminiscent of Brunelleschi's work in fifteenth century Florence, and they rise from high podia which are designed in relationship to the former high box pews. High-set openings to north and south originally housed triple sash windows, replaced by the present over-heavy stone-framed lights in 1883. At the west end is a small organ gallery, with some Jacobean detail, carrying the Renatus Harris organ retained from the earlier church. A careful inspection of the vaulting, with warped binding-arches connecting the central saucer domes with the smaller and lower ones to the aisles, reveal in Christ Church an architect not only in command of the complex geometry of this ceiling, but also—and equally important—able to call on craftsmen of more than average competence. This interior will feel familiar to any visitor acquainted with Gibbs' St Martin in London, built in 1726, and progenitor of many later variations both here and in North America, but the more immediate pattern may have been John Strahan's near contemporary estate church at Great Badminton.[24]

Whilst it is unreasonable to expect that the sashes will be reset to the windows,

[23] N & T Vol II, p. 172.
[24] Pevsner (1), under Great Badminton; also Pevsner (2) for Christ Church and all the other churches.

it would make a vast improvement to this serene space if the stone altar-piece were removed, and the original reredos reinstated fully.

The last of the four churches, and the least known but in some ways the most endearing, is St Thomas, formerly St Thomas the Martyr, and according to Barrett, who was writing at the time of demolition of the mediaeval structure, second only to St Mary Redcliffe in size and grandeur among the city churches.[25]

The surveyor, Daniel Hague, made an inspection in 1789, and reported the structure to be in poor condition, needing a substantial amount of demolition and reconstruction. The parish decided on a complete replacement, and an Act of Parliament in 1790 empowered them to raise the necessary £5000; the intention was a complete rebuilding, including the west tower, but in the event this late mediaeval element was retained, and still fronts the west end rather awkwardly. A local mason/contractor living in the parish, James Allen, was asked to provide a design and to undertake the work. Allen, a carver who had been apprenticed to James Paty, lived in St Thomas Street, and had only recently been disappointed that his scheme for a new St Paul's church had been rejected in favour of that by Daniel Hague, his rival. Little more is known about Allen, except that he undertook some restoration at St Mary Redcliffe, and was responsible for rebuilding much of the church at Winford. In common with many architects and builders he was bankrupted in 1793.[26]

The new church owes no allegiance to its close contemporaries. It was not liberally funded, and externally is rather severe with some use of rendering over rubble rather than good ashlar stonework. Unlike the other new buildings, it has a nave with clerestory of small round-headed windows, and aisles with larger openings trimmed in cut stone. The west end gave little opportunity for display, but the east front, rising directly from the pavement makes a bold classical statement; the centre is crowned by a triangular pediment, below which are two blind panels flanking a generous swag, presumably carved by Allen himself. Below this a strong horizontal moulding returns from the aisle parapets, rising in an arch over a central blind panel containing a small rose window—originally a lunette. The central and side panels are framed by plain pilasters in the form of a Venetian window, all set to a high base. The nave is linked to the aisles by bold swept copings—distant descendants of early Roman baroque,—and the doorways are in classical mode.

What is to be expected for an interior to so bland but dignified an exterior? Entry to the south aisle through its west door, is under a deep gallery on fluted timber columns. This gallery formerly carried the Renatus Harris organ, once again—understandably—brought in from the earlier church, but not installed at the east end, leaving an austere space and stark west wall exposed. The main interior with everything, since 1952, painted white, is a rather ascetic but surprisingly convincing version of Classicism which would not disgrace an Italian or German designer of the time. The nave, with small windows breaking into the plain plastered barrel vault, is divided from the narrow aisles by a five-bay arcade on square pillars to tall plain bases, and the severest of capitals to moulded semicircular arches under a

[25] Barrett, p. 557.
[26] Colvin, entry on James Allen.

strong horizontal base-mould to the vault springing, which has unpainted stone cherubs' heads as corbel supporters to the bay divisions. The sanctuary bay, of the same width but shallower than the remainder, has a vault with simple repetitive decoration expressing the importance of the area. Here is the fine baroque reredos which has been described earlier (p.2).

At the time of the great restoration of the 1880s, when all the churches were subjected to Ecclesiological refurnishing, the box pews gave way to the current benches, and the walls were given a decorative scheme which was subsequently universally condemned, one of the more restrained observations being "... a bad attack of stencillitis ...".[27] This particular round of work cost in excess of £3500, and survived to the middle of this century. The interior is now entirely white, reminiscent of early Jesuit churches in Rome. The oak font of 1793 since 1880 has been used as the lectern. The church is vested in the Churches Conservation Trust, and is accessible only by special arrangement. This is a pity; a worthwhile millenial exercise would reinstate the box pews, relocate the organ, and so far as possible present St Thomas as it was before the "disastrous restoration", thus offering the public a fine building characteristic of this late classical phase, before Victorian interference.

THE BRAIKENRIDGE DIVIDE: 1820 AND AFTER

By the early nineteenth century Bristol's churches, in common with those throughout the country, had experienced a series of transformations or rebuildings, removing them in appearance and spirit far from their mediaeval origins. At this particularly vital time—for much of this would soon be re-transformed—a rich local antiquary and patron, William Braikenridge,[28] was amassing his manifold collections, including the work of a large group of artists who recorded the streets and buildings of the city. In the decade from 1820 to 1830 many hundreds of drawings, principally good and accurate water-colours, were produced, and amongst them the churches figure as a major source for study. Settings, exteriors, interiors, and details of monuments, stained glass and heraldry were carefully drawn and coloured. From these drawings the interiors may be recreated as they were then, but subsequently almost all of them have seen fundamental change.

The extent of this change can be understood by contrasting James Johnson's 1828 interior of St James[29] with a photograph from the same viewpoint in 2000 (Figs 4, 5) In Johnson's drawing the nave is dominated by the broad and very fine baroque reredos, backed by an east wall completely covered by a wall painting, the sanctuary decently contained by a twisted-baluster rail, perhaps also of the early eighteenth century, but possibly a Laudian rail from a hundred years before. To the left—north—side is a pulpit with great suspended tester, all placed two bays west from the altar, and the preaching space is filled with high-fronted pews at two levels,

[27] Dening, p. 129.

[28] Stoddard: Sheena Stoddard, Curator of the Braikenridge Collection in the City Art Gallery, also wrote her Doctoral dissertation on Braikenridge—a copy may be consulted in Bristol University Library.

[29] Braikenridge M 2808.

Fig 4. Interior of St James's Church 1828.

facing inwards in the style of a college chapel. Opposite the pulpit a window is provided with a curtain which can be lowered so that the preacher shall not be inconvenienced by strong light in his eyes raised to heaven. The ceiling is a plastered barrel vault. Today the architectural container is easily recognisable, but the plain east wall, located here when the priory church was divided to give the parishioners their space, has been replaced by a new one in Romanesque detail to match the twelfth century main arcading. The reredos has gone also, and on a simple platform of two steps, without altar rails, is a marble altar of the utmost simplicity. The lofty pulpit has given way to a typical late Victorian round version moved one bay to the east, and rows of east-facing pitch-pine bench pews fill the congregational space, continuing into the south aisle chapel except for a space at the west end providing a baptistry complete with Norman font. The north aisle is narrower, and, until recent re-ordering, opened to a second aisle through an arcade with aggressive polished granite columns with Byzantinesque capitals: these columns remain visible, but the second aisle has been enclosed to provide usable spaces, and in so doing the interior has been enhanced. The plastered ceiling has also gone, and now the roof timbers are all exposed. This serene setting is relatively recent, having been established by the Little Brothers of Nazareth in 1992, and this wonderful oasis of peace in the heart of a great city is lovingly used for its proper liturgical purpose.

The contrast in St James is characteristic of the differences in church arrangement between 1830 and later Victorian times, as substantial restorations were

Fig 5. St James, nave in June 2000 (photograph-author).

undertaken mainly in the 1880s. By this time the Gothic Revival, which had begun as a somewhat light-hearted return to mediaeval pattern-making, had become entrenched as a serious moral issue in the minds of the churchmen and their architects, who were obliged to work in the "correct" mode of—usually—fourteenth century gothic design. The story of the development of the Revival was engagingly told by Kenneth Clark in his "Gothic Revival", published in 1929, and still eminently readable; we do not need to repeat its developing course here. Almost every Bristol church was rearranged and refurnished to meet Tractarian dictate, and there are many references to the nature and cost of the work done. For example, in 1877 work costing £2150 was done in St Mary-le-Port, and was adjudged as having been "... judiciously conducted ..."; it included opening up a mediaeval window for centuries covered by an adjoining building, a new font, introduction of an eagle lectern formerly in the Cathedral, and new pews in Dutch Oak; these last, in Nicholls and Taylors' view appear to have ends more than 1.5m high—surely a draughtsman's error in drawing human figures to the wrong scale! The baroque reredos was retained. The work to Christ Church, included a new portico to Paty's tower, window replacement, removal of the reredos, and repewing, and in 1883 was thought to amount almost to a rebuilding. St Augustine's main restoration had been undertaken a few years earlier; in St Peter the pews of 1698, represented in Johnson's view of 1828 (Fig 2), were replaced with "modern seats", and Temple Church, now alas a hollow ruin, received a ". . . judicious restoration . . ."[30] in 1872, after what was then described as thirty years' misuse.

Similar comments could be quoted for most of the churches — St John alone escaped—and what was established at this time generally remained with little variation at least until 1939. Interiors and liturgy tended to be based on this late Victorian upheaval and return to something approaching at least the outward forms of mediaeval practice, until 1945, and sometimes beyond. One of the only two of our churches which is still a parish church in the full sense is St Stephen (the other being St Mary Redcliffe), and it is likely that if Worcestre could now step in he would feel at home, as it is still laid out largely on Tractarian principles. Externally it looks as it did at the end of the fifteenth century, soon after its completion, although closer inspection will reveal that much of the stonework, and certainly the window mullions and tracery, have been replaced, but without altering the detail. The four open-work pinnacles to the tower, of a specifically "Somerset" pattern, had to be rebuilt after the great storm of 1703 (which also blew down a chimney stack in the Bishop's Palace in Wells, killing Bishop Kidder and his wife as they lay in bed); three of the pinnacles fell, causing extensive damage. By the 1970s they were again in a tenuous state—lacy stonework of this kind is cruelly treated by the English climate, but decay was compounded by traffic and industrial pollution—and replacement was essential. By this time the strength of the conservation movement led to arguments about the appropriate way to restore, natural stonework being preferred, but in an attempt to avoid the cost of a further replacement in sixty to seventy years' time (the normal time-span for major stone repair up-dating), it was suggested that reinforced glass-fibre structures might be more sensible; the synthetic material would be indistinguishable from the real at ground level, and ought to last very much longer. The pilgrim may exercise his own judgement by examining what was done: is it stone, or glass-fibre? The previous major tower restoration had been in 1909, before this was a re-pewing in 1844, and a major restoration by C F Hannm in 1876; it was at that time the baroque reredos was at last taken out, to be replaced by a carved stone "mediaeval" reredos, still in-situ, but concealed by a hanging.

Stepping down into the south porch with its fan vault, our visitor might wonder about the change in street level over five centuries, but entering to the north aisle he would see a familiar-looking font under the tower to his left, and a church vessel decorously filled with lines of east-facing, close-set pews having carved ends with modest detail which he would recognise. Looking around he would be saddened by the white walls and general lack of colour in windows and on statues and tombs— just a touch of brightness to the painted and gilt angels at the capitals to the arcades. Most noticeable, however, would be the absence of the rood and rood screen, which in his time was the only means of definition for the chancel and sanctuary, separating celebrants from parishioners, since the architectural space of nave and chancel is here continuous. The Edney gates and screen in the north aisle, although of the eighteenth century, would not jar, as wrought ironwork of this delicate kind was often used in mediaeval churches. He would admire the wide, austere

---

[30] St Mary-le-Port: N & T Vol II, p. 229, and interior view, p. 227; Christ Church: Gomme, p. 188.

stone altar with deep top slab to chamfered edge, nobly set on two wide steps in the sanctuary, and behind it a fine rich hanging filling the space below the big east window, but would be happier with the carved stone reredos which it conceals (the decaying stonework having led to the need for temporary concealment). The altar is set forward, so that the celebrant may face the congregation—a post 1945 action. A simple brass rail encloses this sanctuary before which inward-facing choir stalls in mediaeval form are fronted by a prominent Victorian carved stone pulpit, and a fine latten eagle lectern. The chancel and sanctuary are carpeted, again a recent innovation, covering the tiles, which remain visible in the central and side aisles. Three more steps descend to the nave with its familiar pews. In the north aisle are two deep fourteenth century tomb recesses, but here the change in floor level would be evident, as the original level is exposed, some half metre below the modern floor, at the tomb of Edmund Blanket and his lady. Monuments of a later date, especially the large early Renaissance tomb to Sir George Snygge, 1617, would be disconcerting, because of their strange roman detail, and this one placed where there should be a side-altar in a chapel enclosed by parclose screens; displayed Royal Arms, as here in painted carved stone, are mandatory post-Reformation items.

It is fortunate that at St Stephen the post-war "liturgical revival" had minimal impact; by retaining the "traditional"—that is nineteenth century mediaeval revival—version of the interior, we are given the opportunity to worship in and appreciate a particular kind of churchmanship which has a long pedigree, and makes optimum use of this late mediaeval building. The Braikenridge collection represents St Stephen only sparsely.[31] But it is clear that, like the other churches, it must have gone through the refitting and re-ordering of three centuries before being established in its present state.

DESTRUCTION AND REVIEW: THE LAST SIXTY YEARS

Although many of the churches were damaged by bombing in 1940 and 1941, when Bristol suffered horribly, only St Augustine disappeared completely, and that through demolition in the 1970s. St Nicholas looks untouched, but three others present varying approaches to partial retention. Of St Mary-le-Port the tower alone still stands, unfortunately rather wrapped around by post-war building, but at least still visible; a splendid John Piper painting captures its dignity immediately following the bombing. St Peter and Temple Church, on the other hand, remained as burnt-out shells, and offer differing but salutary lessons about capitalizing on the historic past.

Temple church was evidently one of the finest in the city (Fig 6), but was entirely gutted; there is an apocryphal but credible story that soon after the bombing the troops making the clearance were of the opinion that the dangerously leaning tower should be demolished, but local wisdom reassured them that it had been thus for several centuries, and it was saved. James Johnson's 1828 view shows the scale and impressiveness of the interior—still, of course, then in its pre-Tractarian layout,

---

[31] Folio X, Nos 751–761.

Fig 6. Interior of Temple Church looking East 1828.

though like all the others updated later. The outer walls were stabilised, with some interior reinforcement to remaining arch divisions, and interior cleared, leaving the "noble ruin" now an important part of the townscape. When new office buildings were constructed in the '70s, a splendid opportunity was presented to celebrate the church, with its attached churchyard and trees, but the planners and architects entirely ignored the chance, and both new buildings, which are of course much higher and bulkier than the remaining seventeenth century buildings at the west end, offer their car parks, escape stairs and rubbish disposal courts towards the church, relegated to a place of insignificance in the hierarchy. A more thoughtful approach would have provided both the church and the office users with a happier environment. It may be argued that the earlier timber-framed buildings, including the Shakespeare Inn, and now open to Victoria Street, equally present backs to the church, but at least their scale was such as to be clearly subservient to the church. This is a view little changed for probably more than 250 years, and the ruined state of the church is not appreciated without walking through the gate and passage way opposite the tower entrance.

St Peter also lost its complete interior, and was similarly stabilised—using the "clearly differentiated from the original" SPAB approach to conservation, rather than trying to match mediaeval work. Before the Blitz the church, like most of our group in Bristol, rose from a light urban weave of streets and buildings founded on mediaeval predecessors; Rowbotham's drawing of the north side of the church with its surroundings (Fig 7) shows this, and evidently the general scene was very close to this until swept away by the bombing. Immediately to the south was a major mediaeval hospital, in timber framing with multiple gables, and the small churchyard had been enclosed in the eighteenth century by the iron railings visible between the church and its rectory. Ironically, the whole church came close to demolition in 1643, because of its proximity to the Castle—then unslighted—and only the approach of Rupert's army apparently prevented this from happening. The late twentieth century view (ca 1970) from Bristol Bridge (Fig 8) emphasises the fundamental reshaping of the setting and surroundings; the city decided to make St Peter's ruins a memorial to the 1939/45 war, and an inscribed stone plaque set in the west wall to the right of the main doorway reads:

IN/MEMORY OF THE/CITIZENS OF BRISTOL/AND/SURROUNDING AREAS/WHO DIED/IN THE BLITZ/DURING/THE 1939-1945/WAR

Set dramatically above the great Pennant stone retaining wall to the river, the surroundings have not been rebuilt to a tight domestic pattern, but have been developed with imagination, enhancing both the church ruin, and its generous enveloping open space of Castle Green. To the immediate south of the church, on a level terrace overlooking a lower level of the Green, is a fine herb garden, and at the east end an ornamental canal-like feature in the best tradition of the landscape garden. Before the tower is a large forecourt well paved in stone, with to its south a broad flight of stone steps leading to the riverside walk. The walling enclosures are all in the traditional grey squared rubble stone, rising as safety barriers to a height which enables them to be used for seating, capped with broad rounded copings in cast stone; these are not only boldly scaled to the generous surroundings, but are carefully textured so as to enrich the ensemble, whilst offering little promise to vandal-

Fig 7. St Peter's Church and Vicarage 1828.

ism. On the north side, adjoining the busy road serving the Broadmead area and car parks, is an extensive parade ground, which for most of the time is unused and appears rather desolate. There is a need here for some catalyst to bring it into the whole composition; in the Netherlands this would be achieved by setting up a close-set row of lofty flagstaffs, complete with flags or pennants. Why are we so demure about this sort of display? Something could easily be done here at minimal cost for

Fig 8. St Peter, from Bristol Bridge, ca 1980 (Photograph – author).

maximum civic impact, and it might bring home to passers-by more immediately how much effort has been entrained in re-creating this large unit of townscape. At the same time, the area perhaps needs more activities using the spaces so created, and it is a great pity that vandalism and its threat necessitates the closure of the interior from general access; it looks sad and abandoned as a result.

Until 1945 the churches were arranged to suit the Victorian canon, with furnishings from the Gothic Revival. Nearly sixty years later, however, there are but two designated as parish churches. A disastrous and rapid metamorphosis was occasioned by the bombings, but after the war some less destructive movements led to further change:

(a) There was renewed interest in liturgical arrangements—the so-called "liturgical revival";

(b) Increases in population, and relocation of communities entailed parochial redistribution;

(c) New church legislation, especially the Pastoral Measure of 1968, made possible more open consideration of the disposal of church "plant";

(d) Conservation, rather than restoration, became the watchword in dealing with fabric.

These movements are not peculiar to Bristol, but all have a bearing on recent changes there, and to a degree are interdependent. The liturgical revival sought to free churchmanship from the perceived trammels of a Tractarian interior, especially in rethinking the worship area to allow for a degree of flexibility of the sort enjoyed by the late mediaeval church. Fixed parallel rows of pews, and a more or less distant altar in the chancel would yield to removable chair seating, with the altar brought forward, either within the chancel, under a crossing, or even into the nave. A favoured corollary was the setting aside of part of the west end of the church as a "social space" for gatherings after the service, coupled with a need for a kitchen and sometimes toilet spaces. This sort of reorganisation was sometimes carried through—often against the wishes of the more elderly members of a congregation—with insufficient understanding of motives or intentions. Through careful consideration and discussion the modifications sometimes made it possible to keep the church open and in use throughout the week, rather than for the limited occasions of formal services.[32]

In most of the Bristol churches, because they were being taken to other uses, this was not done; at St Stephen the altar was brought slightly forward so as to enable a west-facing celebration, but in St Philip and Jacob the altar was brought out from the deep and relatively inaccessible chancel to a wide carpeted sanctuary platform in front of the chancel arch. At the same time the north choir aisle was enclosed and two small rooms provided, whilst the deep chancel can be closed by a curtain and separately used. The pitch-pine pews were retained in the nave and aisles, except for the front rows, as was the Jacobean pulpit and font-cover, and Victorian stone font. Some extra accommodation was also built into a new wing attached to the south-east corner of the church. The church, surrounded by a large square churchyard, principally used for car parking, is an invaluable illustration of the importance of individuals over systems. St Philip is effectively a church without parishioners, but the incumbent, Malcolm Widdecombe, developed a special form of churchmanship which has seen the church filled by a young and enthusiastic congregation over several decades; it remains to be seen whether this will outlast his tenure.

Demographic changes inevitably lead to too many churches in some areas, and not enough in others. Although in the late twentieth century there is a movement of population back towards the city centre, for decades the opposite occurred. Consequently several churches faced small or non-existent congregations, and the buildings could become an embarrassment to the Diocese. One of the objectives of the Pastoral Measure was to make it simpler to cope with church redundancy; before this it was difficult to take a church "out of service", but now it could be effected by following established procedures. In essence the Measure suggested three possibilities in redundancy; suitable alternative use, vesting in a special holding body, or demolition—this last clearly an act of desperation to be avoided if possible. The

---

[32] In 1975 the author was architect for a major re-ordering in St Mary's, Yate. This, *inter alia*, enabled the church to be kept open most of the time during the week.

central churches are all of such historical interest that demolition has not been considered for any of them.

The Bishop's Commission, whose results were published in June 1968, looked at eight central churches[33] (one of these, St George, Brandon Hill, not part of the current study) and was constrained to recommend that several were likely in due course to become redundant. St Michael and probably St Philip and Jacob might be offered for alternative use; St John would be vested in the Redundant Churches Fund; St Stephen with Christ Church and All Saints would become one benefice. All Saints, a complex building historically, but like all the others mainly at that time fitted out in late Victorian terms would be the Diocesan Resource Centre, with Christ Church occasionally used and available for recitals. St James, it was hoped might be a chaplaincy centre for the hospitals group. St Thomas was not among the eight, but, as has been seen, also was vested in the Churches Conservation Trust. In the event most of these recommendations have been carried out; interestingly only in this last year of the century has St Michael formally come through to redundancy, and for the moment St Philip and St Jacob is still active.

Five churches—the victims of bombing—were not, of course, in the remit of the Commission. It is significant of twentieth century attitudes that only one of those five was eventually demolished, and this in the interests of a secular development, but it reflects the importance of the "Conservation Lobby" which has grown rapidly since the war. Now great efforts are made to retain buildings, and if necessary to reconstruct them on "correct" principles rather than condoning loss or rebuilding. The movement in fact has a pedigree stretching back to William Morris and the establishment of SPAB, but gained enormous impetus after 1945 when the country had been awakened by the loss of many buildings of historic value which perhaps had not been sufficiently appreciated before. Now there are many statutory or voluntary bodies taking an interest in proposed alterations to new buildings and their settings—English Heritage, local and national planning authorities, amenity societies, DACs, SPAB, the Georgian Group, Victorian Society, Twentieth Century Society—some or all engaged in the ever-lengthening process of consultation and consent. The post-war institution of "Listing" also has played a vital part in enlarging understanding of the historic fabric of England, and became more rigorous in the last three decades of the century. Although for long the Church claimed exemption from some of the implications of Listing—stemming from Archbishop Randall Davidson's successful arguments in the Lords in 1912—church buildings are often in the prestigious Grade I or II* category, and, since 1975 when state cash became available to help in church maintenance, the same rules apply as for secular buildings. Before this, and since the thirteenth century, the Faculty system, latterly monitored by the DACs, had secured some measure of constraint on unwise alterations to the fabric and furnishings of parish churches. No longer may an unfashionable baroque reredos be summarily consigned to the scrap-head, no longer ancient or less than ancient furnishings and fittings be cast out in favour of the latest fashion—unless allowed through due process of consultation—and good natural stone may not be patched up with cement or artificial stone. But perhaps a synthetic material may be used for worn-out pinnacles?

[33] See "Eight Bristol Churches" (n 19, sup).

IN CONCLUSION

It would be unfair to end on a querulous note. Many extra controls, not all of them solely concerned with the church, may seem inhibitory; how much better, some will say, when the parish priest with his congregation (but primarily the former) could alter, extend, refurnish or otherwise modify his church as new liturgical dictate or an unexpected legacy made possible. We now enjoy a variety in both church structure and interior arrangement occasioned by the great changes which have occurred over four hundred and fifty years which has made it possible to undertake this review, but through examination of historical evidence we also appreciate that much of great cultural and artistic quality has disappeared through those same years, especially in the earliest decades. Add to this the summary loss of some churches through warfare, and it is clear that, even though change and liturgical progress ought not to be prevented through an exaggerated reverence for the past, it is important to be able to give time for thought and debate before existing evidence is removed, even if this be only time for preparing adequate record for future generations: how very vital that can be is demonstrated by our reference to Braikenridge's drawings. The legislation and conservation checks, abrasive though they may sometimes appear, may cause a delay of five years, perhaps ten in arriving at a resolution satisfactory to most, but what is that in the life of a building already at least six and possibly as much as nine centuries old? The best answer was provided by John Ruskin, paraphrased by William Morris, both of them committed mediaevalists, but both horrified at the cavalier treatment by contemporary churchmen and architects meted out to churches great and small in the late Victorian era:

> "It is . . . no question of expediency or feeling whether we preserve the buildings of past times or not. We have no right whatever to touch them. They are not ours. They belong, partly to those who built them, and partly to all the generations of mankind who are to follow us. The dead have still their right to them: that which they have laboured for . . . we have no right to obliterate. What we have ourselves built we are at liberty to throw down; but what other men gave their strength, and wealth and life to accomplish, their right over does not pass away with their death; still less is the right to the use of what they have left vested in us only. It belongs to all their successors".[34]

[34] Ruskin—"Seven Lamps of Architecture", quoted in Thompson, "William Morris" p. 234.

SOURCES OF INFORMATION

Short Title	Author and Title		
Barrett	Barrett, William	History and Antiquities of the City of Bristol	1789
Bettey (1)	Bettey, J	Bristol Parish Churches During the Reformation	1979
Bettey (2)	Bettey, J	Church and Community	1979
Braikenridge	The Braikenridge drawings collection in the City Art Gallery		
Brown	Brown, P	Eight Bristol Churches	1968
Dening	Dening, C F W	Eighteenth Century Architecture of Bristol	1923
Duffy	Duffy, E	The Stripping of the Altars	1992
Gomme	Gomme, Jenner & Little	Bristol: an architectural history	1979
Ison	Ison, W	Georgian Buildings of Bristol	1952
N & T	Nicholls and Taylor	Bristol Past and Present (3 Vols)	1881
Pevsner (1)	Verey, D	Gloucester: the Cotswolds (Buildings of England)	1970
Pevsner (2)	Pevsner, N	North Somerset and Bristol (Buildings of England)	1958
Stoddard	Stoddard, S	Mr Braikenridge's Bristol	1981
Stone	Stone, G F	Bristol as it was and as it is	1909
Winstone	Winstone, Reece	Bristol in the 1940s	1980

And, of course, the churches and those caring for them in various ways.

IX

"The Book of Your Own Heart": Some Observations on Women's Spiritual Memoirs in the Eighteenth Century, the case of the Bristol Moravians[1]

MADGE DRESSER

THIS chapter considers some of the 26 surviving autobiographical and biographical accounts of women who turned to the Bristol Moravians in the Georgian era. These "life Stories" were a distinctive feature of Moravian life and were either written by the subject themselves or were written for them upon their death. Often formulaic, and always written from a post-conversion standpoint, these stories vary both in their length and in the level of authentic period information they contain. A number seem to have been copied and circulated for the edification of other congregations. But their virtues, so far as the historian is concerned are first, that they include autobiographical writings of women whose experience would be otherwise lost to posterity; second, that the language and reference points employed in the recounting of religious life tell us much about Moravian values and; third, that they illuminate wider aspects of religious and social life in this period.

Who were the Moravians? Visitors to Bristol in the second half of the eighteenth century might have noticed the small Moravian chapel just across from the city's venerable St James's Church. This chapel was not a product of Old Dissent like the grander Presbyterian edifice at nearby Lewin's Mead, for the Moravians (or the United Brethren) were not in fact dissenters. They had no doctrinal quarrels to pick with the Anglican Church. Indeed mindful of the persecutions they had suffered on the Continent, they were grateful to their Anglican hosts in England and anxious not to alienate existing political authorities. Closely allied for a short period with the Wesleys, they were certainly evangelical in the sense of wishing to promote people's personal conversion to Christ. They claimed descent from a Bohemian religious group which pre-dated the Reformation, and which had reformed in the early eighteenth-century under the patronage of a Saxon nobleman, the Count von Zinzendorf.[2] Although initially viewed with suspicion by some Church authorities in

---

[1] I should like to thank Dr. John Walsh, Dr. Colin Podmore, Dr. Katherine Faull Eze and Dr. Phyllis Mack for commenting on early drafts of this article. Their kindness and penetrating criticisms have greatly improved it, though I retain all responsibility for its remaining weaknesses. Thanks too to Nicholas Lee and Michael Richardson of the University of Bristol Library, Special Collections and the staff at John Rylands University Library and to Janet Halton, formerly of the Moravian House Library in London.

[2] See M. Dresser, "The Moravians", in J. Barry and J. Morgan (eds.), *Reformation and Revival in Eighteenth-Century Bristol*, (Bristol Record Society Publication 45, 1994) pp.107–114.

For a full analysis of the Moravians' relationship to the Anglican Church before 1760, see Colin Podmore, *The Moravian Church: England 1728–1760*, (Oxford, 1998).

England, the Moravians took the decision not to try to wean people away from other Protestant denominations, but simply to promote the wider cause of an actively committed Christian life. Those who were accepted by the Moravian Church itself, first as "Society" members and then as full members of the congregation, had to prove their sincerity and convince the Church Elders that they were willing to submit to its highly disciplined, internationalist and communal structure. Even then, their final acceptance was to be determined by the drawing of lots, a distinctively Moravian practice intended to ensure the Divine Presence had a direct role to play in the regulation of membership.

Moravianism came to England on the crest of the Great Awakening of 1739, though individual Moravians had previously visited England. Well before Bristol's congregation was formally established in 1755, a Moravian Society existed, over-shadowed though it was by the Anglican based and exclusively male religious societ-ies, as well as the Wesleyans. Women seem to have featured prominently as local initiators and as congregation members.[3] Some two thirds of the congregation was female by the late eighteenth century. The 26 life narratives of women converts which form the core of this discussion have been considered in relation to the 11 surviving accounts by male members of the Bristol congregation. These "memoirs" are mainly to be found in the University of Bristol's Special Collection, though material from the John Rylands Library in Manchester, the Moravian House collec-tion in London along with two printed volumes of biographical material published in the nineteenth century have been included. A few, including those selected for special consideration, are relatively substantial pieces in which the voice of the indi-vidual transcends the formulaic. These life stories, then, in conjunction with the fragmentary references in the minutes of the Elders Conference[4] and the ministers' diaries, and the less numerous and usually less fulsome, life stories of their male counterparts, enable the historian to get some sense of what motivated and distingu-ished these women in their spiritual quest.

The evangelists John Cennick, John and Charles Wesley, George Whitefield and Howell Davis are cited by a number of women as inspirational figures. But my own

---

[3] Brother Horn and his wife Sr. Horn were listed by the Church hierarchy as establishing a Moravian Society in Bristol in the 1740's, before a congregation was officially established in 1755.Cf. The Moravian House, London, "The Report of Bishop Johanes von Watteville . . . regarding Brethren's work . . . dated on board the Grampus . . . 13 June 1748, Hasse Provin-cial MS. This was also true for Wiltshire, where Jane Bryant, who later married John Cennick, had been one of the single women of the group of Friends at Tytherton who sent the invita-tion to the Moravians to take over the Wiltshire Societies. Benigna Bryant and her husband who hosted a thousand strong meeting for Cennick at their house in Lyneham in the early 1740's, moved shortly thereafter to Bath where Benigna kept open house for all religious people. This meant entertaining up to 40 people at a time. Bristol University Library Special Collections, Bristol Moravian Collection, Minister's Diary, 23 March 1763, obituary of Benigna Bryant.

[4] Women had an important role as members of the Elders Conference or Committee. See my "Sisters and Brethren: Power, Propriety and Gender among the Bristol Moravians, 1746–1833", *Social History*, Vol. 21, no. 3, (October 1996), pp. 304–329, and also see Gillian Lindt Gollin, *Moravians in Two Worlds: A Study of Changing Communities* (New York, 1967), 67–196 and Beverley Prior Smaby, *The Transformation of Moravian Bethlehem from Communal Mission to Family Economy* (Philadelphia, 1988), p.22.

research suggests that in many instances, women had already been coping with inner-struggles and religious dissatisfaction long before their first exposure to male eloquence. Even those female seekers who were first stirred, awakened and unsettled by the preaching of charismatic male preachers, were often guided, supported and encouraged in their quest by other women.

All the women I surveyed were literate and five of those selected for our particular consideration were highly cultivated. There is an intellectual dimension to these women's lives which one does not conventionally associate with religious conversion narratives. Yet although these women lived in an age of the evangelical revival they also lived in the age of increasing rationalism and during their lives they struggled with varying degrees of intensity to negotiate between their individualistic aspirations as independent, thinking beings and their wish for mystical union and fellowship. One gets the strong impression that these were women of independent dispositions who, despite their oft expressed wish to be "good" found it difficult to conform to the conventional expectations for their sex. Again and again the first generation of sisters describe themselves, or are described by their biographers as being "of a lively turn of Mind", "of a very lively disposition", "of a lively volatile temper" "of a hasty temper", possessed of "a speculative mind", "romantic and self-willed"; "inclined by nature to love applause and not to be lost in a crowd". It might be argued that these qualities were highlighted simply in order to make more dramatic the nature of the conversion. For Moravians emphasised the need to acknowledge one's depravity in order to more completely humble oneself before the Saviour. Certainly the qualities of spiritual submission are de rigeur in the converted, but nevertheless, the women so described come across as characterful individuals. It was, after all, whilst browsing in John Hutton's London bookshop, that the young Esther Sutton was first exhorted by the Moravian evangelist Peter Boehler, to eschew an intellectual approach and to "seek rather in the book of your own heart." Yet, the fact that Esther Sutton was in a shop, leafing through religious books, reminds us that in an age of growing consumption, many of these women "shopped around" various religious denominations, including Catholicism and Deism, before choosing Moravianism. A critical reading of their stories shows these women to be discriminating and active agents in the course of their religious lives. Yet this was not a simple trajectory. As Phyllis Mack contends:

> . . . the confluence of Enlightenment ideas and evangelical theology heightened a tension that had always existed in Christian thought, between the desire for passivity and self-annihilation on the one hand, and the urge toward self-transformation and world transformation on the other. By the late eighteenth century this tension had begun to generate a new kind of psychic energy: a spiritual agency that was infused both by supernaturalism and by modern habits of self-analysis, emotional discipline and personal development.[5]

If both the autobiographies of men and women increasingly manifest evidence of this tension, the fact remains that the pattern of most women's lives was profoundly different from that of most men. Patriarchal expectations did not make it easy for

[5] Phyllis Mack "Religious Dissenters in Enlightenment England", *History Workshop Journal*, 49, 2000 pp. 1–23.

women who wished to pursue a religious course of life contrary to that chosen by their fathers or their husbands. Childbirth and economic dependence further complicated the picture. The pursuit of religious integrity was particularly difficult for women and the evidence also suggests that their search for religious fulfilment was often precipitated by crises in their personal lives.

We must remember too that the second half of the eighteenth century and the early nineteenth centuries were times of migration and family dislocation. The narratives treated here are full of references to the early death of parents and intergenerational tensions. Implicit in many is the sense of loneliness and anomie typical of the recent urban migrant. The communal support which the Moravians were uniquely well placed to supply made them an attractive port of call for a number of spiritually restless women.

Moravian congregations were rigidly separated by sex and marital status into "choirs". Communal living was highly developed at full-fledged Moravian settlements such as the one at Fulneck, Yorkshire where there were Choir houses for widows and widowers. Bristol was a city congregation rather than a self-contained settlement, but even here, Single sisters and, more briefly, single brothers each had a communal living and working space, though not all single members lived in it. There was also an "oeconomy" (i.e. a school where girls were taught an occupation) at nearby Kingswood which seems to have been administered, at least in part by the Bristol congregation.[6] A few of the Bristol women lived in the single sisters' communal "choir" house which was overseen by a female "labouress" who ministered to the needs of the single sisters.[7] A number of the memoirs expressed their

---

[6] *A Concise Historical Account of the Present Constitution of the Unitas Fratrum or, Unity of the Evangelical Brethren who adhere to the Augustan Confession* translated and with a preface by the Rev. B. La Trobe , (printed by M. Lewis, Paternoster Row, London, 1775), pp. 2–52.

[7] The Moravian church paid "labourers" to do its holy work. Though the term "labourers" usually refers to ministers, it also is used to refer to ministers' wives (who were expected to minister onto the women), as well as to the assistant workers with the various single sex groupings known as choirs. These assistants were, like the ministers and their wives, peripatetic, travelling not only throughout the country and often abroad. In Bristol, for example, the first labourer for the single sisters choir, one Rosina Roemer was born in Augsburg; she was succeeded by Sally Cennick, John Cennick's sister. After her stint in Bristol ten years she travelled constantly on the Brethren's behalf working with Single Sisters in London, Fulneck (Yorks), "the North", Germany and Belfast, Bedford and Zeist in the Netherlands where she was made an "Accoluth" and Deaconess. The rest of her life was spent first in Germany and then in England, where she ended her days amongst the single sisters of Yorkshire. Olsen who succeeded Cennick as Single Sisters' "labouress" in Bristol came from Denmark. Members of the congregation, were constantly travelling to other west country and Welsh congregations and some ministers and other congregation members, female as well as male came from all over the Britain. Of the women's choir, that of the single sisters was the largest and most active. Agnes Purchase (1729–1767) had less genteel contacts, her life story suggests she was of middling or lower middling rank. We know that she had heard Whitefield and Cennick preach when they came to Exeter. She subsequently resolved to go to London on her own on what seems to have been a religious quest. She makes no mention of her economic circumstances saying only that "Providence" had led her to lodge with a Moravian couple, the Hurlocks. Sister Hurlock took her to the Fetterlane Chapel where though she was much stuck by the preaching she was left without the assurance of conversion. In some desperation she went on to seek out "the Fellowship of the Sisters". Conversion seems to have followed for she soon joined the society, and shortly thereafter the church itself. In that

appreciation of having a woman "labouress" and of what we might call the aesthetic sensuality of Moravian services. Moravian women cut a picturesque figure in their distinctive cornered caps with their colour-coded ribbons which varied according to their age and marital status. Spinsters' caps were adorned with pink ribbons. Married sisters wore blue ribbons in their caps and widows white ones and special female-only services attended the award of such ribbons.[8] The emphasis on singing, on special childrens' services, and on other single sex ceremonies including ritual footwashing was commented upon appreciatively in a number of the memoirs. When the blind daughter of a Welsh clergyman, Jane Morris, first took Communion in 1756, the physical rituals which succeeded her initiation had a particular impact on her:

> ... what I felt at the Pedilarium [footwashing] and enjoyment of this highest Good, cannot be expressed ...[9]

Nevertheless, the theme of intellectual independence as well as of female fellowship feature as an important theme in the memoirs I have selected. Take for example the life story of Elizabeth Skrine, the daughter of the Rector of Oakham in Surrey.[10] Written by her Stepdaughter, Sr. Barlow, the account is a detailed one and its tone suggests the two women had a close and affectionate relationship. Such a surmise is supported by the congregational records, which show the two often acted in concert when making loans to the congregation. Skrine, who, as we have seen, was later to become the "Chief Benefactress" of the early Bristol congregation was described by her step-daughter as being of a "serious turn of mind." This description is not surprising when one considers that by 42 years of age, Elizabeth Skrine, who was then a "strict Church woman" had been twice widowed, survived a serious case of

---

same year Agnes Purchase moved into the Single Sisters Choir House in London and later to the one in Bristol where she herself worked as a religious guide to the older girls. Widows Choir houses were limited to larger settlements but the Bristol ministers' diary occasionally alludes to the Widows' meetings and we are told in 1792 that the widows labouress, a Sr. Shepley who attended to "their various wants and distresses with a tender and maternal heart."

   [8] The sisters dressed uniformly in the quiet colours of grey or brown, with white for festival occasions; and each wore the white cap or schnepplehaube (cornered cap) which has become so familiar through their portraits. All the caps were tied under the chin by a ribbon bow of different colours to distinguish the choir. The children wore the red ribbons; the older girls light red; the single sisters, pink; the married women blue and the widows the white bow. . . Theses ribbon bows were of great importance and quite a ritual of their own. The older girls, who wore the light red ribbons, were invested with the pink bow of the single sisters by the Deaconess of that choir in the solitude of her room upon the occasion of their entrance into that choir. When a single sister entered into the happy state of matrimony, she went to the ceremony wearing her cap tied with its pink bow. Immediately after the pastor's wife, who was always Deaconess of the married sisters took charge of the sister, retired with her to the vestry, and invested her with the dignity of the blue bow. After which they rejoined the company, and all repaired to the place where the feast was spread . . .
And when the sad occasion came to wear the white bow of widowhood, it was the Deaconess of the widows who put the symbolic ribbons in its place . . . Elizabeth Lehman Meyers, *A Century of Moravian Sisters A Record of Christian Community Life* London 1918.
   [9] BULSC,BMC, Minister's Diary, 8 July 1776.
   [10] BULSC, BMC, Minister's Diary, 17 November 1763, account of Elizabeth Skrine.

small pox and had lost 2 of her three children. By 1739 she set up house with her daughter-in-law who had also been twice widowed.

She certainly was highly literate. Skrine, we are told, came to hear of the Moravians when a woman friend, one Mrs. Edwin, a prominent London Moravian with ties to the Court, gave her von Zinzendorf's *16 Discourses* "which she much approved of in a doctrinal way . . ." (Mrs. Edwin, noted by Hutton and the Countess of Huntingdon was a rather dour character who according to Hutton "cast gloom" on those around her.)[11]

An assiduous attender of sermons, Skrine was particularly moved by the preachings of one Bishop Hall who, as she related in a letter to a woman friend,

> dissolved my stony heart at once and put an End to reaching after or desiring any Earthly happiness.[12]

Diane Willen's observation that women in particular turned to their pastors ". . . to cope with grief and bereavement, (and) prepare for death . . ." seems apt in Mrs. Skrine's case as well.[13] When she heard John Cennick, she was sufficiently impressed to invite him to stay at her house in Warmley which he did for the greater part of the winter sometime in the early 1750's and where, presumably, he was able to preach. But it would a mistake to see Skrine simply as the creature of male preachers, for there was much in her life and religion which was female-centred. For a start, Skrine's widowhood conferred on her an independence, which married women, even those from gentry backgrounds did not enjoy.[14]

Family concerns took Skrine to Bristol and then to Bath, where it was perhaps her contacts with Mrs. Edwin which led her to enter "into a (short-lived) Family-Connexion with Lady Huntingdon and one Anna Grinfield." Lady Huntingdon was, of course, the leader of a methodist movement and she, employed George Whitefield as minister and had her own chapels in Bath and Bristol.

When (unspecified) "family circumstances" necessitated their separation, Elizabeth Skrine returned to Warmley. There are no further references to the Countess, but it is clear that Skrine kept up her friendship with Anna Grinfield who had since become a Moravian. It was whilst visiting Sr. Grinfield in 1761, that Skrine and her stepdaughter joined the Moravians and became members of the Bristol congregation. Her conception of the Godhead as an androgynous trinity is of especial interest of how women may have reshaped patriarchal theological beliefs.

> " 'I see God as my Father, my dear Savr as my Bridegroom, and the H[oly] Ghost as my Mother . . .'[15]

[11] See Daniel Benham *Memoirs of James Hutton*, (London, 1826) and Anon. (but probably Aaron Crossley Hobart Seymour), *Life and Time of Selina Countess of Huntingdon* (2 vols.), (1893), vol.1, p. 174.

[12] BULSC, BMC, account of Elizabeth Skrine.

[13] D. Willen, "Godly Women in Early Modern England", *Journal of Ecclesiastical History*, Vol. 43, 4 (October 1992) p. 570–1.

[14] Martha Claggett (b. 1691), a noted hymn writer briefly resided in Bristol sometime in the mid-eighteenth century and her friend Charles Wesley remarked in his journal that this mother of 11 children had been "much threatened by her (aristocratic) husband" presumably for her religious views.

[15] BULSC, BMC, Memoir of Elizabeth Skrine.

readers that she was a docile and affectionate child, but that the voice of kindness and affection, had as she put it, "seldom met my ear":

> left to my own entire guidance or subjected to severe control . . . (I) became self willed, impatient and violent, and extremely romantic.

At 16 after her mother's death, she and her sister turned to Catholicism. Despite their entreaties, their father was informed of their apostasy, and as a result, she says, she and her sister "suffered great persecution and harsh treatment,"[25]

> books were "poured upon us," "Bishops, priests and deacons sent to convert us", though, as she tartly opined, "few had any understanding either of their own religion or that of the Roman Church."

She and her sister remained stalwart, reading much and corresponding with learned Spanish Jesuits. She hated hypocrisy and recalled her disgust at discovering that the ex-Benedictine monk turned Anglican clergyman, to whom her father had sent her, "secretly preserved a crucifix and a consecrated host."

Like Clarissa Harlowe, Leonora and her sister had too much "affection" for their father to publicly profess their differences and so agreed to keep their Catholicism a secret. But even after he gave up trying to convert them he

> forbad us to go to church and we were almost shunned by the rest of the family.[26]

When her father died, she was 19 and her memoirs maintain guiltily that the shock her religious rebellion had occasioned had helped to shorten his life. Her father, however, had a shock in store for his maverick daughters, for:

> . . . on opening his will, it was found that *our faith* had diminished our *property*[27]

Thus disinherited, she became "her own mistress" and met her sister in London at the house of some Unitarians. For some years, following the French Revolution, London had been a hotbed of intellectual radicalism, much of which centred around Unitarians like Richard Price and freethinkers like Tom Paine and Mary Wollstonecraft. 1794 was the year of the famous treason trials of artisan members of the London Corresponding Society. So it was no surprise to learn that Leonora Knapp was introduced there to:

> atheists and deists-philosophers and republicans. (Where) I soon imbibed other principles, and shutting up my Bible, I discarded all revealed religion,, and became a professed deist and republican.
> . . . It was the time of political plots, and treasons and I entered into them and disseminated rebellious papers, and gave myself up to the cause of so-called liberty.[28]

During this time she committed various though unspecified forms of evil, professing in retrospect to have been very unhappy but without the means to leave her

[25] Ibid.
[26] Ibid.
[27] Ibid.
[28] Ibid.

lodgings. By 34 thanks to circumstances again undisclosed, she became a woman of some fortune, and

> set out on a career of fashion and dissipation. I had the life of a fine lady and was followed by the rich and the learned.[29]

All was not pleasure and frivolity however, she retained her enquiring nature and:

> desirous of improvement in intellectual attainments, I continued to assemble around me persons celebrated for science, for art, for general talent. I held literary converszaone and devoted myself to scientifical pursuits, mixed with (song writing) and fashionable amusements.[30]

This life must have accorded her some respectability for in 1817 Charles Wesley and his family came to see her and one of their daughters "her dear and invaluable friend" unable to convert her to Methodism, suggested she "should never be happy" until she joined the Moravians. Although she hated the idea she later did attend their chapel when visiting Bristol. She entered as they were in "the midst of the litany" relates:

> "I was struck with the look of peace that pervaded their countenance, and the simple unaffected piety so different from anything I had every seen before ... (she wept) my heart was melted."[31]

The following Sunday she stayed for the Children's service, a Moravian innovation that found particular favour amongst female visitors:

> I was delighted, and reflected with bitterness on my own lost hours of childhood[32]

Her path was not yet completed, for she had to get the approval of the minister— the use of the lot for admitting new members was formally suspended in 1818 so the power of admitting new recruits to the congregation seems to have been transferred, at least in part, from the Elders Conference where women and men presided.

So Leonora Knapp had the first of several interviews with Dr. William Okeley, the minister of the time. It was a tellingly gendered encounter between two intellectually minded people who had both renounced a freethinking rationalism after considerable spiritual struggles.

Okeley, a second generation Moravian had been educated at various Moravian academies in England and the Continent but resigned from the academy at Fulneck in Yorkshire "for his sceptical views" and was apprenticed to a surgeon at Bedford before studying medicine at Edinburgh, then a hotbed of Enlightenment thinking. He published a book on psychology which Moravians considered to be an "infidel" book. He was undergoing some sort of personal crisis and regained his faith in his late twenties, in the late 1780's a few years before Leonora Knapp was to lose hers. In a dramatic and undoubtedly painful gesture, he bought up and burned all copies of his book before returning to Fulneck. He went onto lead a peripatetic existence

---

[29] Ibid.
[30] Ibid.
[31] Ibid.
[32] Ibid.

as a Moravian minister, marrying at 43 despite his recurring illhealth. When Okeley came to Bristol in 1824, he was 56[33]; Knapp was in her early 40's

She was taken with Okeley's preaching.

> My confidence (in) . . . him led me to open my heart and show all its corruptness and seek advice from him as I could not have done from any other.[34]

But Okeley, who had felt impelled to burn his own books in order to expunge his sense of sin, was horrified by the confessions of Leonora Knapp's worldly ways.

> And it our Saviour's will that in this brother, I met with such obstinate rectitude, such an unshaken determination to sift and prove me, such a faithful zeal for the interests of the whole community, that though I was the sufferer, I honoured the spirit that guided him.[35]

It is not clear whether it was Knapp's political or sexual sins, which so revolted him. But his offensive remarks to another congregation member, the Bristol born singer Harriet Hughes, "whose beautiful voice 'proved a Snare to Her' and led her into worldly company",[36] who temporarily left the congregation as a result, suggest he was particularly sensitive to fleshly rather than political misbehaviour.

In Knapp's case, the rest of the sisters and brethren seemed more accepting of her application, but though she resided in Bristol, Okeley told her to try another congregation.

Knapp appears to have internalised Okely's condemnation, it was a judgement from Jesus. How could I have accepted, she asks in her memoirs:

> reception (into the Bristol congregation) while a principal member opposed me from conscientious motives, and could not feel united with me as a member of that little family from want of confidence.
>
> . . . During this painful experience I have been taught by my Redeemer to see more clearly my own exceeding sinfulness—my . . . idolatory—my inordinate pride of heart . . ..[37]

Some of the most eloquent testimony comes from women who were as adolescents, extremely preoccupied with a sense of their own unworthiness and lack of direction. This preoccupation was expressed in religious terms and left them susceptible to those people whose own way of life seemed both virtuous and happy. The Moravians often had a cultic appeal for the distressed and lonely. The spiritual certainty and fellowship they seemed to exude had a special appeal to those directionless souls whose own family relationships were disrupted or troubled. The special dress and demeanour of the Moravians, proved particularly attractive to the spiritually vulnerable.

---

[33] John Rylands Library, Moravian collection, Workers in the Moravian Church 1068.
[34] BULSC, BMC, Leonora Knapp Memoir.
[35] Ibid.
[36] Moravian House, Benham Collection, *Extracts from the London Archives of the United Brethren* (London? 1850), entry under "Harriet Hughes."
[37] BULSC, BMC, Leonora Knapp memoir.

Margaret Tucker a Barnstaple girl born in 1755 recalled in her memoirs the loss of her father when she was five and the loss four years later of an Aunt who had "cared for her with love and tenderness". She had gone to school as a child and then was taught by a governess who clearly felt anxious about her moral welfare, warning her that "there was no middle path for me: that if I deviated at all I should go far astray."[38]

In her early teens she seems to have entered a crisis period, wondering at the hypocrisy of her elders and peers who in her estimation, "talked of goodness without practising it"; and determining that:

> I would *do*, as well as talk. Here I soon failed both inwardly and outwardly, renewed my resolutions, broke them again; and by this means kept my Pride continually on the rack.[39]

"In the midst of my confusion", she went on to recall, "the thought often occurred to me: 'Are there no people in the world, who both *know and do the will of God'? Is every body tost about as I am?*[40]

At 14, in 1769, she was apprenticed to the first milliner in Bath, one Mrs. Brett. Mrs. Brett was a Methodist, her husband was Moravian. It was Margaret Tucker's first encounter with evangelicals and she was somewhat suspicious of the latter, citing the publication a few years earlier of an anti-Moravian tract by Bishop Lavington.

Yet, when she met the Moravian sister Anna Grinfield she recalls being

> ". . . struck at first sight as having something peculiarly heavenly in her appearance, and . . . thought 'Surely the Lord dwells in her heart by faith' Oh that he were as certain of my own Salvation as I think I am of hers."

Later,

"When I saw a Brother or a Sister, I concluded that they were each one exactly what the Hymns etc. described, and I felt a veneration for all and for each one, which led me to think I was not worthy to speak to them

And still later, when

> I saw the Sisters, one and *all* for the first time without bonnets, and I was struck with reverential awe, every countenance appeared so open, the primitive plainness, the happy look, made a deep impression on my mind, and I thought, Ah it seems if the very heart might be read in the countenances, the beauty of the Lord God is upon them, here is no concealment: all is clear, the Spirit of God witnesses in those that they are born again. Ah dear Saviour! baptise me also into thy death! Set thy seal on my heart also!

Margaret Tucker herself was later to prove similarly impressive to Mary Anne Schimmelpenninck, the daughter of the highly intellectual Galton family who were intimates of Priestly, Boulton and Erasmus Darwin among others. In 1801, at 23 she found herself in Bath with her parents and was in a depressed state of mind. A

---

[38] BULSC, BMC, Margaret Tucker memoir.
[39] Ibid.
[40] Ibid.

thoughtful and intelligent young woman, she had been much affected by the religious commitment of her cousin Catherine Gurney with whom she had first stayed when she was 18. At 20, though still not a believer, she and her cousin were discussing existential issues. Like Leonora Knapp, she did not flourish in the milieu of progressive radicalism. She was disquieted by the unhappiness she observed amongst her parent's intellectual and talented circle whilst musing deeply on the seeming meaningless of life. Impressed by the relative serenity of her mother's Quaker friends, she and her cousin briefly came under the influence of Mr. Pitchford, a Roman Catholic and friend of the Quaker Gurney family.

It is hardly surprising that a person of her sensitive and serious temperament did not enjoy the social round at Bath, though contemporaries attest that she made quite an impression there.

Her depression and internal conflict must have been exacerbated by the stiflingly doll like image her mother advised her to cultivate in polite society:

> Above all things enter into no investigations with any body; no abstruse speculations, no referring to principles in common conversation, unless your opinion be asked: and then give it clearly *once*; but make no effort to maintain or enforce it, unless some wise and older person lead the way to an argument; and then put an end to it as soon as you can with a jest ... say very little about what you think, and take care to *think* as little as possible ...
>
> If young men are present, talk to them as much as you please, but always sit in the circle with the ladies.[41]

The narrative of her published biography has many of the hallmarks of a standard conversion story. One particular morning when she escaped the Pump Room and, we are told, fled to a nearby bookshop where, overcome by feelings of "wretchedness" and "deep unhappiness" she broke down in tears. She recalled her surprise when, on looking up, she found a "pleasant appearing women" in the room:

> She was looking at me earnestly, and said, in a sweet and gentle voice, 'I am afraid you are much afflicted, is there anything I can do to assuage your grief?
> 'Oh!' I replied, 'can you do anything for a wounded spirit, who knows not where nor how to obtain peace?'

It was the Moravian Margaret Tucker, who had found Mary Anne Galton in tears. Tucker advised her that the Saviour was her only remedy and that though she was other wise much occupied she would be happy to spend two hours a week with her reading the Bible. Mary Anne, though pleased, was too much a prisoner of convention to accede immediately. But coincidence or providence led her to take up lodgings in the very house where Margaret Tucker lived with a Moravian family (the Hazards in whose bookshop they met). Much to her own surprise, both Margaret Tucker and the Hazard family accepted her, Margaret Tucker read Scriptures to her, one of the Hazard daughters sat by her sickbed and sang hymns to her, she was profoundly impressed by the happy and loving family atmosphere she encountered:

---

[41] Mary Anne Schimmelpenninck, (Christiana C. Hankin, editor), *The Life of Mary Anne Schimmelpenninck*, (2nd edition London Longman Brown Green, Longmans and Roberts 1858), p 299. Thanks to Janet Brewer of Bristol for this reference.

"It surprises me very much that you should be so kind to me; for you cannot like me; I am so disagreeable." They replied, "You mistake; it is not your being agreeable or disagreeable that we regard, we look upon you as a field our Lord has given us to cultivate, and we do not ask if there are few or many weeds ...."[42]

This account, which was part of her biography based on her own memoirs, edited by her relation Christiana C. Hankin and published by a London firm, though it contains many of the expected features of a conversion story—manages to convey a convincing sense of misfittedness and angst one associates with young adulthood.

Mary Anne went on to marry a Dutch businessman living in Bristol. She retained a close association with the Moravians throughout her life, especially after the rift with her parents. She became prominent in evangelical circles by the 1830's as a religious scholar and as an author of anti-slavery and anti-Catholic pamphlets.[43]

Female converts, then, had to negotiate their right to exercise their particular religious beliefs in a variety of family situations. Both male and female converts had to deal with relatives and partners whose attitudes could range from the supportive or the indifferent through to the downright hostile. But women were of course, much more closely constrained by the wishes of their husbands and fathers than men were by those of their wives and parents. The spiritual perseverance exhibited by the first generation of Moravian women, certainly belies the notion of a passive female religiosity. The intellectual dimension of many of their life stories, shows that amongst a certain section of the educated Anglican and Quaker elite, women as well as men struggled to reconcile the contesting calls that rationalism and spirituality made on their minds and hearts.

[42] Schimmelpenninck, *op. cit.*, 310.
[43] See my, *Slavery Obscured: a Social History of the Slave Trade in an English Provincial Port*, (Continuum Press) forthcoming.

X

A Brief Encounter: Sydney Smith in Bristol

JOHN ROGAN

ON 5th November 1828 a sermon was preached in Bristol Cathedral by the Reverend Canon Sydney Smith before the Mayor and Corporation which had a profound effect upon civic relations. Smith was a well-known figure in both literary and political circles, but one who had languished in the ranks of the clergy. However, that was about to change with his arrival in Bristol. Lady Lyndhurst, wife of the Chancellor of the Exchequer, wrote to him on 24th January 1828: "My husband has just informed me that he has nominated you to a vacant stall at Bristol; and he was willing that I should have the pleasure of first communicating to you this good news. I need not say how much it has delighted me."

He was 57 and had waited a long time to become a dignitary of a church in which he had not wanted to serve as a clergyman. His father Robert had retired from business, got married, left his bride—the vivacious, attractive daughter of a French refugee—at the church door so that he might wander the world. Thereafter he moved in and out of nineteen residences, coming to rest at Bishops Lydeard in Somerset. The family seem to have been happy enough, and acquired a reputation for being argumentative. Two boys went to Eton and two to Winchester: Sydney and Courtenay. There they acquired such a reputation for winning prizes that fellow students resolved never again to compete against them. Sydney went on to New College, Oxford as a Scholar and later as a Fellow. During that time he stayed in France, joining a Jacobin Club for the sake of personal safety but becoming an able French scholar.

Thereafter he needed to establish himself in a career. His own wish was to read for the Bar or become a physician. His father forbade both, declining to put up the necessary money to enable Smith to enter either profession. He was told he could become either a tutor or a parson: Sydney did both. Much has been made of this decision. It could be argued that he lacked a vocation, but that is to use a language which was uncommon at that time. Smith approached Holy Orders rather like gentlemen did in the novels of Jane Austen. It was a profession of usefulness in which prayers were read, the sick visited, and there was participation in the legal and social life of the local community. There was little emphasis upon the notion of separation or of caste. To approach the sacred ministry in this way did not imply any lack of belief in the Christian faith. That was accepted, not doubted. It was as true of the clergy as of the laity.

The most succinct statement of this state of affairs comes from the pen of J A Froude (b.1818), Regius Professor of History in the University of Oxford, who learned a great deal about this from living in the parsonage of his father who was both a parish priest and an archdeacon. He wrote, "Doctrinal problems were little thought of. Religion as taught in the Church of England meant moral obedience to the will of God. The speculative part of it was accepted because it was assumed to be true". "People went to church on Sundays to learn how to be good. . . It was not worth while to waste time over questions which had no bearing on conduct and could be satisfactorily disposed of only by sensible indifference." "Christianity had wrought itself into the constitution of their (the people's) natures. It was a necessary part of the existing order of the universe, as little to be debated about as the movement of the planets or the changes of the seasons."

This describes Smith's obedience to his father's command in honourable terms but it also explains his theological outlook, ministerial style and activity. No-one can read his sermons without realising his grasp of the fundamentals of the faith, his sincere attachment to them and to the Established Church, and his willingness to proclaim them.

Perhaps it is in his strictures upon Methodism that his religious outlook can be clarified. In his articles for *The Edinburgh Review* he criticised them for their doctrine of particular providence. Neither he nor the Established Church thought that God was continually intervening in all the small change of life. Their approach to religion was emotional and heavily dependent upon "inward impulses". They spoke much of faith but little of works; they lacked teaching about "practical righteousness". In short, they attempted to make people more religious than was possible with the constitution of human nature. Their preachers and leaders were uneducated artisans: "consecrated cobblers". An ironmonger was all very well as an ironmonger; when he became a leader and teacher he overreached himself. "Are we to respect the poor when they wish to step out of their province and become teachers in the land?" Smith stood on the foundations of 18th century theology and of Archdeacon Paley in particular. Smith's religion was "manly, sober, rational religion", marked by "unobtrusive piety which fills the heart with all human charities and makes a man gentle to others and severe to himself." Such religion is "an object of universal love and veneration".

It was at a later time that doubts were expressed about the credal basis of Smith's faith, but by then the religious climate had changed. The Tractarians stood firmly upon a credal basis protected by the authority of the Church Catholic, not deeply enmeshed in the fabric of society but rather standing over against it, brandishing its apostolic mandate. Meanwhile Methodism flourished, to be a major force both in religion and society. Smith's faith was depressed by the twin forces of Evangelical fervour and Catholic faith and practice.

Sydney Smith became a clergyman and served at Netheravon in the diocese of Salisbury. There the squire was Mr Hicks Beach. In a short time Smith became tutor to Michael, the squire's son. It was intended that they should travel abroad but because of the Napoleonic Wars touring on the continent was impossible; Scotland was decided upon instead. The pair moved to Edinburgh, the heart of the Scottish Enlightenment—the Athens of the North. Smith never neglected his duties. His pupil worked to an exact routine. They got on well together; indeed Smith related well to the whole family, so much so that a second son followed when the first left. In his free time Smith preached occasional sermons in the Charlotte Chapel which were later published. He mixed freely in literary circles and won a reputation as a preacher. Dugald Stewart who heard him declared that Smith gave him "a thrilling sensation of sublimity never awakened by any oratory."

He became an original member of the Friday Club and through his association with people there was one of the founders of *The Edinburgh Review*, along with Francis Jeffrey, a Scottish Advocate, and Henry Brougham, later Lord Chancellor of England. It proved to be a great success but stood clearly on the side of liberalism in a conservative world. "The French Revolution", wrote Froude, "had frightened all classes out of advanced ways of thinking and society in town and country was Tory in politics and determined to allow no innovations upon the inherited faith." The *Review* took a measured view of the French Revolution! Smith acted informally as the editor of the first three issues and his contributions over the years remain the liveliest. However, his wit on grave subjects did not always persuade people of his seriousness of purpose. In the end, as others with a light touch have found, humour is not found to rest comfortably with acceptance of serious commitment. He was a tolerant, broadminded man who believed in freedom but disliked fanaticism (or enthusiasm).

The Edinburgh Review expounded views which received short shrift in many quarters. Smith won literary admiration but secured no tangible reward. He left Edinburgh and took his chance in London, though he continued to write for the *Review* until he came to Bristol. Then he gave it up, believing that a church dignitary should not write for such periodicals. In the capital he preached a little in various proprietary chapels and filled them to overflowing. His income was erratic and insufficient; something more was needed. It came in the form of a benefice at Foston-le-Clay, a little distance from York. He put a clergyman in to do the duties and settled down to lecturing and preaching in London. Then church reform overtook him. No priest had dwelt at Foston for 150 years. In 1808 the Archbishop of York directed him to reside in his benefice under the new clergy residence act. It was a great shock; but he moved with a good grace to life in the country, which he described as a healthy grave.

Despite his isolation from the metropolitan life which was his natural habitat and metier he bent his energies to pastoral ministry. The parsonage was rebuilt. He farmed his glebe, learnt to ride (not very well), got up his law and sat on the bench whilst acquiring a great reputation for reconciling parties in dispute. J A Froude described the style and expectations of both people and parsons at this time:

"The average English incumbent of fifty years ago was a man of private fortune, the younger son of the landlord perhaps . . . His professional duties were his services on Sundays, funerals and weddings on weekdays and visits when needed among the sick. In other respects he lived like his neighbours, distinguished from them only by a black coat and white neckcloth and greater watchfulness over his words and actions. He farmed his own glebe; he kept horses; he shot and hunted moderately and mixed in general society. He was generally a magistrate; he attended public meetings and his education enabled him to take a leading part in county business . . . If he was poor it was still his pride to bring up his sons as gentlemen; and economies were cheerfully submitted to at home to give them a start in life—at the university or in the army or navy."

In general that is a good description of Smith's life and style; save only that he did not hunt and his father who could, would not provide for him. Making ends meet and getting an adequate, secure income were the major concerns of many clergymen, especially those who lacked a patron. We hear much of this from Smith because of his literary talent. There were many others who were less articulate but who had the same anxieties.

The Tory years passed as he resided at Foston with occasional forays to London and Edinburgh. He had secured an entrée into the Whig social circle based on Holland House, but no tangible benefits came his way. Then the government fell and the Whigs came in. Lord Grey was supposed to have remarked soon after taking office that now, at last, he could do something for Sydney Smith. The letter from Lady Lyndhurst was the result.

His letters show his delight in the appointment. On 17th February 1828 he wrote to Lady Holland to say that he had an "extremely comfortable prebendal house; seven-stall stables and room for four carriages". Its aspect was to the south, and from the windows he could see the masts of the West Indiamen in the harbour. He was perfectly happy even though his family were not with him. "The novelty of the place amuses me." There is evident delight in what has come to pass; then the wit takes over. "The little dean I have not seen; he is as small as the bishop they say. It is supposed that the one of these ecclesiastics elevated on the shoulders of the other would fall short of the Archbishop of Canterbury's wig. The Archbishop of York is forced to go down on his knees to converse with the Bishop of Bristol, just as an elephant kneels to receive its rider." The little dean was, however, a man of some standing. Dr Henry Beeke was a Fellow of Oriel College and Professor of History in the University of Oxford. He was also well versed in matters of finance and was regarded as something of an expert on the newly introduced Income Tax. Other chapter members must have satisfied Smith's social sense. Canon Henry John Ridley was a relative of Lord Eldon. Canon Francis Randolph may have been deaf and tottering but he was good-natured, obliging and a relative of the Duke of Bedford. Smith would surely be comfortable with them.

Of the politics of his colleagues he said nothing; he spoke merely of their kindness. His appointment at Bristol meant that he could acquire a benefice which was in the gift of the Dean and Chapter. This was a common practice at the time and continued to be so for a good deal of the 19th century. A residentiary canonry did not require permanent residence in the Close; only attendance during periods of residence, during which the Canon was responsible for the life and worship of the Cathedral. Quite apart from anything else it was a way of providing an adequate stipend, even though it entitled a clergyman to more than one source of income and the payment of a clergyman to do duty when the benefice holder was away. Thus the Reverend John Eagles, whose monument is in Bristol Cathedral as a tribute to literary work, particularly as an art critic, was curate for a time to Sydney Smith at Halburton. Through the kindness of Lord Lyndhurst, who had been instrumental in getting him to Bristol, he was able to resign Foston and secure the benefice of Combe Florey near Taunton.

Now at last Smith was financially secure after years of occasional fees and a modest stipend. He wrote, "I have been very poor the greatest part of my life and have borne it as well, I believe, as most people." Moralists, he said, have extolled the evils of wealth and station, but the acquisition of guineas was an occasion for happiness. There is a realism about his comments both about his financial circumstances and those of the clergy as a whole. His *Thoughts on the Residence of the Clergy* published in *The Edinburgh Review* long before, in 1803, are candid, matter of fact and not worldly.

The move came soon after the death of his son Douglas from a long and painful illness. Like some bereaved parents he felt the desirability of a move away from painful scenes of memory. Combe Florey refreshed his spirit, as Bristol had renewed his sense of being appreciated. "This is a beautiful place", he wrote, "a country most beautiful and fertile." There he resided, coming to Bristol for his residences and business. He had also decided that winters should be spent in the prebendal house. He was set fair for ministry.

5th November is an important date in English history. It was the date of Gunpowder, Treason and Plot, and also the date on which William, Prince of Orange landed on the south-west coast to lead the opposition to James II. The events were commemorated in orders of service which were added to the 1662 Book of Common Prayer. There were not only bonfires but services which were attended by civic dignitaries, who expected to hear a sermon reaffirming the validity of the values enshrined in the outcome of those events. In both cases they were to the disadvantage of Roman Catholics. As time passed after the separation of the Church of England from the Holy See, the position of Roman Catholics became more and more difficult. This was made worse by the action of Pope Pius V when in 1570 he issued a bull that not only declared Queen Elizabeth to be a heretic but went on to excommunicate all those who were loyal to her. Further, he deprived her of her kingdom and absolved her people from all oaths of loyalty to her. It had dire consequences. The security of the kingdom was endangered by the prospect of rebellion. The rising that did, indeed, occur resulted finally in the execution of Mary, Queen of Scots. But for most Roman Catholics the problem was how they could ever take an oath of loyalty to the monarchy. That problem lasted for a long time. Meanwhile there were English martyrs and dissident groups, one of which—on its own initiative—tried to blow up Parliament and the Royal Family. The restrictions on Roman Catholics were increased. Some efforts were made by the kings to alleviate their lot, but an anti-Roman furore was easy to fan. This reached its height in the so-called Popish Plot and the passing of the Test Act. By this the holder of every public office was required to receive the Eucharist according to the rites of the Church of England, swear the oath to the Act of Supremacy and Allegiance, and renounce the Doctrine of Transubstantiation. It drove Roman Catholics, including the heir to the throne, from public life. From 1673 onwards this remained the law, and though there might be winking at it informally in local life, it was enforced nationally.

The biggest difficulty on this account lay with Ireland. There English colonisation had faltered and the Reformation had failed. It was a country with some semblance of independence, but it was subordinate to the English Parliament and it was administered in the interests of a small English Protestant minority. "The great misfortune of Ireland is, that the mass of the people have been given up for a century to a handful of Protestants, by whom they have been treated as Helots, and subjected to every species of persecution and disgrace" wrote Smith. He then listed their disabilities: they could hold neither civil nor military office, they could not vote, they could not be a member of a corporation, nor practice either the law or medicine. Further, a younger brother turned Protestant could cheat his elder brother of his inheritance. A Roman Catholic could not either purchase land freehold nor acquire it on a long lease. And there were further restrictions itemised by Smith in his *Edinburgh Review* article of 1820.

Clearly Ireland was a place where there was chronic burning resentment. There could be no presumption of loyalty to the joint kingdom of England and Scotland. Whenever the time was ripe, trouble might be expected. On 1st February 1793 the French Republic, on the full tide of revolutionary ardour, declared war on Britain. Ireland could be an Achilles heel. There was already in existence the United Irishmen, who stood for the complete separation of Ireland from Britain. The French could help them as they had assisted the American colonists twelve years earlier, with signal success. Help was indeed sent, but proved to be no more effectual than aid to the Jacobites earlier in the century. There was aid but no success. The rising collapsed after the Battle of Vinegar Hill on 21st June 1798.

There were profound effects. British control of Ireland needed to be secured. On 1st January 1801 by Act of Parliament Ireland was brought into union with Britain. Ireland was to send 32 peers and 100 commoners to London. The Church of Ireland was amalgamated with the Church of England to bring secular and ecclesiastical life in both islands together. However, the continued Protestant minority rule could not be justified in the new circumstances and every effort was needed to win over Irish loyalties against French temptations. Some concessions to Roman Catholics were needed. Pitt, the Prime Minister, proposed some degree of emancipation. George III refused to accept them. In his view they were contrary to his coronation oath, and he was right.

His great-grandfather had been brought in to wear the Crown precisely to safeguard this Protestant anti-Roman Catholic polity. The Elector of Hanover leaped over the heads of more than fifty others to sit upon the throne. Though not an Anglican but a German Lutheran, he was Protestant and that was what mattered. English society and political life had been defined by Protestantism. It was what had marked the English out; not least in their wars against first Catholic Spain and then Catholic France. The normal order of succession was altered so that this Protestant bedrock of English identity was secured. Roman Catholicism was associated deeply and strongly, in the English mind, with disloyalty and sympathy with France, the Vatican, and with devoted attachment to the House of Stuart. Despite the inevitable association of Jacobitism with Catholicism, the old adversary James Edward (the Old Pretender, James III) never wavered in his religious allegiance, though conversion to Anglicanism might have wrought considerable political advantage. If his great-grandfather had thought that Paris was well worth a Mass, he considered the Mass worth the throne of his kingdom. However, as long as the Jacobites led by a Roman Catholic posed a threat to Protestant English and Scottish political life, fellow Roman Catholics were bound to labour under disabilities and suspicion. Not until the total defeat of Charles Edward, the Young Pretender, at Culloden in 1746 could there be amelioration of their circumstances. It was bound to take time. In the aftermath of the rising of 1745 there were punishments and penalties which bore hard upon the Scottish Episcopal Church and the Roman Catholics of Scotland. Within a few years, however, it was evident that Jacobitism was dead as a political force. James died in 1766; Charles in 1788; Henry lingered on but was a Cardinal of the Roman Church. The line was dying out.

Yet the suspicion of Roman Catholicism lived on and was easily fanned into riot. In 1780 anti-Roman Catholic petitions began to flow into the House of Commons. Lord George Gordon was psychologically flawed: he did not believe that major political figures were true Protestants. The mob in London stirred. The Gordon Riots ensued. They were the worst of the century. Whatever else they displayed, it was clear that anti-Roman Catholic feeling was potentially virulent. In a sense they were profoundly conservative and patriotic. They were one more affirmation of one of the principal bases of Englishness: Protestantism.

Ireland, however, did require careful handling. The problem caused by the presence of an overwhelmingly Roman Catholic population in one of the constituent parts of the new United Kingdom could not be ignored. Rule by and for a tiny Protestant minority could not go on.

However, the preoccupations of the long war with Napoleon took precedence. After it, the debate about the position of Roman Catholics in Anglo-Irish society took place in the media and not in Parliament. Sydney Smith was prominent in that controversy. Within six years of the Union of Ireland with Britain he had published *The Letters of Peter Plymley* (1807 and 1808). They aroused great interest and more than 20,000 copies were sold. Readers had little difficulty in identifying their true author, and Smith never sought seriously to disguise himself.

The letters were a sustained argument in favour of Roman Catholic emancipation; not merely on account of Ireland but because of his view about toleration and freedom of expression. There was no Roman conspiracy against the state. "I love the Church as well as you do; but you totally mistake the nature of an establishment, when you contend that it ought to be connected with the military and civil career of every individual in the State." "Common justice and common sense combine to demolish such exclusiveness. The establishment should stand on its own merits and live by its own endeavours. If the coronation oath forbids the toleration of Roman Catholics, why have the laws been relaxed in favour of Dissenters? If the king is obliged to receive the advice of his parliament about public affairs, by what right does he exercise private judgement in this important matter? Should Napoleon make successful inroads into Ireland, should we hear any more of the sacredness of the coronation oath? The appeal to history is two-edged. As many people were put to death for their religious opinions under the 'mild Elizabeth' as under 'bloody Mary'. "Time has softened Catholic as well as Protestant". "Whatever your opinion may be of the follies of the Roman Catholic religion, remember they are the follies of four millions of human beings, increasing rapidly in numbers, wealth and intelligence, who, if firmly united with this country, would set at defiance the power of France. If they are alienated from Britain, they would threaten its security." "Why are we to endanger our own Church and State, not for 500,000 Episcopalians but for ten or twelve Orange families, who have been sucking the blood of that country for these hundred years past?" Britain has had compassion "for the victims of all other oppressions, except our own."

The argument is not confined, however, to prudence in relation to the threat in Ireland from the French. There are matters of justice and civil rights. He argues that the effect of the penal laws extended beyond, perhaps, what was intended. It is more than a matter of exclusion from certain offices and dignities. Exclusion "carries with it a certain stigma which degrades ... and the very name of my religion becomes odious". This he writes is particularly striking in England. The argument of the University of Oxford that Catholics are the enemies of liberty is unsustainable. It is mistaken zeal to associate one religion with freedom and another with slavery. Smith punches his point home; but many patriotic Britons did make the link.

Whatever may be thought about the errors of Roman Catholicism, there was no case now for forbidding its practice and for excluding its adherents from public life. They should enjoy the rights and privileges of citizens, at least equal to that of Dissenters. Arguments may be mounted about its doctrines and practices, but that is as far as opposition should go.

Ireland was a major factor in this debate. However, there were changes in general attitudes to Roman Catholicism during the first two decades of the 19th century. The defeat of Napoleon had laid to rest the fear of Catholic France. Protestant England was secure and could afford to take a broader, more relaxed attitude, now that it was the victorious arbiter of Europe. Whatever the law said, Roman Catholics had served in the army and navy. An increasing number of intellectuals were more understanding and sympathetic. The burgeoning Romantic Revival was revealing afresh the colour and vigour of the Middle Ages in which a Catholic tradition reigned supreme. By the early 1820s the argument for the inclusion of Roman Catholics in the political life of the country had been won. It was regarded as the most prudent strategy. The cause had won over a significant and influential number of members of the House of Commons. The cabinet also contained supporters of the cause. Progress seemed to depend to some extent upon the degree of support which could be secured in the political nation as it then stood.

There was opposition. In March 1825 there was a meeting of the clergy in Cleveland and Yorkshire to consider the subject at which Smith was present and spoke. The argument that Catholics could not be believed upon their oath was ridiculous. It was their fidelity to their oath that had kept them out of public life for so long. Next, that Roman Catholicism was to be opposed because it was unchanged and unchanging was untenable. The world had moved on from the 15th century. Nobody called the Church in Scotland a persecuting church now, on account of what it did and said in 1646. The proposition that the government was essentially Protestant leads to an analysis of the word: Presbyterian, Swedenborgian, Episcopalian, Ranting, Methodist? Essentially one of them? In fact, in this Protestant government Catholic peers and commoners sat for over a century. Those who argue the danger of emancipation must answer the question: What danger? They can find none. Catholics did not rebel in 1715 or 1745. Smith then laid before the meeting a petition in favour of emancipation. It secured two votes in addition to his own; it was lost by a large majority. His first effort was during March 1825 in Cleveland; his second in the East Riding of Yorkshire in the following April. That too failed.

In 1828 Daniel O'Connell was elected Member of Parliament for County Clare. He was a Roman Catholic elected to the Westminster parliament with all the anti-Roman Catholic legislation still in force. The largely reactionary cabinet of the Duke of Wellington was plunged into a crisis. Under the Test Act O'Connell could not sit. But if he did not there could be serious trouble: civil war in Ireland was feared. Could the government afford to face down its own Ultras? That depended upon a judgement about the state of public opinion. While anti-Roman opinion in

England may have been shrinking, it was still significant and where it still existed seemed to be sharper in sentiment. That sharper reaction seems to have been stimulated by the rising tide of Irish immigration. In the 1780s there were about 40,000: by the 1831 census there were about 500,000 (5 per cent of the labour force). They were concentrated in northern and Scottish cities and were mainly male, young adults, illiterate, unskilled and able to undercut the wages of British-born manual workers by an acceptance of lower pay. In some places the indigenous population felt that it was being swamped. All these cities petitioned against emancipation. Glasgow sent in 21, bearing 24,000 signatures; Manchester's had 22,000; Dundee had 53 petitions with a claim from a newspaper that virtually every Protestant in the city signed. The petition from Liverpool was so large that the porter in the House of Commons could barely lift it.

Bristol also petitioned against emancipation, with 38,000 signatures. It was against it, as vigorously as it had been against the abolition of the slave trade. Both reforms were regarded as inimical to the interests of the city and county.

The size and number of these petitions indicate that the movement had secured support not only from the manual classes but the middle class community as well. In many ways this might be considered odd, having regard to the increasingly relaxed attitude that the educated commercial and professional classes took towards Roman Catholicism. This showed that it was no longer regarded as either a political or religious threat. People seem to have petitioned on the basis of "not so much from what they knew, as from what they felt". Linda Colley writes that they regarded Protestantism as a vital part of who they were now and "the frame through which they looked at the past. The evidence suggests that many ordinary Britons who signed anti-Catholic petitions in 1828–9 saw themselves, quite consciously, as being part of a native tradition of resistance to Catholicism which stretched back for centuries and which seemed, indeed, to be timeless." She points out that resistance to emancipation was marked especially in the West Country. Activists remembered the rising of the Protestant Duke of Monmouth against the Roman Catholic James II in 1685. Both Frome and Taunton commemorated, at this time, those who had suffered death on account of their support of Monmouth. The Prince of Orange had landed in the south and moved towards London through the south-west, gathering support as he went. The Bishop of Bristol had been one of the seven bishops who petitioned James, an action which precipitated the revolution of 1688. The south-west was Protestant.

That was the background to the outlook of the Mayor and Corporation of Bristol as they processed to the Cathedral on 5th November 1828 to hear a sermon from the new Canon Sydney Smith on the occasion of the celebration of the nation's merciful and gracious deliverance from Roman Catholic treason and oppression in 1605 and 1688. The scene was set for confrontation.

Relations between the Corporation and the Cathedral had been brittle from time to time. There had been arguments about the design and location of seating for the Councillors and their wives, about how the Sword of State should be carried and where it should be placed in the Cathedral. There were other disputes about protocol: should the civic party wait to be fetched by a cathedral party or should they make their own way to the church? Once in their seats, should the preacher go immediately into the pulpit to speak or should the service continue in the normal way? Could the service start if the Mayor and Corporation were not present, because they were late? These disputes had been spread over a considerable period of time, but they betokened a certain uneasiness with each other.

Did the Councillors know what manner of clergyman was to preach before them? Sydney Smith was a well-known figure, not as a churchman so much as a significant journalist; a publicist of the first order. *The Peter Plymley Letters* had received notoriety (as well as high sales) and *The Edinburgh Review* was one of the most important and well-known periodicals of the day. On the other hand it was the journal of the Whigs, and that party was the circle in which Smith moved. A conservative, Protestant, traditionally-minded Council might well have known a little about him, but they might not have taken the full force of his outlook and principles. They went placidly along to the Cathedral.

Smith, on the other hand, knew very well what the Council was like. It was "the most Protestant corporation in England". He was determined on his course. "All sorts of bad theology are preached at the Cathedral on that day, and all sorts of bad toasts drunk at the Mansion House. I will do neither the one nor the other, nor bow the knee in the house of Rimmon", he wrote to Henry Howard. "Bad theology" means addresses which took a jingoistic, triumphalist tone over the Gunpowder Plot and the deliverance of 1688. As he had indicated in his writings, neither the Church nor society could remain locked in the past, with the bitterness and hatred of previous centuries dominating attitudes and practices in the present. Ireland has been the location of so much of that spirit.

The Corporation must have known that they would get a well-delivered sermon. Though Smith wrote his addresses out *in extenso* and read them from his manuscript, he had, nonetheless, a lively manner of delivery—punching the cushion from time to time and, he said, disappearing periodically in a cloud of dust. He was established as a distinguished preacher and speaker. Catherine Crowe related to Smith's daughter: "Although we went to the Cathedral long before the doors were open, we found a crowd already established there; and when the doors were opened, it was a rush like entering the pit of a theatre on the night of a new play" to get the best seats. Henry Cockburn wrote, "He held the manuscript in his hand and read it exactly as an ordinary reader holds and reads from a printed book; but the thoughts had been so well considered, the composition was so proper, and the reading so quiet and impressive, that I doubt if there were a dozen dry eyes or unpalpitating hearts in the Church." Smith himself thought that Anglicans could learn from the Dissenters' manner of preaching, though he distrusted their emotionalism. More animation was called for in the preachers of the Church of England. "A clergyman clings to his velvet cushion with either hand, keeps his eyes riveted upon his book, speaks of ecstasies of joy and fear with a voice and face that indicate neither, and pinions his body and soul into the same attitude of limb and thought, for fear of being called theatrical and affected ... We have ... persevered in dignified tameness so long, that while we are freezing common sense ... the crowds are feasting upon ungrammatical fervour and illiterate animation", delivered with "the genuine look and voice of passion." "Why are we natural everywhere but in the pulpit?" There seems to be some hidden admiration for the sermons of illiterate Methodist cobblers. He is not to be taken too seriously, therefore, when he declared of his own preaching, "I have the pleasure of seeing my audience nod approbation as they sleep."

Sleep they did not on 5th November 1828. The ceremonial of the services perhaps made him feel a little self-conscious, which expressed itself in his humour. He described himself as processing "preceded by a silver rod, the very type of dignified gravity . . . they say I am a severe, solemn-looking man." The sermon he produced was not written specially for the occasion. It was one which had been prepared for a congregation in York in 1825 on the theme of Religious Charity. He adapted the text, and it remained one of his favourites and was published in his collected works. This recycling of sermons was a common practice. They were adapted for a particular occasion; and this was one.

It was in the Bristol form that it was printed. The text was Colossians chapter 3, vv 12–13: "Put on, as the elect of God, kindness, humbleness of mind, meekness, long suffering; forbearing one another, and forgiving one another." Smith began by recalling the reason for the service, declaring how good it was to see "the magistrates and high authorities of the land obedient to the ordinances of the Church", setting forth an example of gratitude and of serious devotion. It was also, he declared, a day for "honest self-congratulation that we have burst through those bands which the Roman Catholic priesthood would impose upon human judgement . . ." "It is impossible that any candid man should not observe the marked superiority of the Protestant over the Catholic faith" in its emphasis upon the authority of Scripture, its discouragement of "vain and idle ceremonies", and discernment of the place of clergy as advisers and guides rather than as "masters and oracles". Protestantism "encourages freedom of thinking upon religion".

Then the argument turns to toleration and charity. "I hope, in this condemnation of the Catholic religion (in which I most sincerely join its bitterest enemies) I shall not be so far mistaken as to have it supposed that I would convey the slightest approbation of any laws which disqualify or incapacitate any class of men from civil offices on account of religious opinions. I regard all such laws as fatal and lamentable mistakes in legislation; they are mistakes of troubled times, and half-barbarous ages. All Europe is gradually emerging from their influence." He went on to say that this was not because he was attempting to convert his congregation but to protect himself from misrepresentation; but again he asserted "I should be to the last degree concerned, if a condemnation of theological errors were to be construed into an approbation of laws which I cannot but consider as deeply marked by a spirit of intolerance." It would be an abuse of his privilege of preaching to seek to convert his hearers to his own views.

He said that he would go on to treat of charity and forbearance in religious matters only and not in general. He would declare general principles. "What you choose to do, and which way you incline upon any particular question are, and can be, no concern of mine." To attempt that would be "the height of arrogance". Religious charity was at odds with religious violence. There will always be differences of opinion. It may be an evil but it is there to be lived with. Lack of charity here hardens error and provokes recrimination. We should hear not only critics of some cause or institution but also attend to what people may say in their own defence. There are limits to intolerance. "To listen to enemies as well as friends is a rule which not only increases sense in common life, but is highly favourable to the increase of religious candour." The Scriptures distinguish between laudable zeal and lamentable zeal. "The object is to be at the same time pious to God and charitable to man; to render your own faith as pure and perfect as possible, not only without hatred of those who differ from you, but with a constant recollection that it is possible in spite of thought and study that you may have been mistaken—that other sects may be right—that a zeal in his service which God does not want, is a very bad excuse for those bad passions which his sacred word condemns." In fact the differences between the sects is less than the furious zeal of partisans suggests. "I have thus endeavoured to lay before you the uses and abuses of this day; and, having stated the mercy of God's interference and the blessings this country has secured to itself in resisting the errors and follies and superstition of the Catholic Church, I have endeavoured that this just sense of our own superiority should not militate against the sacred principles of Christian charity. That charity which I ask of others, I ask also for myself. I am sure that I am preaching before those who will think (whether they agree with me or not) that I have spoken conscientiously and from good motive and from honest feelings on a very difficult subject—not sought by me but devolving upon me in the course of duty—in which I should have been heartily ashamed of myself (as you would have been ashamed of me) if I had thought only how to flatter and please, or thought of any thing but what I hope I always do think of in this pulpit—that I am placed here by God to tell the truth, and to do good." He concluded by quoting from memory Jeremy Taylor, who in his *Holy Living and Dying* records a rabbinical story. Abraham received a visitor, but before offering him hospitality said "Let us worship the Lord our God." The visitor replied that Abraham's God was not his. He would worship his own God in his own way. Abraham, enraged, put him out of the tent, only to hear from within a voice which said, "Abraham, Abraham! Have I borne with this man for three score and ten years, and canst thou not bear with him for one hour?"

The tone of the sermon is charitable and moderate. There are no fireworks or striking phrases, let alone witty thrusts. The preacher is modest in his personal claims. He deals with general principles. Roman Catholic Emancipation is the illustration of his fundamental point. Yet his support for that cause is clearly, if unprovocatively, stated. The language is quite different from the speeches delivered in Cleveland and the East Riding on the same subject. However Smith, despite his pulpit disclaimers, did aim to provoke. The letter to Howard which has been quoted already makes his intention clear. The Corporation were to be challenged about their Protestant exclusiveness, in the name of Christian charity. He wrote to Lord Holland telling what he had done. In his letter he quoted what he thought to be the heart of the address, which was an appeal for Catholic emancipation.

His civic hearers were not deluded: they had been challenged. They disagreed with the preacher. "They stared at me with all their eyes. Several of them could not keep the turtle on their stomachs." He wrote to E J Littleton, "I told you I would make a splash in Bristol . . . I let off in the Minster no ordinary collection of squibs, crackers and Roman candles . . . In short I gave the Mayor and Corporation . . . such a dose of toleration as will last them for many a year." Catherine Crowe remarked that at Clifton and Bristol he was more wondered at than liked. "All their prejudices were against him; they were totally incapable of appreciating his talents or comprehending his character." Whether there were uncomfortable moments at the civic feast, or whether he declined to drink toasts of which he disapproved we do not know. But the Mayor and Corporation had made up their own minds about the sermon. They resolved not to go to the Cathedral again; not on such a day for such a service. St Mary Redcliffe would do instead. The brittle relationship had fractured again.

In a sense, the sermon was a shot too late. Smith preached on 5th November 1828, but the government of the Duke of Wellington, provoked by O'Connell's election, had decided to face down its own Ultras and proceed with emancipation. The Test Act had been repealed already on 9th May 1828. Smith made no reference to it. The Council must have known by the time of the service that their views were not to prevail in national politics. Four months afterwards the Emancipation Bill went through: Roman Catholics were given the right to vote and to sit in Parliament. They were eligible for any public office, except that of Lord Chancellor and Lord Lieutenant of Ireland. In return they had to swear an oath denying that the Pope had any power to interfere in the domestic affairs of the United Kingdom. They were to recognise the Protestant succession, as laid down by Act of Parliament, and they were to repudiate any intention of upsetting the Established Church.

Bitterness hung on in local church and state relations. Smith moved to St Paul's Cathedral as a Residentiary Canon at the end of 1831. His former colleagues were left with the task of mending the fences. London was Smith's scene. He was a metropolitan figure once more. All his witticisms about the chapter at St Paul's could not disguise his immense pleasure at—in a sense—coming home. There in the capital his talents found full rein. He relished his speaking and enjoyed the plaudits. But as time passed he became more and more critical of the life of the Church of England. He disapproved of the Ecclesiastical Commission, as his *Letters to Archdeacon Singleton* showed. He had learned to play the old system, which was in sore need of reform, as both Peel and Bishop Blomfield saw. He thought it should be left alone.

But the organisation and style of the Church of England in Smith's day were vulnerable to radical criticism. This came in the form of the *Extraordinary Black Book* which exposed the tremendous differences that existed in the stipends of the clergy. What was the use of a Church which took so much and gave so little? The utilitarian argument was put with force. A convincing answer was required. Though Smith thought him a worthy man but without two grains of common sense, Thomas Arnold had grasped, at least, the nub of the problem. Smith showed no awareness of the profound changes taking place in society as the urban and industrial revolutions proceeded apace. Cities like Manchester, Liverpool and Birmingham grew, together with their satellite towns, and had no satisfactory ministry provided for them by the Established Church. It was in these places that Methodism and the Free Churches generally made such significant inroads. They cared for the industrial working class, and they were prepared to use the capacities of ordinary artisans to whom they gave appropriate training.

Just after Smith's death in 1845 the Religious Census of 1851 showed that in the north of England more than half the population attended a Free Church, if they attended a church at all. The strength of the Church of England was in the south: in the smaller county towns and new suburbs and in fashionable spas like Cheltenham and Bath. In Preston the majority of people who went to church were Roman Catholics. Smith's interest lay in the national political scene and in the criticism of major issues: Parnell and Ireland; Indian Missions; Charles James Fox; Female

Education; Game Laws; Spring Guns; Bentham and Prisons; just to take some titles from his contributions to *The Edinburgh Review*. There is nothing that touches on the radical economic and social changes of the time which other authors like Coleridge, Ricardo, Malthus and Arnold addressed. In this sense he is a traditional Whig; in favour of freedom and tolerance on the basis of the social and political *status quo*, managed by their magnates. He was no more sympathetic to the Tractarian Movement, as it gradually unfolded a pattern and idiom of church life and priesthood which was, in many ways, the opposite of his own.

Combe Florey remained dear to his heart. There was never a backward glance to Bristol, except once. In 1834 he heard that John Kay was to be Bishop there. It brought home to him that he would never be a bishop. Whether he could, realistically, have hoped for a bishopric in his early sixties may be doubted. He said he would have liked the opportunity to refuse one. A witticism or a sincere recognition, in his heart of hearts, that episcopacy was never the ministry for him?

NOTE

The main source of information about Sydney Smith is to be found in two volumes:

(i) *A Memoir of the Revd Sydney Smith* by Lady Holland (his daughter) in a Selection from his Letters edited by Mrs Austin.

(ii) *The Works of the Revd Sydney Smith*, with his own introduction. New edition London 1869. Longmans the publishers presented a copy to the Chapter of Bristol Cathedral.

The most popular biography is *The Smith of Smiths* by Hesketh Pearson. First published in 1934; published by Penguin in 1948. Pearson is mainly interested in Smith's character and wit, for which the letters and reported conversations are more important than the literary works, all of which have a tone of high seriousness.

Selected Letters of Sydney Smith ed. N C Smith with an introduction by Auberon Waugh, Oxford 1981. Again the interest is upon character and wit. Waugh is particularly interested in Combe Florey, which is his own home.

Britons by Linda Colley, London 1996 (paperback), originally Yale University Press 1992. Professor Colley makes clear how important Protestantism was in promoting an English sense of identity. Her section on Catholic Emancipation is most useful, and I am indebted to her for the background to this question.

The Oxford Counter Reformation: Short Studies on Great Subjects, vol. 4, J A Froude, London 1883, is an excellent account of the ecclesiastical climate in which Smith grew up. It also shows clearly why Smith would be unsympathetic to the Tractarians.

Sayings of Sydney Smith by S A Bell, 1993.

Sydney Smith by G W Bullett, 1971.

Sydney Smith by O Burdell, 1934.

Sketch of the Life of Sydney Smith by S J Reid, 1971.

Sydney Smith by G W E Russell, 1994.

XI

Christian Missionary Work Among the Seamen and Dock Workers of Bristol 1820–1914

M. J. CROSSLEY EVANS

> "Wind, hush your cry On the deep;
> Waves, be at peace, Tempest cease!
> For the world is so tired, Go to sleep!
> Seamen, sail home To the west,
> Furl, furl your sail, Night is best,
> In the harbour at home There is rest!
> Heart, do not fear, God is near!
> Rest in His arms, That is best,
> In the harbour of Heav'n There is rest!"
> "In Harbour" from *Songs for Music* (1913), by F. C. Weatherley

We need look no further than the eighteenth and nineteenth century sea shanties to find some of the traditional vices to which our seamen were exposed. The famous windlass and capstan work song sung by all hands on deck asks:

> "What shall we do with the drunken sailor,. . .
> Early in the morning?"

The only suggestions that are made are:

> "Put him in the long boat 'til he's sober, Pull out the plug and wet him all over!
> Put him in the scuppers with a hose pipe on him",
> and "Heave him by the leg in a running bowlin".

Or take this popular halliard shanty:

> "Oh! whisky is the life of man,
> Whisky made me pawn my clothes,
> And whisky gave me this red nose.
> Whisky killed my poor old dad
> And whisky drove my mother mad
> Whisky up and whisky down
> And whisky all around the town
> Oh! Whisky here and whisky there
> Oh! I'll have whisky everywhere."

Which was sung to the refrain of "Whisky for my Johnny".

In a shanty entitled "The Girls Around Cape Horn" we are told of the Spanish girls:

"that love a Yankee sailor when he goes on a spree;
He'll dance and sing and make things ring, and his
money he'll spend free
And when his money it is gone, on him they won't impose;
They far excel those Liverpool girls who will
pawn and steal his clothes."

The shanty songs are full of sailors' molls: there are "black-eyed Susan", "all those ladies now on land", "pretty Sukey" who walked "near to where our frigate lay" but would not "steer the marriage course", "scornful Sue", "the lass that loved a sailor", and "pretty Polly" to name but a few.

They were probably little better, or worse, than the one who lived in Plymouth town "and she was mistress of her trade", to which the chorus was:

"A-roving, a-roving,
Since roving's been my ruin,
I'll go no more a-roving with you false maid."[1]

Drink and women were two of the hazards of a seafaring life which were sufficiently enjoyable to be celebrated in song. Others, however, had nothing to commend them. The end of the eighteenth century and the beginning of the nineteenth, have been called the dark days of the mercantile marine; marked by misery, hardship and degradation. It was said that "the merchantman then was often a den of iniquity, cruelty and privation", and the press-gang, the crimp and the sponging house were amongst the lesser evils to beset a seaman's life.

In the nineteenth century the system of crimping was universal in every port, and the newly-returned sailor was viewed as fair game for every species of petty crook and moll. Crews were rarely paid until they had been in port for two or three days after the end of a voyage. Until they were paid they were generally penniless and housed by boarding masters who posed as the seaman's friend. Freedom, temptations of every kind, gin, and women were plied upon them under the guise of hospitality. On pay day they were presented with a bill which not only itemised the food and drink they had consumed and the bed they had shared, but all the furniture and articles, real and imaginary, which had been broken in successive brawls, and the expensive new clothes they had purchased. Before long the seaman was reduced to pawning and beggary, and forced through hunger and need, to take ship once more. The unlucky ones might find themselves in sponging houses kept by bailiffs as a place of preliminary confinement for debtors, or in a house of correction as a result of drink-induced violence.

If life on the shore was full of danger for the nineteenth century seaman, life aboard ship was more so. Harsh discipline meted out by masters who were not uncommonly drunk, ships' biscuits riddled with weevils, rotting meat, and loneliness were the common lot. Many voyages lasted for twelve months or more; boredom, poor weather, danger from storm and tide, a lack of female company, all had to be endured. Whilst evils at sea could not be lessened by the Christian missionaries, they set themselves the task of improving the lot of the seaman on land, and this

[1] R. Baker & A. Miall, *Everyman's Book of Sea Songs*, (1982), pp. 64–65 & ff.

paper will look at some of the organisations which flourished in Bristol and the work that they undertook among these men and their families between 1820 and 1914.

Briefly, we should consider the shipping in Bristol in the early nineteenth century. In the 1830s the port was visited by numerous West Indiamen, a small number of East Indiamen, Irish packets, American and Australian emigrant ships, and vessels from as far away as the Baltic and Newfoundland.[2] As the century progressed, steamships became more and more important. Captain John Irving (1779–1865), an early supporter of the Bristol Seaman's Friend Society & Bethel Union, sometime circuit steward of the King Street Wesleyan circuit, trustee of Portland Chapel and West India merchant,[3] was one of the most important ship owners in the port of Bristol. A small number of merchants such as the Daniels, Irvings and Hilhouses controlled most of the mercantile shipping in Bristol, but many small investors, shopkeepers and gentlemen in the city, owned part shares in various vessels.

The formation of a floating harbour in 1809 boosted trade, and the century saw a continual improvement in the quality of the docks in Bristol which culminated in the creation of the docks at Avonmouth, opened by Edward VII almost a century later.

The port of Bristol extended for most of the nineteenth century to include the islands of Flat and Steep Holme, and Aust in Gloucestershire. The missionary work undertaken by various organisations dealt with the city of Bristol and at a later date with the shipping off Portishead, Kingroad, Penarth Road, Steep Holme, Flat Holme, Pill, and Avonmouth.

Missionary work among the seamen of Bristol was a direct result of the Evangelical Movement's desire to address the evils to which our seamen were exposed. During the nineteenth century it attracted wide support from churchmen and women of all denominations, as well as from those whose livelihoods were directly or indirectly dependent upon seamen. Whilst the moral and spiritual improvement of seafarers was the main objective of all the societies engaged in this work, the habits of thrift, self-improvement and above all, Temperance, were inculcated with unremitting zeal.[4]

Of the numerous societies active in Bristol in the nineteenth century, three were of particular importance: the Seamen's Friend Society and Bethel Union, the work of which spanned between the period 1820 and 1903; the Seamen and Boatmen's Friend Society, which commenced work in Bristol in 1871; and what became the Missions to Seamen. The first two were interdenominational, and the latter was attached to the Established Church. Although there were a number of other comparatively short-lived societies engaged in similar work in Bristol during the period 1820–1914[5], none were as important, and the record of their activities is largely

---

[2] *The Bristol Record Society*, XV, (1950), pp. 1 & ff.

[3] He allowed the Seaman's Friend Society to purchase their first ship to be used for missionary purposes, the hulk *Aristomenes*, at £150 less than it was valued. A.J. Lambert, *The Chapel on the Hill*, (Bristol,1929), pp. 70, 90–92.

[4] For an overview of the subject, see J. Press, "Philanthropy and the British Shipping Industry 1815–1860", *International Journal of Maritime History*, I, part 1, (1989), pp. 107–127.

[5] The other societies were: 1. *The Naval and Military Bible Society* The Revd. Roald Kverndal upholds the claims of this society to be the "precursor of organised maritime mission". It was founded in 1779 and its object was to distribute Bibles among British soldiers and seamen in

confined to entries in the annual *Bristol Directory*. By 1903, of the five missionary agencies which had worked on behalf of seamen in Bristol in the second half of the nineteenth century, only two remained.[6] This paper will concentrate on the work of the first two, the Seamen's Friend Society and Bethel Union, and the Seamen and Boatmen's Friend Society, and on the life of the flamboyant Revd. Leonard William Parry (1872–1955) who was the leading missionary in Bristol in this field from 1899 until the outbreak of the Great War, and whose papers were saved from destruction by Mrs. Gill Hodder, a former secretary of the Clifton and Hotwells Improvement Society.

THE MISSIONS TO SEAMEN

The Revd. Dr John Ashley (1799–1886) is credited with founding The Missions to Seamen. In 1835, he was on holiday in Clevedon, and took a day trip out to the islands of Steep Holme and Flat Holme, which were then in the parish of St Stephen's, Bristol. Whilst there, he was concerned with the lack of evident means of providing spiritual comfort and solace for the local residents, the lighthouse keepers and the fishermen. Subsequently, he founded the Bristol Channel Mission.[7] The Society of Merchant Venturers granted him twenty guineas in April 1839 towards the cost of purchasing a vessel from which he could conduct services.[8] A small committee met to co-ordinate the work of Dr Ashley in bringing the Gospel to seamen

the Royal Navy "to spread abroad Christian knowledge and reformation of manners". It is not found in the Bristol *Directories* after 1867. 2. *The Merchant Seaman's Bible Society* The Merchant Seaman's Bible Society was founded in 1819 in London. It was dedicated to visiting ships, distributing tracts and reforming the manners and morals of the crewmen. An Auxiliary society was founded in Bristol in 1820. The treasurer of the Society in the 1840s was Councillor Peter Aitken (1798–1877), an Anglican and Conservative banker who lived at 34 Richmond Terrace. The secretaries were Mr. J.K. Bragge, who ran a young gentlemen's boarding school in Richmond House, near Clifton parish church, and Mr. Charles Metivier, of 3 Bellevue, Clifton. The auxiliary disappears from the *Directories* after 1865. Both Messrs Aitken and Metivier were involved with Dr. Ashley in the work of the Bristol Channel Mission in 1843–4. Mr. Peter F. Aitken is listed as treasurer of the Auxiliary of the Mission to Seamen in Bristol in 1862 and 1868. I am not sure if this is the same society as the Bristol Marine Bible Association mentioned by the Revd. R. Kverndal op. cit. p. 147, which was formed as an auxiliary by a zealous Bible Society collector, John James Beard, who was later active in the foundation of the Bristol Ark. 3. *Seamen's English and Foreign Bethel* The origins of this organisation are unknown to me. In 1878 it ran a mission hall in St. George's Road, Hotwells next to Prospect Row. The missionary, S.D. James, last appears in the *Directory* for 1891. In 1892 there was no missionary, but the work was stated to have been conducted "in connection" with Pembroke Congregational Chapel, Oakfield Road, Clifton. The last record of the mission is in the *Directory* for 1894. 4. *The Royal National Mission to Deep Sea Fishermen* Founded in 1881 by Mr. Ebenezer J. Mather. An auxiliary was founded in Bristol shortly afterwards. For a history of the organisation, see L.W. Hawkins, *Fishermen's Mission: Royal National Missions to Deep Sea Fishermen: The Bethel Ships*, (1992).

[6] Draft letter from the Revd. L.W. Parry to Andrew Carnegie, 5 April 1905 in the possession of the author.

[7] L.A.G. Strong, *Flying Angel: The Story of the Missions to Seamen*, (1966), pp.18 & ff, L.A.G. Strong says it was founded in 1837 and re-named the Bristol Channel Seamen's Mission.

[8] P. McGrath, *The Merchant Venturers of Bristol*, (Bristol, 1975), p.438, based on H.B. 18, p. 318, 12 April 1839.

and fishermen. Amongst the members of the committee were Alderman Charles Pinney (1793–1867), Mr Thomas Porter José (1802–1875), a well-known tobacco broker and Danish consul who served as mayor of Bristol between 1864 and 1865,[9] and the Revd. John Hensman (1780–1864), the revered evangelical Anglican, who was successively curate of St Andrew's, Clifton, minister of Holy Trinity, Hotwells, and the first vicar of Christ Church, Clifton.[10]

Dr Ashley is often held up as an Anglican hero. Unfortunately, the minutes of the Mission show him to have been a man of great pride, and very difficult to deal with. The committee had fitted a ship called the *Eirene* (Peace) which travelled from Portishead to Clevedon, from Clevedon to Pill, and from Pill to Steep Holme. We find Dr Ashley complaining that the captain of the vessel was sulky in manner, had conducted himself "very improperly", and neglected prayer amongst seamen on board the ship. Dr Ashley received a salary of £200 a year, which compared very favourably with the sums of money which were paid to many curates. Dr Ashley was not prompt in completing his reports for the committee. We find in April 1844, when the Mission had been in progress for three years, that one of Dr Ashley's numerous female admirers had promised an additional £50 a year to augment the chaplain's salary, which was felt by some of his supporters to be inadequate. Dr Ashley was a man of hot temper, and unstable temperament. Shortly afterwards he engaged in a newspaper correspondence with a Mr Bryant, which was published in the *Bristol Journal*. The secretary of the Society was requested by the committee to use his best endeavours to ensure that the arguments between the two were patched up. The chaplain was requested to abstain at present from visiting Lundy and Caldy Island, and to confine himself to the stations that were specified in the Society's first report. Mr Bryant, once the situation was fully explained to him, withdrew his letter of criticism. Dr Ashley was unwilling to make a similar compromise, and all the efforts of the Revd John Hensman to act as arbiter were in vain. The situation spiralled out of control, with Dr Ashley withholding the payment of subscriptions to the treasurer. Dr Ashley's behaviour resulted in individual members of the committee resigning throughout 1844. They included Alderman Charles Pinney in October. Numerous clergymen used their best efforts to try to persuade Dr Ashley to take a more reasonable line. Unfortunately, he would not be mollified and threatened to publish the correspondence between himself and the committee in various Bristol newspapers. The Society held an annual general meeting in the Committee Room of the Prince's Street Assembly Rooms on 5th December, 1844. The leading members of the committee resigned with effect from the last day of the year, and in spite of the fact that Dr Ashley had packed the meeting with female supporters who were keen for the work of the Society to continue (on Dr Ashley's terms), it appears

---

[9] A.B. Freeman, *Bristol Worthies and Notable Residents Past and Present* 1st Series, (Bristol, 1907), p. 51.

[10] At different times, the committee included: Messrs. *Thomas Kington*, Treasurer; Dr. *Ashley; Charles Pinney*; Samuel Worrall; *George J Hadow*; James George; *Peter Aiken*; Isaac Cook; Capn. Richard Drew; *W.C. Bernard* (One of the Elder Brethren of Trinity House); the Hon. Capn. Irby RN; Capn Jenkinson RN; Lieut-Col. Sir Digby Mackworth, Bart; *Charles Metivier*; the Revd. Charles Buck, Rector of St Stephen's; *Major General Marshall*; Rear Admiral Poulden; *T.P. José* and the Revds. *J.B. Clifford*, Joseph Haythorn, *John Hensman, John Hall, William Hunt, H. Livius*, and *Horatio Montague*. The active members in 1843–4 are in italics.

that the Channel Mission collapsed.[11] Officially we are told that "energy and enthusiasm drove him to serve the men who had such need of him", and that in 1850 the effect "of such work in all weathers was bound to have its effect upon a man who was never strong". In fact I have not been able to find any concrete evidence for the survival of the society in any form between 1845 and 1850. For reasons which are not apparent, Dr Ashley seceded from the Established Church in 1876 whilst curate of Somersham in Suffolk.[12] The work begun by Dr Ashley was restarted in the Bristol Channel in 1855 firstly by the Revd Clement D. Strong on a seventy foot iron built yacht called the *"Glow Worm"*, and later by the Revd Robert Buckley Boyer. The first public meeting of the Missions to Seamen held in March 1857, announced that there were five chaplains working in the Bristol Channel, the Isle of Wight, Milford Haven, Swansea and Cork. Scripture readers were appointed in a number of other ports.[13] From that date onwards the Missions to Seamen assumed prominence in the lives of sailors throughout the port.

Dr Ashley's life and work is currently being researched by a Bristol graduate, Miss Rhoswen Charles, a former secretary to the Missions to Seamen. Until her study of Dr Ashley's journals for the period 1841 to 1843, and other papers, is completed, much of his work will remain shrouded in inaccuracy, mystery, and myth. A recent pamphlet by Mrs Josephine Teague, entitled *The Missions to Seamen Church and Institute* (undated) makes an invaluable addition to the information available on the work of the Missions in Bristol between 1880 and 1940.

THE SEAMEN'S FRIEND SOCIETY AND BETHEL UNION

The most influential and long-established society dedicated to the conversion of seamen in Bristol during the nineteenth century was the Seamen's Friend Society and Bethel Union. The main force behind this organisation was a former seaman, known as Bo'sun, or the Revd George Charles Smith (1782–1863), who had served in Nelson's navy and fought at the battle of Copenhagen. He had later been ordained as a Baptist minister, and resided in Penzance. His concern for the lack of Christian support and encouragement for the seamen in the navy, both merchant and royal, assisted in the formation of the Bethel Union in London in 1817, which provided spiritual consolation to the seafarer and the first seamen's church, known as the Ark, which was dedicated in 1818. His colourful appearance in naval uniform, complete with medals, attracted considerable attention, and he was often followed through the streets by large groups of enthusiastic children and street urchins. He was fearless in his pursuit of the sinner; combing rough quays, sordid lodging houses,

[11] The whole sorry story is contained in the Bristol Channel Mission Minutes 1843–1844, Bristol Record Office, MS 12168 (18) ff. 1–53.

[12] G.D. Burtchaell & T.U. Sadleir, *Alumni Dublinensis*, (1935), p. 24, the rather inaccurate account of his life in F. Boase, *Modern English Biography* IV, (1908), p. 183, *The Times* 1st April 1886, p.1, The Revd. R. Kverndal, *Seamen's Missions Their Origin and Early Growth*, (Pasadena, 1986), pp. 381–394 recounts his work for the Missions to Seamen.

[13] The Revd. R. Kverndal, op. cit. p.389; G.A. Gollock, *At the Sign of the Flying Angel*, (1930), pp. 69–70.

and the questionable places of pleasure frequented by seamen.[14] Soon, he was requested by a number of friends in Bristol to come and speak to local supporters of the movement. When he preached at Old King Street Baptist Chapel in Bristol not a seat was to be had inside the chapel, and the disappointed crowds tried to scale the outside of the meeting house so that they could hear him through the windows.[15] On 27th July 1820 a committee was formed and on the 4th August 1820, the Great Room in Prince's Street was hired so that a public meeting could discuss the aims and objectives of the London Society. We are told by the report that was published in the *Evangelical Magazine*, that a large number of women were present. The chairman "expressed his regret that so much apathy should have hitherto prevailed with respect to the sailors, to whom the nation was so much indebted." The aims of the Society, which were to improve the morals and the religion of sailors, were outlined by the speakers, who included the Revd William Thorp (1771–1833), the Independent minister well-known for his opposition to the emancipation of Roman Catholics;[16] the Revd Thomas Connolly Cowan (1776–1856), formerly an Anglican curate at St Andrew's, Clifton, who had seceded from the Established Church to form his own congregation, which had built Bethesda Chapel on Brandon Hill; the Revd Thomas Steffe Crisp (1788–1868), the assistant minister at Broadmead Baptist Chapel, and later principal of the Baptist College 1825–1868;[17] and a number of Royal Navy officers. The Revd William Thorp was the minister of Castle Green Independent Chapel from 1805 until his death. A powerful and popular preacher, his support for missionary work among the seamen in Bristol was invaluable in attracting the laity to the cause.[18] Another influential supporter, and a friend of Wilberforce and Cobden, was the Revd Thomas Roberts (1780–1841), formerly of Brixham, Devonshire, who became the Baptist minister of the Pithay Chapel in 1808, and in 1817 presided over the movement of this meeting house to larger premises in Old King Street.[19] For some years he had been a sailor, and suffered shipwreck in his mid-teens.[20]

Following the success of similar ventures in London, it had been decided that a floating chapel should be established in Bristol. The intention was to create a Bristol Ark. A former warship, the *Aristomenes*, was purchased and transformed into a floating chapel, which could seat between 800 and 1,000 people. It was opened on 29th

[14] The best extant biography of Smith is to be found in the Revd. R. Kverndal, op.cit., especially pp. 113–132, Bristol Record Office, MS 40556, p. 127.

[15] The Revd. G.C. Smith was a well-known visitor to Bristol, whose activities were much disliked by the Established Church. For his efforts to preach at the St James's Fair, Haymarket, in 1823, an annual scene of vice and disorder, see Smith's *Bristol Fair but No Preaching*, in six parts (London, 1824), He began his work for the Bethel Union by having five weeks of preaching on board ships in the harbour. The Revd. R. Kverndal, op. cit., p.171, shows that he considered founding a mission in Bristol in 1817 & p. 224 that the Wesleyans opened an Ark in May 1818 on board a merchantman in the harbour.

[16] The Revd. I. Jones, *Bristol Congregationalism, City and County*, (1947), pp. 14–15.

[17] N.S. Moon, *Education for Ministry: Bristol Baptist College 1679–1979*, (1979), pp. 42–44.

[18] The Revd. N. Caston, *Independency in Bristol: with Brief Memorials of its Churches and Masters*, (1860), pp. 64–74.

[19] J.G. Fuller, *The Rise and Progress of Dissent in Bristol; Chiefly in Relation to the Broadmead Church*, (1840), p.252.

[20] The Revd. B.J. Gibbon, *A Child . . . A Hundred Years Old*, (Bristol, 1909), p.16.

August 1821, and the Revd. Thomas Roberts preached the morning service. Shortly afterwards a second society, the Clifton, Hotwells and Pill Seamen's Society and Bethel Union was formed and the *Mary* of New York was purchased with a view to similar conversion into a floating chapel. *The Sailors' Magazine and Naval Miscellany* for July 1824 (edited by the Revd G.C. Smith) gives a detailed account of its transformation. During the latter part of 1823 and the beginning of 1824 the *Mary* was converted by a number of shipwrights in Hotwells to form a model for all future floating chapels "for convenience, lightness, free ventilation, accommodation and appearance, without anything extravagant". In the Clifton Ark, the middle deck was removed and lowered. The work of the shipwrights was to convert the whole of the ship into a chapel with extensive galleries, a pulpit, and a reading desk. It was the intention of those who built the Ark that sailors and their families should be induced to attend worship together. It was also intended that the officers, captains, ship owners, merchants and their families should worship in the gallery of the Ark, so that the seamen and all those who were interested in the work of shipping in the city should be together as a family. The loss of the cabin in the creation of the chapel meant that a poop was built on the quarterdeck, which acted as a vestry for the minister. Washing facilities were also provided, and it was intended that a newly made great cabin would be used as a committee room and library. Even at this early stage, those who were involved in the work of the Clifton Ark were intent on encouraging seamen to save their money, and a savings' bank and seamen's register were created. The main body of the ship had free seats for approximately 500 people. After the cost of the ship had been paid, the Society and its subscribers were required to find an additional £800 to pay for the cost of furnishing the ship. Many poor families in Hotwells "strained every nerve to contribute their mite towards her" and worshipped there regularly.[21]

On the 2nd June 1824, the *Mary* was dedicated to the worship of God. *The Sailors' Hymn Book* was appointed to be used as the chapel's hymn book. Bo'sun Smith travelled from Penzance to conduct the opening service and the sermon was preached by the Revd Thomas Crisp.[22] The Clifton Ark had three regular services on board each Sunday after its opening. A lecture was held on Wednesday evening; a prayer meeting was held each Friday evening, and on Sunday mornings at 7am. It was agreed that once a week a Bethel meeting would be held on the deck of some ship or packet boat which was visiting Bristol. It was also intended to supply the Ark with a visiting minister from a distance to Bristol once every six weeks. It was hoped in this way that many people would be attracted to hear preachers who were known in Bristol only by their reputation. The Clifton Ark was moored on the Mardyke, following the refusal of the Society of Merchant Venturers to allow it to be moored in the Floating Dock where it would be inconvenient.[23] It was regarded by the dis-

---

[21] The Revd. R. Kverndal, op. cit., pp. 224–226.

[22] Another minister who took an active part in the opening ceremony was the Revd. John Wooldridge (died 1840), who was for some years a missionary with the London Missionary Society in Jamaica. He was an independent minister of the Gideon Chapel, Newfoundland Street, between 1822 and 1831, The Revd. N. Caston, op. cit. pp. 156–7.

[23] P. McGrath, *The Merchant Venturers of Bristol*, (Bristol, 1975), p. 438, based on H.B. 15 p. 401, 7 May 1824.

which were situated at a distance from Bristol. His involvement with the Bristol
Bethel ship spanned the period from 1820, when he joined the first committee and
took an active part in the work of the Bethel companies, until his death in 1895.
He was one of the Society's vice presidents for many years.[29]

The hulk *Aristomenes* was the first of a number of ships owned by the Bethel Union.
It was overhauled in 1832, and in 1844 condemned and sold to be broken up for
£215. The replacement was H.M. bombship *Aetna*, which was purchased from the
Admiralty, re-fitted at a cost of £1,539 and moored at a new site at the Grove, near
Queen's Square. The ship's seating was increased to hold 800 *circa* 1870, but it was
condemned and sold in 1883. The mission's work went into partial abeyance for
eighteen months until the committee found a suitable replacement, although services were held in a meeting room at 59, Broad Street. *The Jungfrau*, quondam
Gloriosa was purchased in Liverpool in February 1885, and became the fourth and
final Bristol Bethel ship. The Society continued its work until 1903, when the Dock
Board required the mooring for other purposes and no alternative site for the ship
could be found. In due course the affairs of the society were wound up and the
residual sum of £75 was given to the Bristol branch of the Seamen and Boatmen's
Friend Society.[30]

The Seamen's Friend Society and Bethel Union employed its own missionary from
1836 onwards. The most influential was a former sailor, Simon Short (1824–1901),
who was first associated with the Bethel ship in 1846, and served as superintendent
of the mission for almost forty years from 1859 onwards.[31] Mr Short signed the
pledge in his eighteenth year. In his early years as missionary he preached both to
the sailors and to the navvies working on the new railways. "He would climb the
deck of a ship, or mount a wagon in front of a public house, and with clarion voice
proclaim the blessings of temperance and the truths of the Gospel. Sometimes he
was thrown into the water, or had his coat torn to shreds." In the early 1860s he
organised temporary sheds on quays and railway cuttings to serve the workmen hot
non-alcoholic drinks. He opened a coffee tavern in West Street in 1862, and later
a cocoa boat in the floating harbour. Soon the popularity of his work enabled him
to open and manage similar rooms elsewhere in Bristol. Between 1876 and 1881
he was called away from Bristol by his numerous admirers and asked both to establish the coffee tavern movement in Liverpool, Newcastle-on-Tyne, Bradford, and
elsewhere in the north of England, and to promote the principles of total abstention.
In Bristol he established the Workman Public House Company to run a number of
tea, coffee, and cocoa refreshment rooms, and upon his own account he ran a coffee
and cocoa tavern at numbers 11 and 12 High Street. He founded the National
Coffee Tavern Association of which he became president and was known as "the
father of the coffee tavern movement". His work to improve the lot of the seafaring
and working man was recognised by his appointment to the Bristol Board of Guard-
ians, and, after his death, by a drinking fountain erected close to Holy Trinity

---

[29] For Ashmead see M.J. Crossley Evans, *By God's Grace and to God's Glory: An Account of the
Life and Times of Buckingham Chapel, Clifton, Bristol 1847–1997*, (Bristol,1997), pp. 3 ff.

[30] *35th Annual Report for 1903*, (1904) and *36th Annual Report for 1905*, (1906).

[31] *Western Daily Press*, 19 March 1901.

Church, Hotwells, the scene of much of his pioneering mission work on behalf of the Seamen's Friend Society and Bethel Union.

In 1899 Mr Short was succeeded as missionary by Mr Edwin Taylor. At this time the mission was holding three week night services, two Sunday services, a Pleasant Sunday afternoon and a meeting of a Band of Hope on Wednesday evenings. When the space occupied by the *Jungfrau* was required by the Dock Board, Mr Taylor, his workers and congregation joined the Seamen and Boatmen's Friend Society. They were joined by five members of the committee of management, who augmented the committee of the new parent body. Mr Taylor took over the responsibility for the Terrett Memorial Hall in Hotwells, and, after refurbishment, the hall was re-opened for the use of seamen on Good Friday 1903. The resignation of Mr Taylor in July 1905, when he accepted a post in Reading, brought to a close the long association of the Seamen's Friend Society and Bethel Union with the port of Bristol. Mr Thomas Ozora Elworthy, a printer and stationer, who had served on the old committee for over half a century, remained on the committee of the Seamen and Boatmen's Friend Society until at least 1911.

THE BRISTOL SAILORS' HOME

Many members of the committee of the Seamen's Friend Society and Bethel Union were involved in the formation of the Bristol Sailors' Home. The first committee of this Home included the aforementioned Thomas Pethick, and Mark Whitwill (1826–1903), a vice-president of the Seamen's Friend Society and Bethel Union, who worshipped at Highbury Congregational Chapel and served as a councillor for St Philip's from 1870 to 1891. He was a justice of the peace, a former chairman of the Chamber of Commerce, a ship owner and ship broker who played an active part in the formation of the Bristol Children's Hospital, and was sometime chairman of the Bristol School Board. Other leading members of the committee included Messrs. Charles Hill, the ship builder, Philip Miles, one of the local members of parliament, and Lieutenant Kemball, who was one of the secretaries of the Merchant Seamen's Bible Society for the Port of Bristol, and one of the secretaries of the Seamen's Friend Society and Bethel Union.

At a meeting held at the offices of the Marine Board in Prince's Street on 16th September 1851, it was determined that a Seamen's Home should be built in Bristol. The existing societies involved in missionary outreach to seamen worked together to do all that they could to provide assistance to raise subscriptions for this worthy venture. A house in Queen Square was purchased for £1,300, which provided good quality accommodation at a reasonable rent for seamen between voyages, and cut out the unacceptable practices of boarding-house owners. The committee ensured that lavatories were provided and that water and gas were laid on. The house was provided with 52 iron bedsteads, 52 coconut fibre mattresses and pillows, linen, blankets and other necessary items. A cook and steward were employed, and a list of rules were drawn up. The cost of board and lodgings for men was 13s. a week, or 2s. a day, and for boys 10s. a week or 1s. 6d. a day. The amount of washing per week which was allowed for was: 3 shirts, 1 pair of trousers, 1 flannel waistcoat, 1 pair of drawers, and 2 pairs of stockings. The Seamen's Home assisted seamen to save money, and encouraged them to open an account with a savings bank. Swearing and improper language was not acceptable, and drunkenness was not tolerated. No smoking was allowed in the dormitories. Prayers were held each morning at 7:45am. Numerous local lodging and boarding-house keepers were concerned by the amenities provided by the new Seamen's Home, and in order to ensure that their supply of visitors was maintained, they adopted a system of boarding vessels outside the Cumberland Basin offering cards encouraging seamen to stay with them. The committee who ran the Seamen's Home took action against this, and were obliged to employ an agent in Pill, who would board the vessels and give seamen details of the Seamen's Home, before they reached the city, thus circumventing the wiles of the lodging-house keepers. It was suggested that the river pilots should be encouraged to tout for the Seamen's Home at a remuneration of 1s. per head for all seamen they induced to enter into the Home.[32] There were some problems in the early days of the Home because numerous social distinctions were observed amongst seamen, and in 1853 we find the mates in the Seamen's Home objecting to eating their meals in an open dining room with the ordinary seamen. Consequently it was necessary for the committee to give instructions for one table to be separated from the rest of the room by a curtain, so that the mates and other officers could eat in privacy. Lieutenant William Henry Kemball RN (1793–1853) was the first superintendent of the Seamen's Home. It was generally the case that the masters of the Seamen's Home were chosen from officers, either in the Royal Navy, who had inadequate pensions as "half pay" officers, or former captains of merchant ships. Captain John Freeman Saunders (1795–1866), who was appointed superintendent of the Home in 1853, had sailed for thirty-seven years out of the Port of Bristol.

THE PILL SEAMEN'S MISSION

By the 1870s, Mark Whitwill (1826–1903) was also vice-president of the *Pill Seamen's Mission*, which was established in 1871, and had as its president, the Revd Frederick William Gotch (1808–1890) of the Bristol Baptist College. The Pill Seamen's Mission employed a missionary, Mr Shepherd, a visitor, Mrs Emma Shepherd, and a Bible reader, Mrs Cox, who took an active part in sustaining missionary work amongst the families of seamen.

THE WORK OF THE SEAMEN AND BOATMEN'S FRIEND SOCIETY IN BRISTOL AND HOTWELLS 1871–1912, WITH PARTICULAR REFERENCE TO THE SUPERINTENDENCY OF THE REVD LEONARD PARRY

The Revd Leonard Parry lived firstly in Hotwells and then in Clifton for a total of twenty-four years, between 1900 and 1927. As superintendent of the Western Division of the Seamen and Boatmen's Friend Society between 1899 and 1912, and the first secretary of the National Sailors' Society between 1912 and 1914, his name

---

[32] Bristol Record Office, MS 40311/G1, Minutes of the Seamen's Home 1853–1860, f.51, 7th June 1853.

would have been familiar in almost every household in the city due to his innovative and aggressive missionary and pastoral work among the seamen and the dock workers of the city. How many people have heard of the Revd Leonard William Parry today or know that his wife, Jessie, is commemorated on a marble plaque set into the garden wall of the Manor House in York Place, Clifton? Even the focus of his work, the Terrett Memorial Hall, no longer exists. This building, erected in 1893/4 opposite the lock to the Cumberland Basin, was, according to the Bristol *Directories*, swept away between 1953 and 1956 in the clearance of properties which was the prelude to the erection of the Hotwells fly-over. During Mr Parry's lifetime, his work in Hotwells and Clifton Wood was consigned to oblivion, and his manifesto for the Bristol Municipal Elections in November 1947, whilst mentioning his work in Bristol in the 1890s, remained silent about the most significant part of his life's work.

Who was he and what was the nature of his work? I will try to answer these questions from the evidence available to me. Firstly, who was he? In 1947 F.W. Leat, the chairman of the Bristol Liberal Committee for the city of Bristol told the electors of St James's ward that Mr Parry was "a grandson of one of Bristol's leading freemen and business men." Joseph Colston Parry, his grandfather, was in fact a boot and shoemaker during the 1860s, in modestly comfortable circumstances, resident at 34 Broad Street. Joseph Parry was the father of a numerous family, of whom two are important to our story: a daughter, Catherine Colston Parry (1829–1862), and a son, Julius Colston Parry (1832–1898), who was the father of our subject.

At the age of sixteen in 1845, Catherine was converted to evangelical Christianity by hearing a sermon by the Revd David Morgan, curate of Holy Trinity, St Philip's. His ministry changed the course of her life. She was confirmed, and became a Sunday School teacher at the Hannah More Sabbath School. She later commenced a school of her own, ran bazaars and employed her needle in the service of numerous worthy causes. In 1857, she left the Church of England and became a member of the United Brethren or Moravian Church, prior to her marriage to the Revd Samuel Hartley Reichel, the Moravian minister at Kingswood. She opened a Sunday School in Kingswood, and established a Dorcas Society for the poor. In a brief, but happy married life, of just over four years, she bore her husband three children, but never recovered from the effects of the birth of her last child. She died in the spring of 1862 from the combined effects of "pulmonary congestion, and great debility", at the age of 33.[33] Greatly loved within her domestic circle, and sincerely mourned, the life and death of Catherine Reichel, formerly Parry, influenced the lives of all those with whom she came into contact, living and dead, including her brother Julius, sometime accountant and station master, and her nephew.

Leonard was one of Julius's numerous children. He was born at Bishop's Lydeard, near Taunton on 18th March 1872, where his father was employed in a clerical capacity on the railway. In 1886 he began work as a drapery assistant in a shop in Exeter.[34] Whilst there, he became involved in the YMCA, which was to play an

[33] A manuscript account of the life and death of Catherine Colston Reichel, written *c.*1863 by her husband, the Revd. S.H. Reichel, and in the possession of the author.

[34] L.W. Parry, Copy Letter Book 25/8/1934—18/2/1935 p.19, letter to Messrs William Whiteley Ltd. 26 September 1934.

important role in his later life. In about 1890 he moved to Bristol and continued his business training, firstly in the Barton Warehouses, and latterly at Baker, Baker, in Wine Street.[35] Although only employed in relatively humble positions in both establishments, he made numerous business acquaintances which were to be of use to him in his later career.

At the age of twenty-one in 1893, Leonard Parry was appointed the honorary secretary of the Youths' Department of the YMCA, whose special mission to those aged 14 to 18 was encapsulated by Archdeacon Sinclair thus: "Our aim, above all things, is that where our youths meet for physical training, for social intercourse, for intellectual equipment, there they should also learn the inestimable blessing of self-control, decision for Christ and His service, the discipline of the imagination and the purification of the desires. Our hope is that they will cultivate noble ideals, sympathy with all good men, and all good things, communion with our Father in heaven, love to Him, and love to men."

To look at how this was achieved it is instructive to read copies of the *Weekly Bulletin* for members in 1898 and the *Youths' Winter Evenings: Pleasant and Profitable, Prospectus (for) 1898–1899*, which contains notices of literary lectures and mutual improvement classes; chess, draughts and association football matches, lectures on such subjects as "Songs of the Sanctuary and how they were sung", "Disarmament and Peace: England's Duty", "The Great Earthquake at Lisbon" and "Time and Time Keepers", some illustrated by lime-light views. There were social teas, concerts with the phonograph, and others featuring songs, piano and violin renditions of such well known pieces as Mascagni's *Cavelleria Rusticana*, whose standard English translation of the libretto was provided by the Bristol-based barrister and lyric writer Frederic Edward Weatherley (1848–1929).[36] The Youths' Department debated the evils of smoking, upheld a strong Temperance tradition, held Sunday evening Gospel meetings, ran a library which was well supplied with papers and periodicals, and held PFEs, Pleasant Friday Evenings with songs and recitations. The YMCA saw the years between 14 and 18 as "ones of danger" and by keeping the young men fully occupied in the evenings the committee hoped to broaden the youths' horizons and win them for Christ.

Leonard Parry's work as honorary secretary of the Youths' Department was so successful that in 1896, after three years in the post, he became a paid official, as the department's general secretary. *The Bristol Evening News* for the 7th October 1898 reveals that although still "only a young man" (he was 26) he had founded a Haven Home at 9 Brunswick Square, St. Paul's, for young men living away from their families. He had begun a youths' holiday savings' bank, and, as an agent for the Economic Life Assurance Society, he encouraged his charges to pay premiums and make financial provision for their futures.[37]

---

[35] Bristol Municipal Election, St James's Ward, 1 November 1947. Manifesto of L.W. Parry.

[36] Weatherley also provided the standard English translation of Leoncavallo's *Pagliacci*, and wrote the lyrics of 1,500 drawing room ballads, including: *Nancy Lee* (1876, music Stephen Adams, alias Michael Maybrick), *They all Love Jack* (1880, music Stephen Adams), *The Midshipmite* (1885, music Stephen Adams), *The Holy City* (1892, music Stephen Adams), *Danny Boy* (1913 to the *Londonderry Air*); and *The Roses of Picardy* (1916, music Haydn Wood). For many years, *The Holy City* sold 50,000 copies a year.

[37] *Youths' Winter Evenings: Pleasant and Profitable 1898–1899*, p. 24.

Many of Bristol's leading citizens were involved in the work of the YMCA, including members of the Wills and Fry families. During his six years working at No. 5 St James's Square, Mr Parry came into contact with many people of influence in the city. It is not known, however, if it was through any of them that he came to be involved with the Seamen and Boatmen's Friend Society. The most likely persons to have influenced him were Councillor Alfred Smith, the treasurer of the Society, who was actively involved in the Totterdown branch of the YMCA, and Mr R.M. Morphett, the secretary of the YMCA, who served on the committee of the Seamen and Boatmen's Friend Society.[38]

On 5th January 1899 the *Bristol Evening News* reported that the High Sheriff of Bristol and Mrs. Charles Wills, would hold an "at home" for members and friends of the Youths' Department on the following evening. This would mark the retirement of Leonard Parry from his secretaryship of the YMCA Youths' Department and celebrate his assumption of the superintendence of the Seaman's Bethel in Guinea Street, near St Mary Redcliffe.

THE SEAMEN AND BOATMEN'S FRIEND SOCIETY

The Seamen and Boatmen's Friend Society was founded in 1846, and aimed to promote "the social, moral and religious welfare of seamen and boatmen" by five means: firstly, by preaching the Gospel on board ship, and in the society's Bethels; secondly, by visiting shipping and boats upon rivers and canals; thirdly, by circulating the Scriptures, the society's magazine, *The Waterman*, and tracts; fourthly, by the establishment of Sabbath Schools, and Bands of Hope for the children of seamen; and lastly by providing coffee and reading rooms.[39]

The Seamen and Boatmen's Friend Society was an ecumenical organisation. Its patrons included at different times, the Bishops of Worcester and Coventry, the Bishops of Manchester and Ripon and leading lay and clerical Nonconformists. Its work in Bristol commenced in 1871. By 1876 it was employing as its superintendent and mission agent the Revd William Hart Coombes, B.A., who carried on his work among Bristol seamen, canal boatmen and their families from his home, 7, Greenbank Terrace, Coronation Road. In 1886 he was succeeded by Mr Edwin Ferguson of Totterdown, who was appointed pastor and superintendent, and in the following year the society acquired the Bethel in Guinea Street, between the Bathurst Basin and St Mary Redcliffe Church. The *Bristol Directory* for 1895 advertised two services on Sunday at the Bethel, prayer meetings on Mondays and Wednesdays and Temperance work also on Wednesdays. In addition to his missionary work, pastor Ferguson ran a coffee and cocoa tavern at 188 Gloucester Road, which he continued after relinquishing the pastorate in 1897. There followed a period of reorganisation at the Bristol station under the Revd John W. Cannings, the parent Society's travelling

---

[38] The Revd. B. Gibbon, *op. cit.*, pp. 43, 49, Mr. Morphett was superintendent of the Old King Street Baptist Sunday School from 1887–1901, the treasurer from 1880–1901, and a Sunday School teacher from 1880. In 1894 he became secretary of the Bristol Young Men's Christian Association, and later became a Baptist pastor at the Burr Mission, Chicago.

[39] *Arrowsmith's Dictionary of Bristol*, ed. H.J. Spear & J.W. Arrowsmith, (Bristol, 1884), p. 160.

and organising secretary, who was based in Birmingham[40]. During 1898 1,670 vessels were visited by the missionary and his helpers, and 2,400 copies of *The Waterman*, 4,300 tracts, and many New Testaments were given away to seamen, dock workers and their families. The parent society was incorporated in January 1899.

By the end of the nineteenth century, the Society had twelve mission stations: four in the north-west; Liverpool, Ellesmere Port, Birkenhead and Seacombe; three in the Midlands; Birmingham, Walsall and Hednesford; Bristol, Plymouth and Bath in the south-west, and single branches in London, and Leeds, all presided over by the general secretary, Joel Cadbury, the Quaker philanthropist, who was based in Birmingham. The Society had a General Committee of Management which met annually in London, and five regional committees.

Although inter-denominational, it was, at least by the 1890s, predominantly Nonconformist and Temperance in tone. *The Christian Million: The Readable Religious Weekly* for 31st October 1902 stated that when the Society's work was extended to Bristol in 1871, it was one of five organisations engaged in similar work. In thirty years the number had shrunk to three organisations, and was soon one of only two.

The Society was re-launched by the reopening of the refurbished Guinea Street Bethel, and an eight-day Gospel Mission led by the new superintendent in March 1899. For this Mr Parry was able to draft into service the Junior YMCA band, and organise testimonies from those who had renounced their past life and turned to Christ.[41] At about this time, the new superintendent was ordained as a United Methodist Free Church minister, which increased his standing within the community amongst whom he worked.

Shortly after Mr Parry's appointment as superintendent and missionary, the focus of the society's work shifted from the Bathurst to the Cumberland Basin. Committed Bible Christian Methodists or Bryanites, Councillor, later Alderman, William Terrett[42] and his wife, Sarah Mary (1836–1889), played important roles in founding the White Ribbon Temperance Army. They were largely responsible for building Redcliffe Crescent Chapel, York Road, New Cut, Bedminster in 1877, and their family raised a thousand guineas towards its cost.[43] Mrs Terrett died on the platform after giving a Temperance address in "her own dear Mission Hall," in Princess

---

[40] The 55th *Annual Report* of the Society for 1900 (1901) reports in the inside cover that the Society's work was begun by Mr. Cannings in Leeds in September 1899. He first took services in a small room at 10 Warehouse Hill, which subsequently became a reading room, and formed a local committee, which took over financial control on 1st January 1900. The Riverside Mission Hall, on Warehouse Hill, was opened in February 1901. The Revd. J.W. Cannings resigned from the Society in October 1903, upon accepting the pastorate of a Baptist chapel near Leicester, the 58th *Annual Report* for 1903 (1904), p.5.

[41] *The Waterman*, March 1899, XVIII, No. 4, p. 38.

[42] For Councillor Terrett, see *Bristol in 1898: Contemporary Biographies* (1898), I, p.72, Councillor Terrett and his wife were monomaniacs on the subject of Temperance. The diary of the Revd. Laurence Henry Byrnes (1822–1902), pastor of Pembroke Congregational Chapel, Clifton from 1869–1890, recounts that at a large church meeting on 2 November 1887 Mr. Terrett "got up and assailed me for not being a tea-totaller and quite spoiled the meeting for all useful or spiritual purposes". MS Journal, in the possession of the author. It is just possible that the journal entry should read Terrell and not Terrett.

[43] *An address delivered by Mrs. W. Terrett . . . on the occasion of her laying one of the memorial stones of Redcliffe Crescent Chapel, Bedminster, on the 22nd October 1877*, (Bristol, 1877).

Street.[44] The debt on the church, when coupled with the subsidy needed to run two Gospel halls erected in the memory of his wife, placed great financial strains upon Councillor Terrett.[45]

The Terrett Memorial Hall, opposite Cumberland Lock, was built in 1893/4 to commemorate Mrs Terrett's Temperance work. It had a large new hall which seated 400, a vestry and a caretaker's house attached, together with a debt of £745 1s 3d outstanding on the building. Sympathetic to the aims of the society, Councillor Terrett promised £100 towards the liquidation of the debt if the local committee of the Seamen and Boatmen's Friend Society raised £350 towards its purchase by 1st June 1901.

The affairs of the society were in the hands of a local committee of nine men, who in 1901 numbered amongst its members, Councillor William Terrett; Captain Henry A. Butt MN, (the father of Dame Clara Butt), a shipbroker, leading Temperance advocate, and chapel steward at Redcliffe Crescent Methodist Church; and Councillor Alfred Smith, a coal factor and ship owner who was Bristol's lord mayor between 1905 and 1907. All were active in the various branches of the Methodist Church (which was not finally re-united until 1932). R.M. Morphett, the secretary of Bristol YMCA, was a leading Baptist layman, who was superintendent of Old King Street Baptist Sunday School from 1887 to 1894; Mark Whitwell Junior, a leading shipowner, was a member of Highbury Congregational Chapel,[46] and the Revd John Leon Thomas, Congregational pastor of Wycliff Chapel, Totterdown from 1898 to 1908, later became secretary of the Religious Tract Society in the West of England.

At this stage it is worth considering the character of Councillor Alfred Smith (1843–1920) in more detail. He was the Society's treasurer from before 1899, and became chairman in 1905, retaining the office for the remainder of Leonard Parry's involvement with the Society (until at least 1912). He played an important role in the affairs of the Society throughout the Edwardian period. In 1900 his daughter, Jessie Kate, aged 32, was married to Leonard Parry, a not unhandsome man of 28, without money or family, but with prospects. Thereafter, through thick and thin, Councillor Smith was bound to Mr Parry for the sake of his daughter's happiness and security, and for the good of his grandson, Alfred Leonard Parry (1901–1983), whose birth permanently impaired his daughter's health. It was through Councillor Smith's extensive business contacts in Newport and Cardiff that the society was able to extend its work there from 1905 onwards.[47]

Councillor Smith was an active worker for the United Free Methodist Church. In

---

[44] For her life see the Revd. F.W. Bourne, *Ready in Life and Death: Brief Memorials of Mrs. S.M. Terrett, founder of the White Ribbon Gospel Temperance Army*, (1893), which is the most odious book of its kind that I have ever read!

[45] The church struggled against a crippling debt, which was only cleared in 1926, fifteen years before it was destroyed by enemy action. It was rebuilt after the war.

[46] *Western Daily Press*, 6 December 1921, *Bristol in 1898: Contemporary Biographies*, (1898), I, p. 97. He was a member of the local Marine Board, president of the Chamber of Commerce, consul for Belgium, vice consul for Uruguay, CBE, JP (1912), and sometime conservative councillor. He was a supporter of the Sailors' Home.

[47] From an early stage in his marriage, Mrs. Parry's monies were at her husband's disposal, and he borrowed freely from her, and through her, from her father.

1872 he was so moved by the sight of ragged children playing on a piece of open ground on Oxford Street, Totterdown, that he determined to found a Sunday School and mission. By June 1875 he had erected a building, and the following September he had a school of 140 with seventeen teachers, a secretary, and a librarian. For 34 years he remained superintendent, and devoted his energies to teaching the Gospel of Christ to the young. He was also founder of Oxford Street Methodist Church, and remained a continual and munificent benefactor to it during his long life.[48]

Although the major influence on the work of the Seamen and Boatmen's Friend Society in the 1890s and 1900s was Methodist, through the work of members of Redcliffe Crescent and Oxford Road Churches, the officers and congregations of Pembroke Congregational Chapel in Oakfield Road, Clifton; Hope Congregational Chapel, Hotwells; Zion Congregational Chapel, Bedminster Bridge; and Wycliff Congregational Chapel, Totterdown, were also active supporters of its work.

I will place the work of the society in the Edwardian era under a number of headings, and consider each briefly.

PASTORAL WORK

During the 1900s the country relied increasingly on the mercantile marine for the supply of its foodstuffs and for the export of its industrial products. The opening of the Avonmouth Docks in 1908 by Edward VII heralded the influx of an even greater number of sailors into the port of Bristol. Some were discharged in the port, and others travelled here from all over the country, from London, Southampton and Liverpool (often by foot), to find employment with one company or another, in one of their respective steam ships or sailing vessels. The annual reports of the society record the number of seamen helped to Cardiff or Newport each year, enabling them to find suitable berths where ones were not available in Bristol. From 44 cases in 1902, the number rose to 100 in 1903, to over 120 in 1905, and reached 200 in 1906. Mr Parry reported that due to the stagnation of trade in 1906, many thousands of seamen had been thrown out of employment, a state of affairs which affected everything from the barge to the liner. The large number of cases of want in such a crisis were well beyond the capacities of voluntary organisations. In one port alone, on one evening, over 200 men sought refuge in mission premises. In the Newport branch, between 11th December 1905 and 25th January 1906, 109 destitute seamen were offered free beds, and 76 were given free meals.

To help alleviate the cases of want among seamen in Bristol, in March 1900, Mr Parry started to provide free Sunday teas at the Guinea Street Bethel. These were moved to the Terrett Memorial Hall the following year. The cost of the simple tea was defrayed through the kindness of friends and donations from Joseph Storrs Fry (1826–1913), the philanthropic cocoa manufacturer. The water police were briefed to send the destitute for cups of tea, and were given tea-tickets to distribute to

---

[48] Anon, *Oxford Street United Methodist Sunday School 1872–1922*; *Short History of the Oxford Street Methodist Church, Totterdown, Bristol: Celebration of Jubilee 1875–1925, and Diamond Jubilee 1875–1935*, (Bristol, 1935), Alderman Smith wrote a number of hymns for the use of his Sunday School, some of which were harmonised by the well-known Bristol conductor, Mr. George Riseley.

deserving cases. In 1903 it was estimated that 500 seamen had been given free teas, a third of whom were in a destitute condition. The missionary reported that he had talked five men out of suicide, one of whom, a German, who had been assisted by him over a period of three weeks, produced a loaded six-chamber revolver, and tried to shoot himself. Another sailor, after 26 hours without food and in a desperate and distressed condition, was intercepted at the Grove by a water policeman who prevented him from drowning himself. The seaman was duly sent for tea and a square meal in Hotwells. Each Sunday, the free teas were followed by Gospel services and testimonies. The work continued until May 1910, when it was suspended through lack of funds.

Visits to sailors, dock workers, and their families who were unwell, were undertaken by the missionary and a team of volunteers. In 1902, 3,250 visits were made, garments were distributed to the needy and the provisions left over from the Sunday teas given to those in want. Portions of Scripture were read to the bed-ridden, the illiterate, and those in need of company, compassion and support.

MORAL AND SOCIAL IMPROVEMENT

a) Sunday School

The Sunday School was run at the Guinea Street Bethel for the children of seamen and dock workers. Each August there was a Sunday School outing on one of Messrs. P. and A. Campbell's Steamers, such as the *Westward Ho* or *The Britannia*. These boats took approximately 100 people, without charge, to Clevedon, Portishead or Weston, where they spent the day crabbing, fishing, playing games, and holding a service on the esplanade, accompanied by a portable harmonium. It should be remembered that for many children this was the only holiday that they had each year. In 1910, the committee expressed the intention of opening a Sunday School in Hotwells.

b) Mothers' Bright Hour, later called the Women's Bright Hour

Mrs Parry and a small number of supporters organised these meetings at Guinea Street from 1900 onwards, and at Hotwells from 1901 onwards. Seamen's wives and widows were encouraged to meet together. By 1910 the Wednesday evening meetings at Hotwells were supported by ladies from Pembroke Congregational Church in Oakfield Road, and attendance often numbered 75. In the summer the members of the Mothers' Bright Hour joined the Sunday School outing to Clevedon or Weston.

c) A Young Women's Sewing Group and a Christian Endeavour Society

A Young Women's Sewing Group and a Christian Endeavour Society were both established. The Christian Endeavour Society encouraged the young to read the Bible daily, to pray and put their religion at the heart of their lives. The Young People's Society of Christian Endeavour was begun in July 1900 under the aegis of Miss Jessie Kate Smith (1868–1937), Alderman Smith's daughter, who later married Mr Parry. The Society came to England from America in 1887, and a National

Union was formed in Bristol in 1896. The ten principles of the movement were effectively expounded by Miss Smith who won many young people for Christ through her work with the young.[49]

d) *Pleasant Sunday Evenings (PSEs)*

Pleasant Sunday Evenings (PSEs) were introduced by Mr Parry and widely advertised. They were based on a form with which he was familiar from his work with the YMCA. Evening entertainments consisted of recitations, vocal and instrumental music, and an address, usually on a Temperance theme. Had we been fortunate enough to attend the 166th PSE on 14th May 1903, we would have heard Miss Mitchell play *Grand March* on the pianoforte, Mr Reynolds sing *Mona* and Mr Hussey recite *The Beggar*, as well as listened to Mr Veale's Temperance address. The early phonograph was pressed into service for entertainment and attracted considerable support from those unable to purchase one for themselves.

In August 1905, Mr Parry secured a fourteen day visit from the Fisk Jubilee Singers from America, one of whom was an aged former slave.[50] Their Gospel message and rendition of *The Prayer Songs of the Slaves* were immensely popular. People were turned away from the meetings, and the visit was extended by a further seven days. The superintendent found 37 men who formed two divisions of a melodeon band to accompany the Jubilee Singers during their services.

e) *Literature*

Boredom and loneliness were two of the enemies which beset seafarers on their long monotonous voyages. To combat them, Mr Parry and his helpers collected a huge number of improving books, tracts, and periodicals, and New Testaments which were distributed to ships moored in the docks. Parcels were sewn up into book bags by volunteers who received hessian for the purpose. Books were given to the society by authors, publishers, well-wishers, and the Religious Tract Society. In 1901 tracts were distributed in 12 languages. By 1902 it had risen to 18: Norwegian, Swedish, Danish, Russian, Lettish, German, Dutch, French, Belgian, Spanish, Portuguese, Italian, Greek, Gaelic, Welsh, Manx, Celtic and English. Some 18,000 copies of the Society's own magazine, *The Waterman*, were also distributed, which in due course was localised and paid for by advertisements. By 1908 the tracts and religious literature were written in 29 languages and dialects.

SPIRITUAL

The Revd Leonard Parry was resourceful, innovative and hard-working as the Society's missionary. By 1901 he was holding services or social activities daily except on

---

[49] The Revd. H.T. Wigley and the Revd. A. Wright, *Jubilee Reflections of the British C.E. Union 1896–1946*, (1946); Various, *The Platform of Principles: For Christ and the Church*, (undated) p. 36, *The Work of the Committees in the Young People's Society of Christian Endeavour*, compiled by the Revd. F.E. Clark, (undated), p.32.

[50] J.B.T. Marsh, *The Story of the Jubilee Singers; with their songs* (new edition, 1885). Fisk University was a missionary institution in Nashville, Tennessee. The singers took an active part in the revivalist meetings of Messrs. Moody and Sankey. For their first visit to Bristol in

Mondays and Fridays. In 1903 over 700 services were conducted, with a number in Norwegian and German. By 1905 he was holding weekly limelight services where stories such as the Prodigal Son and the Pilgrim's Progress were told by means of slide projection.

In the summer months, open air services were held each Sunday on one of the Scottish steamers by permission of the agent, Mark Whitwell Junior, and a harmonium was carried on board ship to assist in worship. In 1900, services were held on the Welsh Back three times a week, conducted by assistants at the Guinea Street Bethel young Christian Endeavours. In 1905 open-air services were taking place each Sunday evening in the vicinity of the Cumberland Basin.

Missions were a regular feature of the activities of the Hotwells Branch throughout the Edwardian period. None, however, could compare with the success of the Revival Services held at both branches in January and March 1905. We are told that the "intense religious feeling existing throughout the country was felt here to such an extent that over 200 conversions were recorded".

TEMPERANCE

Temperance has been referred to on a number of occasions in this paper. The Band of Hope at the Guinea Street branch was active, and members were encouraged to take "the pledge" to abstain from all intoxicating and spiritiferous liquors, and to recruit new members under the banner. The need for this work cannot be better exemplified than by the following letter to the superintendent:

"Norman Cottage
Dec 24th / 08

Mr Parry
    Dear Sir,
I thank you very much for writing me an account of my son Reg. I am very greaved to think I have a child that as sunk so low I have always helped him as far as its laid in my power in fact have distresed myself often for him.I have sent him both clothing and money and I find it pawned for drink as soon as he gets it. Therefore I feel it is wrong to send any moor a man with health strength and a good trade he could earn quite £2 pr week if he liked. To desert wife & children its very dreadful. We all feel it most keanly. He ought to be a comfort to us now instead of our greatest trouble. I am truly sorry for him, but even if I could afford to send him as I have bean doing I feel its Incouraging him in his bad Habbits. I realy cant think what to say to him if I wrote. I must leave him in the Hands of his God. Trusting he will keep him from harm & shew him the Strait way. Dear Sir try & persuade him to live a better life & look after his wife & 2 boys. Then we wold try again to help, but its usless when all goes for drink.
Thanking you for yr kindness
Beleave me
    Yrs Respectfully
    M. Mason   "

1874, see p. 72. The singers were actively supported by the leading figures of the day, such as Gladstone, Shaftesbury, and Spurgeon.

SEAMEN'S AGREEMENTS

Seafarers were frequently in port without any funds, or even clothes suitable to gain employment. In order to help the situation, in 1909 or 1910 Mr Parry devised agreements with destitute sailors to provide them with assistance in one or all of the following ways: "1. Paying for fares from one port to another, 2. Provide board and lodgings at either of their homes in Bristol and Newport, 3. Advancing money for the purpose of clothing". In return the seaman bound himself to repay the society out of his next wages. Human nature being what it is, these agreements were not always honoured. In July 1910 William Smith, an illiterate fifty year old Glaswegian, five feet two and a half inches tall, with a dark complexion, black hair and eyes, and a tattooed dot on his right hand, applied for, and received ten shillings for clothes. The money was due to be repaid from his wages on board the *SS Llangorse* (Messrs. Evan Thomas Radcliffe & Co.) but he failed to join his ship at Newport, and the money could not be recovered. The returns were obviously sufficient to allow the scheme to continue, which it did until at least January 1912. This far-sighted form of giving financial assistance embraced not only seamen, but mess-room stewards, and firemen.

MUSIC AND THE MISSION

Temperance addresses on their own would have attracted few auditors from the class of person for whom they were designed, were it not for the free-teas and the musical aspects of the Pleasant Saturday Evenings, the watch-night services on new year's eves, and the harvest festivals.

The Edwardian age was one where entertainment was often within the domestic circle, and most family members had musical skills which could be employed at little notice. Consequently, when compiling his weekly programmes, Mr Parry was able to call upon a large number of amateur soloists and pianists from among the voluntary workers for the Society. The pianos at both missions were in constant use.

While the committee members might enjoy rarefied music, Alderman Smith for example was President of the Society of Bristol Glee-Men, they were not exclusive, and believed in improving the taste of their audience. On the other hand, humour was a vital ingredient of the meetings. Consequently duets such as *The Spider and the Fly*, and *Jack and Jill*, and *Mixem's Matrimonial Mart*, always had a place on the programme.

Vocal quartets, trios, duets, solos, and similar groupings on popular instruments such as the banjo, piano, violin, piccolo and mandolin were common. The music was sometimes associated with the immensely popular nigger minstrel concert parties and songs such as *All the Darkies March Away* were greatly appreciated. Mandolin bands, Mr Plucknett's male voice party, glees, part-songs and solos by the Oxford Street Glee Party were all pressed into service at meetings. Boy trebles were in demand to sing "tear jerkers" such as *Little Hero, Britannia, The Pride of the Ocean* and *The Lads in Navy Blue*, which appealed to the seamen's sentimentality. Other popular rousing songs such as *Boys of the Old Brigade* were calculated to vary the mood of the meetings.

The words of Fred Weatherley's ballad, *They all Love Jack*, were on everyone's lips, and the tune was whistled in streets, on quay sides, and on board ships throughout the country. Phrases from the song were used in addresses at the mission stations and in the annual reports of the Society:

"They all love Jack, For his heart is like the sea, ever open, brave and free, and the girls must lonely be 'til his ship comes back; but if love is the best of all that can a man befall, Why, Jack's the King of all, for they all love Jack!"

Other "catchy" tunes and poems were freely adapted, for use in the station, such as Rudyard Kipling's *The Absent-Minded Beggar*.

No musical evening at the missions would have been complete without its recitation, which was chosen for its stirring or improving qualities. Such was *How Horatius Kept the Bridge*. Music hall recitations, like *In the Workhouse: Christmas Day*, by George R. Sims (1847–1922), and *The Green Eye of the Yellow God*, by J. Milton Hayes (1882–1940), would have been felt to be too racy for religious meetings.

The phonograph, then a novelty, was a feature of these Pleasant Saturday Evening gatherings from 1900 until as late as 1908, by which time phonographs were becoming more commonly used. Selections of music such as *The Suwanee River, The Story of the Fox and the Goat*, Handel's *Largo*, the laughing song *Old, but awfully tough! Ora Pro Nobis, Jerusalem*, and the immensely popular *Holy City* with words and music by the greatest musical partnership of the age, Fred Weatherley and Stephen Adams, exactly caught the mood and the taste of the Edwardian era.[51]

Hymns played a vital part in worship at the mission. Many of the hymn-sheets used both staff and the tonic sol fa notation developed by the Congregational minister, the Revd John Curwen (1816–1880). The latter made vocal singing in congregations, Sunday Schools and families much easier. Tonic sol fa can be said to have played a huge part in the immense popularity of singing in the Victorian and Edwardian eras. For choice, most hymns sung at the mission were rousing, full of hope and Christian valour; some dealt with the sea, and some were by the American evangelists, Dwight Moody and Ira Sankey,[52] or associated with the later Torrey-Alexander Mission. The work of the mission stations followed the well tried means used by the Wesleys, the Revds. Augustus Toplady (*Rock of Ages*), Isaac Watts, and John Newton in the eighteenth century. Music was a handmaiden assisting in the worship of the Creator, and many of the hymns sung, although now largely forgotten, proved that the devil didn't have all the good tunes!

THE SOCIETY'S AUTUMNAL MEETING, 1908

The Society's five day autumnal meeting in 1908 represented the high point of Mr Parry's superintendence of the Western Division. It began with a garden party at Alderman Smith's home, Brooklea, St. Ann's Park, and was followed by a concert at

---

[51] For an excellent over-view of the subject, see: R. Pearsall, *Edwardian Popular Music*, (1975); for individual composers, *The Oxford Companion to Popular Music*, ed. P. Gammond, (1991); for the collaboration between Weatherley and Stephen Adams, H. Simpson, *A Century of Ballads 1810–1910: Their Composers and Singers*, (1910), pp. 192–197.

[52] For an excellent account of their missions see: the Revd. W.H. Daniels, *D.L. Moody and His Work*, (1875).

the YMCA hall in Totterdown. On Sunday there was a water church parade, and church services were held at the Terrett Memorial Hall and elsewhere. Public meetings were held the following day in the Lord Mayor's Council Room in the Council House, where an appeal was made for "a higher life of enthusiasm and purity, and higher and yet holier desire to reach the erring". The afternoon was taken up with a general committee meeting at the YMCA, in St. James's Square, which was followed by a public missionary meeting. On Tuesday, a devotional meeting was held, which was addressed by Charles R. Parsons, who spoke of his conversion half a century before and gave an autobiographical address entitled "How Christ came to Bristol". Parsons was one of the most revered figures in the Temperance and Nonconformist community in Bristol at the time. He founded the Old Market Street Wesleyan Methodist Bible Class in 1880, which enjoyed great success in winning men and women for Christ, and he established Wesley Hall in Barton Hill. At one time the Male Bible Class numbered 800 members, and his books: *The Man with the White Hat*, *The Little Woman in Grey*, *The Vicar of Berrybridge* and *Purity and Power* were printed and read in their thousands. By 1900 it was reported that nearly three million of his books and tracts had been distributed.[53] In the afternoon delegates travelled by break to Avonmouth to view the Royal Edward Dock which had been opened by the King in July[54] and the afternoon and evening was occupied with cutting the first sod for the new reading room and by another missionary meeting. The final day was devoted to visits to the mission stations in Newport and Cardiff by steamer, courtesy of Messrs P. & A. Campbell. Mr Parry was presented with a fountain pen by delegates and missionaries, and the meeting was celebrated by him in a truly execrable poem entitled "Ready, Aye! Ready", published in the Society's paper, *The Waterman*. This was the age of boys and girls committing poems to heart and reciting them in school and within the domestic circle.

THE NEWPORT (MONMOUTH) BRANCH 1905–1911

Alderman Smith had close commercial links with the town of Newport. The Board of Trade returns for 1904 showed that 18,434 men were either engaged or discharged in the port and this number did not include those who were engaged in the coastal trade. There was undoubtedly work for the society to be done there and after an invitation by a number of residents, a station was opened at 34 Commercial Road in December 1905, which acted as a Sailors' Rest, Coffee Bar, Reading Room and Mission. At the same time the branch assimilated the South Wales and Foreign Sailors' Gospel Book Mission, and a local committee was formed which was superintended from Bristol. In the first year over 800 free beds and many free meals were given to destitute seamen.

The costs involved were considerable, and in 1907 it was reported that the station had a deficit of £90 18s 0d, although it had been possible to furnish the new home completely. A missionary, Mr Wilson Fraser, was appointed, and as a result of his work among the sailors and their families, attendance at Sunday services increased

---

[53] C.R. Parsons, *The Story of Old Market Street Bible Class*, (1900). The substance of his address is probably to be found in C.R. Parsons, *These Forty Years 1878–1918*, (Bristol, 1918).
[54] *The Daily Mirror*, 10 July 1908.

and the Reading and Recreation Room was well supported. Mrs Fraser, who had a Salvation Army background, acted as matron, and in common with lady workers for the Society in Clifton and Bristol, often gave Sunday evening Temperance addresses to the men.

Godfrey Charles Morgan, 1st Viscount Tredegar (1828–1913), a substantial, generous and enlightened landowner in South Wales, and a veteran of the Charge of the Light Brigade at Balaklava, lent his support to the endeavour, as did successive mayors of Newport and Lewis Haslem MP. Lord Tredegar's surviving correspondence with Mr Parry is terse in the extreme, and in a speech he once described a philanthropist as "an old gentleman, probably with a bald head, who tries to make his conscience think he is doing good all the while he is having his pocket picked".[55] Mr Parry used his name with gusto and the society's documents proudly proclaimed Lord Tredegar's patronage.

By the close of 1908 the station reported that 5,687 beds had been made up during the year, of which 3,628 had been paid for, 1,400 had been supplied on credit, and 659 had been given with meals freely to those in destitution.[56] Notwithstanding the valiant efforts of the committee, the missionary and the superintendent, the station's total liabilities including several outstanding accounts, had risen to £182.5s.1d at the end of 1909.[57] During 1910 the trade situation was very poor and labour trouble at the docks resulted in over 1,500 free beds being given to destitute seamen, which increased the station's liabilities.[58] In spite of the need for this social work amongst the destitute in a land of plenty, and considerable financial problems, there were elements hostile to the work of the Society in South Wales. In September 1910 *The Western Mail* contained a letter entitled "A Protest and a Warning" attacking the "Sailor Saturday Collections" in Barry. The protest came from representatives of the Missions to Seamen and the British and Foreign Sailors' Society. In reply, Mr Parry noted that the latter society had no branches in either Newport or Bristol but had raised, without protest from the Seamen and Boatmen's Friends Society, £40 in each town to further their work. He stated that he regretted the closure of the Barry District Seamen's Society, due to lack of funds, and that had the finances of his own Society permitted, he would have welcomed an amalgamation. In the face of worsening problems Mr Parry relinquished his superintendency over the station in April 1911.

THE CARDIFF BRANCH 1907–1911

In keeping with Mr Parry's aggressive missionary policy, the work of the Society was extended to Cardiff in June 1907. A committee was formed under the chairmanship of Richard Cory JP and in September a Sailors' Mission Club and Home

[55] See *Wit and Wisdom of Lord Tredegar*, (1911); p.35 quotes part of one of his speeches upon the opening of the Seamen's Mission Church in Newport on 18 January 1887. In *The Standard*, 12 March 1913, it was computed that Lord Tredegar gave away £100,000 a year in charity and donations, and that his annual income was between £365 & £500 thousand.
[56] *38th Annual Report of the Western District for 1908*, (1909), pp. 8–10.
[57] *39th Annual Report of the Western District for 1909*, (1910), pp. 9–10.
[58] *40th Annual Report of the Western District for 1910*, (1911), pp. 8–9.

was opened at 3 Stuart Street, which was well supported by seamen and fishermen. Unfortunately the Western District Committee neglected to have the Home licensed by the Cardiff City Council, as required by an Order in Council dated 26th October 1896.[59] The Home's activities were drawn to the attention of the Medical Officer of Health, Dr Walford, by a number of complaints, of which the following anonymous letter, dated 23rd December 1907, may be typical. "I would draw your attention to . . . the filthy state of the beds and bedding, some, if not all, are infested with vermin . . . the steward in charge turns an *English Sailor* out to make way for a *Foreigner*, this occurred last week three nights in succession. There are men now staying at the mission who owe between three and four pounds each . . . men who have been there for 6 and 7 weeks have a two course dinner while others who have only been there 8 or 9 days had:- $\frac{1}{4}$ basin of soup and a very thin slice of bread." Beds were charged at 6d, 9d or 1s 0d a night, and a half pint mug of tea, coffee, or cocoa, cost $\frac{1}{2}$d.

In October 1908 Dr Walford required the Society to apply for a licence under the Boarding House Keepers' Act. In the meantime they were instructed to refrain from lodging seamen and reminded that they were liable to a fine of £100. The formal application was submitted in December with an aggressive and defiant covering letter to the town clerk of Cardiff from Mr Parry as district superintendent. In December the keeper, Mr Beamish, was summoned before the Cardiff Police Court. Notwithstanding the injunction of the stipendiary magistrate to the contrary, Mr Parry instructed Mr Beamish to keep the lodgers and retain their payments for lodgings, giving receipts for the sums as "donations to the Society". The Society's solicitor was appalled, and the reaction of the Medical Officer of Health predictable. The financial situation of the branch deteriorated to a position where tradesmen's bills were left unpaid.

At a meeting of the Society's General Sub-Committee held in the Cobden Hotel, Birmingham on 9th February 1909, it was stated that the Cardiff press had reported on 27th January the strong condemnation by the Cardiff Health Committee of the way in which the Sailors' Home at 3 Stuart Street was conducted. The seriousness of the situation led to a special General Committee Meeting being called to consider the conduct and the finances of the Bristol District. This was necessary because the financial statement for the year to 31st December 1908 showed that the Society's outstanding liabilities were £206 0s 8d of which the Western District accounted for £152 14s 3d. Statements elsewhere indicate that the total figure was actually much in excess of this.

The situation was aggravated by an article in *Truth* by two of the Cardiff town councillors animadverting upon the uncleanliness of the Society's Mission Home. The Cardiff committee denied the truth of the allegations, but the work of the society was severely damaged, and in March 1909 the Mayor of Bath received, anonymously, a copy of this article just before presiding at a public meeting on behalf of the Society in Bath.

A further application for a licence to keep a seamen's lodging house in March

---

[59] This mistake is understandable. Apparently no such licence was required for the established Cardiff Sailors' Home. The city bye-laws governed the registration of seamen's lodging houses.

was not successful and the Society's solicitor informed Mr Parry that he was unwise "in practically attempting to defy the Health Committee". By April 1909 the possible closure of the Cardiff Home called into question the financial viability of the station. A copy of the society's *Annual Western District Report* for 1909 shows that the committee circumvented the lack of a licence by giving away over 1,000 free beds to seamen, a situation which continued in 1910 and put an almost impossible strain on the branch. In addition, seamen were visited on board ship and close to the shipping offices. The Reading and Refreshment Rooms, which were open between 7:00am and 10:00pm, were heavily used by sailors, firemen, dockgate men and ship's officers, but the deficiency for the Western District stood at £438 0s 1d at the end of 1910. In a letter to the editor of the Cardiff *Western Mail* in September 1910, Mr Parry noted that the deficit of the Cardiff branch was £150. Mr. Parry's superintendence over the Cardiff branch was relinquished in 1911.

The Cardiff Sailors' Mission Club had regular services, thrice on Sundays, daily prayers on Monday and Wednesday evenings, and occasional concerts.

FINANCE

How was this work paid for?

In the first instance it came from subscriptions raised by the missionary, and his supporters. Door to door collections were made, and families, friends and business contacts, were all solicited. In 1900 an army of volunteers, many of them maiden ladies, stretching from the Isle of Wight to Bridgwater, from Salisbury to Minehead and from Penarth to Stroud, raised subscriptions for this work. By this means some £286 out of an income of £363 was raised. Among the most generous subscribers (in 1900) were the Bedminster Coal Company (£5), W.D. and H.O Wills (£4 4s 0d), the Bristol United Breweries (£3 13s 6d), Messrs Elder Dempster & Co. (£3 3s 0d), and Harvey & Sons Ltd. (£2 2s 0d). Occasionally (in succeeding years) the Society managed to secure subscriptions from the Dowager Duchess of Beaufort, the Dowager Lady Tweedmouth and Sir Greville Smyth of Ashton Court. However, neither their generosity, their prestige, or an increase in subscribers could mask the fact that the Society could spend money faster that it could be accumulated. By 1905 the Society's annual financial figures were recording a significant deficit, in spite of showing an increase in subscriptions, and about 1,000 annual subscribers.

Undeterred, Mr Parry pressed the committee to widen the scope of the Society's work. In 1905, he appealed, unsuccessfully, to Andrew Carnegie, the Scottish-American philanthropist, for money to build a Carnegie Sailors' Home and Institute on the site of a number of houses, shops, warehouses and two public houses in Hotwells. Mr Parry stated that the city was in the midst of spending £3m on a new dock at Avonmouth, which would enlarge the number of seamen in the port. At the same time, the city was in the midst of an appeal for a £50,000 extension to the Infirmary and a £10,000 appeal for endowing beds at the General Hospital. The citizens, who were deluged by appeals for monies to aid worthy causes, suffered what may now be called "donation fatigue", and would, or could not, support this visionary project.

Mr Parry's next venture tested his organising skills to the full. He launched a flag day in aid of the Society, entitled *Sailor Saturday* on 24th November 1906. Pulpit notices giving information about the initiative were prepared to be read from every pulpit in the city on the Sunday beforehand. Mr Parry outlined his grandiose schemes to a reporter from the *Bristol Evening News*; these included a home for sailors, a dock labourers' reading room, a coffee room, and a training home for lads. The financial results of the flag day in 1906 are not known, but in 1908 £326 15s 4d was raised in the district by using collection boxes in the shape of a ship. In 1909 the Mayor and Lady Mayoress of Bath gave great support to the enterprise, but Mr. Parry was short of collectors and the Bristol branch raised only £121 0s 6d. The following year saw an increase in receipts by a third, but there was a general feeling that the results had been adversely affected by the results of the General Election.

The deterioration in the Society's financial situation was rapid between 1908 and 1911. As early as 1901 the architect, Mr, later Sir, George Oatley (1863–1950), gratuitously drew up plans for an extension to the Terrett Memorial Hall to include Reading, Recreation, Coffee and Writing Rooms, and a "bathroom, lavatory and twelve bedrooms". The cost was put at £400 with an additional £75 needed to furnish the rooms. Plans remained in abeyance until 1908, when, encouraged by Mr Parry, work on the building began in earnest. The first sod was cut that autumn by Alderman Terrett. Building work was rapid, and the premises would have opened at Christmas-time 1909 had it been possible to furnish them. Some £73 11s 3d worth of materials were given by local firms including: slate, glass, lead, timber, grates, locks, gas-fittings, lavatories, bricks, steel, mortar, and chimney pots. A public meeting held in September 1909 under the aegis of Mr, later Sir, Stanley Badock JP (1867–1945), the High Sheriff of Bristol, solicited subscriptions for the work. Alfred Smith, now an alderman, emphasised that the creation of these much needed facilities would be a boon to dock workers, dockgate men and sailors, because it would mean that there would no longer be any need for them to go to the public house. The hall and its facilities would help to "stem the terrible evil of intemperance", provide social help and fellowship, and bring men to hear the Gospel, and so to Christ.

The Sailors' Rest and Home was finally opened on 5th May 1910 by the Lady Mayoress,[60] with Dr, later Sir, Ernest Cook JP (1855–1945), the principal of the University of Bristol's training colleges, and chairman of the Bristol Education Committee, in the chair. The Reading Room and Restaurant were open between 7:00am and 11:00pm; meals and beds were provided for destitute seamen without charge, and friends supplied the reading room with magazines, periodicals and other improving literature. The increased tonnage of the port of Bristol meant that the facilities were constantly in demand by seafarers.

Mr Parry had been able to use the contacts and knowledge that he acquired in

---

[60] The lady mayoress was the wife of Councillor Christopher Albert Hayes JP (1850–1916), a builder and contractor. He was on the city council between 1904 and 1911, served as lord mayor between 1909 and 1911, and as an alderman between 1911 and 1916. W.G. Neale, *At the Port of Bristol*, II (Bristol, 1970), pp. 239–241. He was a freemason, a member of St. Kena's Lodge, No. 1833, and senior church warden of the Anglo-Catholic church, St. Raphael's, Cumberland Road, see *Bristol Biographies*, II (1899), p. 321. He was the treasurer of the Seamen and Boatmen's Friend Society from 1905 until at least 1912.

business in the 1890s to benefit the Society. Not only had he used them to increase annual subscriptions and furnish materials for the reading room, and sailors' rest, but he furnished the new premises by the same means, obtaining knives, coal boxes, drapery, furniture, pictures, china, paint, wallpaper, and even the timber for the bunks. So far so good. The annual financial report for 1909 showed that the Society needed £400 to clear its liabilities, a further £250 was required to construct the extension and £75 to furnish the new rooms. The committee decided to raise £250 by mortgage and appealed for the balance of £475. In the end the expenses were far greater than expected. The Bristol branch for the year ending 31st December 1910 showed a deficiency for the year of £61 2s 11d with smaller deficits in Newport and Cardiff. The mortgage of £500, as at 31st December 1908, had not been paid and there was now an additional bank loan of £250.

The 40th annual meeting of subscribers and friends held at the YMCA Hall, St James Square on 6th March 1911 cannot have been an easy one for either the committee or the officers. Mr Parry moved a resolution which was resolved *nem con*, which "ventured to ask that all the subscribers double their subscriptions for this year to meet the adverse balance". The Sheriff of Bristol, Mr George Riseley, a friend of Mr Parry's father-in-law, before moving the adoption of the annual report, spoke at length about the value of the work undertaken by the Society particularly in the light of the recent developments at Avonmouth.

THE NATIONAL SAILORS' SOCIETY 1912–1914

What happened next? To be honest, I am not certain. I have not found a report for the Seamen and Boatmen's Friend Society for 1911, or a mention of an annual meeting in 1912. A Sailor Saturday was organised at Barry in June 1911. A note dated 3rd August 1911 states that Mr Parry had relinquished the superintendency of the Newport branch "some months ago". We do know, however, that between January and May 1912, the Seamen and Boatmen's Friend Society split into two parts. This was caused by the refusal of the majority of the committee to increase its number of stations, and its decision to withdraw support for about thirty affiliated missions, which they had been accustomed to assist. One part of the committee, including Alderman Smith, was determined to ensure that the society returned to an even financial footing, even if that meant re-trenchment and the cessation of some of the Society's existing activities. The Revd Leonard Parry, Alderman Terrett and others were determined to realise their grandiose schemes for the welfare of local seamen which had been outlined to Andrew Carnegie in 1905. Spurred by the threat posed to their work by the financial situation, and believing that something needed to be done urgently to support those sailors and dock workers who were in need, they decided to found their own society, the National Sailors' Society. They acted swiftly and decisively. Articles of Association were drawn up, divisions were created with branches in Rotherhithe, Southampton, Swansea, Newport, Cardiff, Liverpool and Sunderland. In many places, committees were set up, premises acquired, and superintendents and missionaries appointed. A Grand Council was self-appointed under Alderman Henry Fuller Morriss JP, who had been Mayor of Bermondsey in 1909 and 1912, and was a former long-standing member of the

Seamen and Boatmen's Friend Society's Committee.[61] It included the Mayors of Southampton, Swansea, Sunderland and West Hartlepool. How active they were is debatable. Alderman W. Howell Davies MP (1851–1932) of Down House, Sneyd Park, chairman of the Bristol Docks' Committee, was an inactive member of the Grand Council of the National Sailors' Society during 1913–1914. His letter to Mr Parry accepting membership of the Grand Council is a model of its kind: "House of Commons, 13th April 1913, Dear Mr Parry, I agree to be a member of your Grand Council, but do not expect me to attend meetings. I am far too busy for that. Yours sincerely, W. Howell Davies." He was a Wesleyan Methodist and served on the committee of the Seaman and Boatman's Friend Society between 1906 and 1907.

In Bristol, Mission Houses were set up at 182 and 184 Hotwells Road, 2 King Street, and at the Gospel Hall, Pill. At the opening of the new Mission House in Hotwells by the Duchess of Beaufort in September 1912,[62] Alderman Morriss stated that the new Society was "out to do a still more aggressive and active work in different parts of the Kingdom". The story of the formation of this society has yet to be told. Its aims and objectives were laudable, but there were inevitable problems with two societies involved in similar work, competing for subscriptions, and holding flag days among the same people. The situation brought hostile press notices, in spite of the new society having raised £541 10s 5d during its first year.

The new society held its first meeting and conference in Bristol between 31st May and 3rd June 1913. Alderman H.F. Morriss, the Revd Leonard Parry, and Alderman Terrett all took an active part. The meeting culminated with a garden party, which Alderman and Mrs Smith were induced to hold for the delegates and the committee. In the surviving photograph of the occasion, the Alderman's stance mirrors the stiffness and coldness, to a degree unusual even in an age of formality, which characterised the tone of his correspondence with his son-in-law. The society's first *Annual Report* probably reveals why Mr Parry's involvement with the National Sailor's Society was a short one. During 1912/3 the Revd. E.H. George, superintendent of the West Wales Division, and Mr Parry received only part of their salaries and the committee expressed the hope that £140 "to which they are entitled, if

---

[61] Alderman Morriss is described in the first *National Sailors' Society Annual Report and Prospectus* for the year 1912./3 as having both largely provided the initiative to found the Society, and as having addressed meetings on the subject of forming a new society in Bristol, Southampton, Newport and other ports. He was president until at least 1914. In his Christmas card for 1913 he describes himself as "a great sufferer in business from the present costly and uncertain system of legalism". He was a good amateur poet, the author of *Poems of Purpose* and a hymn for the Coronation of King George VI (1937), and remained in contact with Mr. Parry well into the 1930s, when he was flourishing as a property developer. He was actively involved with the refurbishment of Wesley's House in London in 1934. Alderman Morriss served on the General Committee of the Seamen and Boatmen's Friend Society from before 1900 until 1911 or 1912. In the 1900s and 1910s he attended St Winifred's Congregational Chapel, Lower Road, Rotherhithe, and was the honorary pastor of their mission hall. In *Wesley's Chapel Circuit Plan and General Directory* for April 1936 he is listed as one of the three poor stewards and as conducting one of the Thursday mid-week services at Wesley Chapel. He then resided in the Garden Village at Woldingham in Surrey.

[62] *Bristol Times and Mirror*, 11 September 1912; *Bristol Evening World*, 10 September 1912. Both note other important projects for the future outlined by Mr. Parry.

funds allow, may be raised as additional income for the new year."[63] It appears the monies were not forthcoming and it is likely that Mr Parry resigned with effect from the end of the Society's year, 30th April 1914.

The work of the Seamen and Boatmen's Friend Society did not end in Bristol and Hotwells following the departure of Mr Parry in 1912, although our evidence for it is largely confined to the recollections of an ever decreasing number of people, and the entries in the *Bristol Directories*. It appears that the Society was obliged to dispose of the Guinea Street Bethel between 1912 and 1913, in an effort to address the dire financial situation in which it found itself as a result of Mr Parry's unrealistic ambitions and hubris. His place as a missionary and district superintendent was taken by a succession of ministers; the Revd Robert Dodds 1913–1920, the Revd A.R. Stevenson 1920–1929, and the Revd George B. Hood 1929 — *c.* 1942, and the Revd Alfred Kay, *c.* 1942 – *c.* 1954, who ministered through the Great Depression, the stagnation of trade in the 1930s, and the Second World War. They continued to use the Terrett Memorial Hall as a Seamen's Rest and Home, and as a base to minister to the seafaring population of Avonmouth.

The National Sailors' Society was incorporated in 1914, and at the time of Mr Parry's departure from the Society provided 17 beds for seamen in 182–184 Hotwells Road, and mission houses at 2 King Street, Welsh Back; Lebeck House, Dowry Square; and the Gospel Hall Seamen's Mission at Pill. By 1917 the general secretary and superintendent was the Revd W. Burton, who advertised that the society provided homes for seamen at different ports, thousands of free meals a year and bedroom accommodation for all seafarers. He remained in post until sometime after 1930.

And what of Mr Parry? In 1914 he moved with his family to 27 Zion Hill, Clifton, where they resided until 1927. We have occasional glimpses of him in these years; in 1916 he nearly lost his hand in an accident; in 1917 he was taking occasional services and was on the circuit of the United Free Methodist Church in Bristol. However, he either neither received or accepted any call to a pastorate, and remained unattached to a particular church. The *Bristol Directory* still referred to him as the Revd Leonard Parry in 1920, but how he lived and employed himself we can only guess. His devoted wife, physically frail, and frequently unwell, received small cheques from her father, entered trade with her husband privately as a draper, and was obliged to take in paying guests to make ends meet. On the strength of her family connections she was frequently called upon by desperate tradesmen to settle her husband's long-outstanding accounts for petrol and other items. The letters addressed by her to friends, which survive from this period, are full of illness, servant problems and the difficulties of finding guests from a suitable background to ensure that the family's reduced circumstances were not made any more painful than necessary. In spite of the manner in which Mr Parry split from the Seamen and Boatmen's Friend Society, when he drew up his will on 27th April 1925 he made provision in the event of his only son predeceasing his wife and remaining

---

[63] As a superintendent missionary employing an assistant, Mr. Parry was entitled to a maximum of £250 p.a. This does not include anything that he may have been paid as general secretary.

unmarried for a trust to be created to fund a missionary to be based at the Terrett Memorial Hall for the benefit of sailors and the Hotwells community.[64]

The situation had changed dramatically by the late 1920s. Mr Parry no longer used his clerical title. He founded a property company which flourished during the Depression, and by the time of his death in Clevedon in 1955, he was wealthy, and a substantial owner of slum property in south Bristol, much of it acquired in the 1920s and 1930s. For me, nothing more clearly shows some of the facets of his character than a passage in a letter to his son, dated 1st October 1942 from Ilfracombe where he was convalescent: "I am now [hob]knobbing with a Barrister from London who is likely to do a local deal in which the Chatterton [his property company] may come in." It plainly reveals his own social origins, and his sharp eye for monetary advantage.

There is no doubt that the Revd Leonard Parry was stubborn, proud and wilful. In his dealings with the branch of the Seamen and Boatmen's Friend Society in Cardiff he left tradesmen's bills unpaid, attempted to circumvent local Acts and planning regulations and showed himself to be capable of guile and downright sharp practice. Ultimately the personal and public ambitions that he nurtured for his work seriously impaired the effectiveness of the organisation that he served. He showed impatience and an unwillingness to allow a lack of financial security to stop him from realising his plans for expansion, and he negated his considerable abilities, energy and enthusiasm. His time at the Terrett Memorial Hall saw a great expansion of the Society's work amongst seamen and docker workers, but his leaving sacrificed much of what he had achieved, and he must have left behind him feelings of bitterness and betrayal. No wonder he decided to make no mention of his work in his election manifesto of 1947, thereby recognising that the "diamond had been lost in the flaw".

ACKNOWLEDGEMENTS

I should particularly like to express my thanks to my grandmother, Dr Isabel Crossley, MB, ChB, DPH (1902–1998), whose father, Captain Hugh McKee MN (1862–1951) was a master with the Charante Steamship Company (Messrs T. & J. Harrison), and who first stimulated my interest in this subject when I was young; to my cousin Lieutenant Vincent Alexander McMillan, RNR, formerly of Canadian Pacific, and to my friends, Mr Louis Anthony Haslett, formerly of Union Castle, and Mr Charles William Wallis-Newport, marine surveyor, formerly of Ellerman's, whose extensive knowledge of nautical history and research into the merchantile marine have always been freely and willingly shared; to Mrs Gill Hodder, former secretary of the Clifton and Hotwells Improvement Society from whom I acquired many of Mr Parry's manuscripts; to my cousins, the late Mr Nigel Bythe Coward (1902–1984) and Mrs Maisie Isabella Coward (1904–1991), who first interested me in the lives and work of the Ashmead family, to my friend, Mr Michael Thomas Richardson, Special Collections' Librarian at the University of Bristol, for reading

---

[64] In the case outlined he also left £60 p.a. to an assistant secretary of the Youth's Section of the YMCA. When his will was proved in 1956 his estate amounted to £33,548. He also owned the freehold premises, Lebeck House, Dowry Square, where the National Sailors' Society held its first meetings in 1912.

through and commenting upon the text, and to Messrs James Marcus Phillpotts and Adrian Kok Wee Koh for preparing this manuscript for publication. The basis of this work is two lectures given by me, the first to the Bristol and Gloucestershire Archaeological Society on the 7th November 1996, and the second to the Clifton and Hotwells Improvement Society on the 21st January 1997.

XII

Contrasting Clerics in Nineteenth-Century Bristol: Dean Gilbert Elliot and Canon John Pilkington Norris

JOSEPH BETTEY

IN THE north-east corner of the nave aisle of Bristol cathedral the recumbent marble effigy of Dean Gilbert Elliot (1800–1891) lies serene in devout medieval fashion. On the adjacent pillar a bronze plaque commemorates Canon John Pilkington Norris (1823–1891), the representation of his stern features gazing directly across the aisle at the Dean. It is ironic that the memorials of the two men should be in such a juxtaposition, since in life they held contrary opinions on most of the issues in which they were involved. They were the most eminent clerical figures in Bristol during much of the later nineteenth century, and both achieved a great deal. The diocese of Bristol had been united with the diocese of Gloucester in 1836, and the clergy of Bristol looked to the Dean and canons of the cathedral for leadership. Dean Elliot and Canon Norris were constantly brought together by their work and common interests, yet in character, churchmanship and attitude they could hardly have been more different. The purpose of this account is to describe the careers of the two men, the major projects in which they were both involved, and to explore the disagreements which arose between them during the twenty-seven years that they worked and argued together.[1]

GILBERT ELLIOT 1800–1891

Gilbert Elliot came from a well-connected family of distinguished soldiers, civil servants and diplomats. Descended from the Elliots, earls of Minto, he was the third son of the Hon. Hugh Elliot who served as ambassador to various German states and in Copenhagen and Naples, before becoming Governor of the Leeward Islands and finally Governor of Madras. It was while his father was ambassador in Germany that Gilbert Elliot was born in Dresden. He attended schools in Norwich and Edinburgh, and studied at Trinity Hall, Cambridge where he graduated B.A. in 1823 and M.A. in 1828. He was ordained deacon in 1823 and priest in 1824. In 1825 he married Williamina, the daughter of Patrick Brydone F.R.S. The marriage produced one son and three daughters. Elliot's career in the Church was assisted by his family connections, particularly with the Russells, the prominent Whig dynasty. He was presented to a succession of wealthy benefices in Kent, Westmoreland and Essex,

---

[1] Most of the sources for this study are in the records of the Dean and Chapter of Bristol cathedral. The records are now in the Bristol Record Office. For a list see Isabel M. Kirby, *Records of the Diocese of Bristol*, 1970.

eventually becoming rector of Holy Trinity, Marylebone in 1846.[2] He was prominent on the evangelical or low church wing of the Church of England, resolutely opposed to the views of the contemporary Oxford or Tractarian Movement within the Church. An impressive figure, with a powerful voice he was an effective preacher and advocate of protestant views. Elliot was also a staunch Liberal. He was active in anti-papal protests and refused to allow the ecclesiastical ceremonial vestments or ornaments which were being introduced into churches by the Tractarians. Elliot's religious views and Whig politics coincided with those of his relative, Lord John Russell, and when Russell became Prime Minister in 1850, one of his earliest ecclesiatical appointments was to present Elliot to the Deanery of Bristol. Elliot was to remain as Dean for the next forty-one years.[3]

As Dean of Bristol, Elliot entered upon the duties of his new position with energy and enthusiasm, taking up residence in the Deanery which at that time occupied an area to the north-west of the cathedral, at the western edge of College Green. He rapidly became involved with Church affairs in Bristol, including the creation of new parishes, educational work, relations with nonconformist congregations and the spiritual welfare of the prisoners in Bristol gaol. He was also concerned about the fabric of the cathedral and the limited accommodation which it provided. Following the demolition of the medieval nave during the early sixteenth century, the proposed re-building had never been carried out. The cathedral therefore consisted only of the chancel, chapels and transepts, although in 1838 the houses which had occupied the site of the medieval nave had been removed. As early as June 1850 Elliot invited no less a surveyor than Isambard Kingdom Brunel to examine some defects in the cathedral. Brunel's hectic life-style and varied business interests are evident from his reply to the Dean's request. Brunel wrote that he was able

> "to give a couple of hours for a cursory inspection to form some opinion of the subject. I can be at the Cathedral at 5 oclock on Tuesday morning next, having to leave Bristol by train to Exeter at 7.50."

The appointment was kept, and Brunel later reported to the Dean that the defects in the cathedral building were not sufficiently serious as to demand immediate action but that "The next or the following generation will probably be called upon for more extensive repairs and restoration." As will be seen, Brunel's opinion based on his rapid survey was somewhat over-optimistic.[4]

Conscious of the dignity of his position and of his family background, Elliot appears to have earned the respect rather than the affection or friendship of his colleagues. He was evidently esteemed within the Church, and he was elected Prolocutor or speaker of the Lower House of Convocation during the period 1857–64. At the cathedral his evangelical views were evident from his refusal to allow a cross, candles or flowers on the altar, or to have a robed choir. He also adamantly prohib-

[2] J.A. Venn, *Alumni Cantabrigiensis 1752–1900*, 1944, Obituary in *Bristol Times & Mirror*, 12 August 1891.
[3] *Ibid.*
[4] R.A. Buchanan, "Brunel in Bristol", in P. McGrath & J. Cannon, eds., *Essays in Bristol And Gloucestershire History*, 1976, 249.

ited the introduction of additional communion services, the observance of saints'
days or any new ritual. While he was Dean the services remained plain, and the
occasional communion services were celebrated without the choir. The clergy wore
simple surplices and academic hoods, but no cassocks; preachers wore plain black
gowns. Like his patron, Lord John Russell, Elliot regarded the Tractarians as agents
of Rome within the Church of England. At a meeting of Bristol clergy in November
1850 he attacked both the Tractarians and the supine attitude of the bishops.

> "What hope have we to countervail this direct effort to lead to Rome if the
> Bishops will not interfere? Is it not high time that the Tractarian treason should
> no longer be permitted to train converts to Rome, that Tractarian presumption
> should no longer be permitted to ride rough shod over the really faithful and
> mourning servants of the church?"[5]

Elliot was autocratic in his government of the cathedral, and in his relations with
the canons and the cathedral staff. In his replies to a questionnaire about cathedral
government, issued by the Cathedral Commissioners in 1879, Elliot laid great stress
on his sole responsibility for the governance of the cathedral, and on his obligation
to "well and truly govern in the Church". He also claimed the right and duty to
"influence, chide, convince, and beseech the Canons and all other officers of the
Church". He quoted from the Statutes that "the power of directing be left wholly
to the Dean".

In addition, Elliot claimed that ". . . the regulation of the cathedral services is
altogether in the Dean, I have never heard it questioned or doubted." According to
Elliot the only duty of a canon "consists in residing not less than three months in
each year and preaching a sermon each Sunday, either by himself or by a fit substi-
tute".[6] In his personal life Elliot suffered a succession of tragedies. His eldest daughter, Mary Elizabeth, died in 1847 at the age of 13. In 1851 his only son, Gilbert,
who was a lieutenant in the Royal Navy was lost at sea, aged 22, and two years
later, in 1853, his wife, Williamina, died and was buried in the cathedral.[7]

In spite of these blows, Elliot continued with his plans to provide additional space
for congregations in the cathedral. He consulted the well-known architect and
church restorer Giles Gilbert Scott. Scott took the view that "the primary demand
is for a nave of the grandest possible capacity" and recommended the removal of
the Tudor screen on which the organ stood, the clearance of many of the choir
stalls and the provision of chairs for the congregation, thus increasing the available
accommodation from some 300 persons to about 1000. Subscriptions were raised
in Bristol and the work was carried out by the Bristol architect T. S. Pope in 1860–
61 at a cost of more than £15,000. Unfortunately this major re-ordering of the
interior resulted in the destruction of most of the beautiful screen or pulpitum
which had been given to the cathedral in 1542, and the removal of the heraldic
pavement from the Berkeley chapel. Elliot also seized the opportunity to remove
and destroy some of the medieval misericords or lively carvings beneath the seats in

---

[5] Quoted by P. Cobb, *The Oxford Movement in Nineteenth-Century Bristol*, Bristol Historical
Association, 1988, 14.
[6] Bristol Record Office, (hereafter B.R.O.) CD/A/7/6/3.
[7] Information from Elliot's memorial in Bristol cathedral.

the choir stalls which he regarded as indecent or improper, although from surviving illustrations they do not seem to have been particularly objectionable. The result of Dean Elliot's work did not meet with universal approval. The bishop of the diocese, Charles Thomas Baring, (bishop 1856–61) whose relations with the Dean and Chapter were already strained, opposed the scheme and refused to preach at the civic service held at the completion of the work on 27 June 1861, while the influential journal *The Ecclesiologist*, although acknowledging the difficulty of providing more space within the cathedral, totally condemned the way in which the scheme had been carried out, and suggested that it would have been far better to raise funds to rebuild the nave. In particular the journal criticised Pope's work in the strongest terms "the pattern and materials are such as would disgrace a railway station, or the showroom of a cheap lath and plaster warehouse", while the verdict on the light screen which Pope had designed to replace the Tudor pulpitum was that it resembled "a gate to a field with the hedges taken away".[8]

While the work on the cathedral was progressing, the Dean decided to leave the ancient Deanery House on College Green alleging that it was unhealthy and unsuitable. For a time the house was used by the Y.M.C.A., but in 1865 it was demolished to make way for the construction of Deanery Road along the north side of the cathedral, providing a new route to Hotwells. The Dean moved to Clifton, living first in Royal York Crescent and later at the Mall.

In 1863 Elliot remarried. The nineteenth-century reticence of the newspapers over personal affairs meant that the marriage was only briefly reported. His bride was Frances, daughter of Charles Dickinson of Queen Charlton on the southern outskirts of Bristol. She was a member of a wealthy west-country family and she had inherited the manor of Queen Charlton in 1838 while still a minor, and later had also acquired an estate at Farley Hill Court, near Reading. Not mentioned in contemporary reports was the fact that she had prevously been married at the age of eighteen to a Scottish landowner, John Geils of Geilston on the Clyde, by whom she had four daughters. This marriage had ended in divorce in 1848 and John Geils was still alive, although the marriage register of Queen Charlton describes her as "Frances Dickinson, single woman". A year earlier, in 1862, Dean Elliot had officiated at the marriage of one of his prospective wife's daughters, Katherine Geils to Robert Brooks of Epsom at Queen Charlton. The Dean's second wife was an inveterate traveller. One of her daughters, Cecile, was married to the Marquis del Moral in Spain, and another daughter, Clotilde, was married to the Marquis Zorudadari Chigi of Siena. After their marriage the Dean and his wife spent a good deal of time visiting these daughters and travelling in Spain and Italy. Consequently, the Dean was away from the cathedral for long periods during the time that the nave was being rebuilt. For his wife, these travels resulted in the publication of two books, *The Idle Woman in Spain* and *The Idle Woman in Italy*. The Dean's marriage to a divorced woman must have caused considerable comment in ecclesiastical circles, and it is remarkable that no contemporary references have been discovered.

Sadly, the Dean's second marriage was not a success and brought great unhappiness to both parties. The evidence for this comes from the correspondence of the

---

[8] J.H. Bettey, *Bristol Cathedral: The Rebuilding of the Nave*, Bristol Historical Association, 1993, 6; G. Cobb, *English Cathedrals: The Forgotten Centuries*, 1980, 40–1.

author, Charles Dickens. Elliot had become acquainted with Dickens while he was rector of Marylebone. It may have been the influence of Dickens which led Elliot to preach a series of powerful sermons at Marylebone appealing for funds to provide education for poor children in the parish. Later, Dickens called on Elliot during a visit to Bristol on 13 November 1851. Dickens had an even closer friendship with Elliot's future wife. After her divorce in 1848, she reverted to her maiden name and called herself Mrs Frances Dickinson. She began to send Dickens short stories, some of which he published. She also appeared with him on the stage in a successful production of *The Frozen Deep*, written jointly by Dickens and Wilkie Collins in 1857. This rich, lively writer and actress, mother of four daughters, seems an unlikely partner for the staid and strictly evangelical Dean who was twenty years older than her. Frances Dickinson's frequent letters to Dickens reveal her misgivings before the marriage in 1863. Afterwards they reveal the break-down in the relationship. By 1869 the rift was so deep that Dickens and Elliot's brother, Frederick, were obliged to act as mediators. Dickens held a long meeting with Elliot at the Athenaeum on 3 August 1869. In a letter to Frances Elliot, Dickens reported that because of disagreements over the marriage settlement, a disputed mortgage on some unspecified property, and allegations that her husband was mismanaging and wasting his wife's fortune, Elliot was considering resigning his Deanery. Such bitter disputes with his wife at the time when the cathedral nave was being rebuilt may explain why the Dean failed to give his whole-hearted support to the project. The marriage survived, but both parties seem to have lived apart for a good deal of each year. Elliot's second wife is not mentioned on his memorial in Bristol cathedral.[9]

The major event in the life of Bristol cathedral was the rebuilding of the nave, which will be discussed later in this chapter. Perhaps stung by the torrent of criticism which had greeted his attempt to improve the accommodation within the cathedral, Dean Elliot remained aloof from the early stages of fund-raising and nave reconstruction. He doubted whether sufficient funds could be raised or whether the ambitious scheme could be completed. He did, however, continue to keep a tight control on all aspects of the services within the cathedral, and was ever watchful to frustrate any attempts to introduce extra services or innovation.

From 1863 to 1897 the bishop of the united dioceses of Gloucester and Bristol was Charles John Ellicott. His relationship with Dean Elliot was never close and was often tense. Elliot was at pains to emphasise the rights of the Dean and Chapter within the cathedral, and certainly did not welcome an episcopal visit. Consequently, the Bishop seldom came to the cathedral; he held his ordinations elsewhere, and found himself involved in several disputes with Elliot over his right to preach in the cathedral. An example of the Dean's attitude and pessimistic outlook is recorded in the life of John Percival who had been the headmaster of Clifton College, Bristol and subsequently was President of Trinity College, Oxford and finally Bishop of

[9] Queen Charlton Marriage Register, Somerset Record Office, D/P/Q Cha 2/1/4; *The Bristol Times*, 7 November 1863; Joy Burden, *Winging Westward*, 1974, 16; E. Walford, *County Families of the United Kingdom*, 1886; G.A.J. Loxton, *Queen Charlton*, 1999, 82; G. Storey, ed., *The Letters of Charles Dickens*, X, 18659–61, 287–9; X, 1862–64; 1865–7. *passim* W. Dexter, ed., *Letters of Charles Dickens*, 1858–60, 1938, III, 734–5. I am grateful to Dr Martin Crossley Evans for drawing my attention to this material concerning Dickens.

Hereford. In 1882 Percival accepted appointment as a canon of Bristol cathedral. Upon arrival to take up his term of residence at the cathedral, Percival proposed to hold Sunday evening services in the recently-completed nave. The suggestion was fiercely resisted by the Dean on the grounds that "there is no pulpit and the Chapter will not provide one" and secondly "because no one will come". The Dean was eventually forced to give way in the face of Percival's enthusiasm. Percival provided a pulpit at his own expense, and the services rapidly became very popular, attracting large crowds every Sunday. As a result of Percival's efforts, 500 extra chairs had to be purchased for the nave.[10]

Much of the Dean's work in Bristol during his later years was concerned with education. He played a prominent part in the movement to found a university in Bristol. It was while John Percival was headmaster of Clifton College during the early 1870s that the desire to create a university for Bristol gathered momentum. Dean Elliot was an early and enthusiastic supporter. He was chairman of the committee to promote a "College of Science and Literature" founded in 1874, and with Percival he was able to involve the influential support of their friend Benjamin Jowett, the Master of Balliol. Jowett had maintained a close friendship with Elliot and his family for many years. During the early 1860s he had seriously considered marriage with Elliot's elder daughter, Margaret, but eventually Jowett's fellowship at Balliol, the Mastership which he obtained in 1870 and his intense but platonic friendship with Florence Nightingale, proved more attractive. Jowett continued to visit and correspond with Margaret Elliot until his death in 1893, and he also corresponded frequently with her father. Thus Elliot was able to enlist Jowett's support for a university in Bristol. Although already more than seventy years of age, Elliot was vigorous in fund-raising and in securing support for the University College. He became the first President of the College, and on his death in 1891 was succeeded by Benjamin Jowett.[11]

Elliot was also closely involved with the foundation of Clifton High School for Girls in 1877 and became the school's first President. He seems to have taken a less active interest in the Cathedral School and rarely attended the meetings of the school's governors.[12]

Dean Elliot died at his house in the Mall, Clifton on 11 August 1891 and was buried in the cathedral churchyard. He had lived to the age of 91 and had been Dean for 41 years. Not surprisingly he had taken little part in civic affairs or cathedral life during his last years. His obituaries in the local papers were at best lukewarm in their references to his achievements, and his colleagues in the Cathedral Chapter recorded his death in their minutes without any comment or expression of regret. The entry in the minutes states only that the Chapter Clerk reported the death of the Very Reverend Gilbert Elliot, Dean of Bristol, which took place on 11 August 1891.[13]

[10] D. Winterbottom, *John Percival, the Great Educator*, Bristol Historical Association, 1993, 7; B.R.O. DC/A/8/16.

[11] J. Latimer, *Annals of Bristol in the Nineteenth Century*, 1887, 474–5; B. Cottle & J. Sherborne, *The Life of a University*, 1951; D. Carleton, *A University for Bristol*, 1984; G. Faber, *Jowett*, 1957, 299–306.

[12] B.R.O. 40170.

[13] B.R.O. DC/A/8/8 Chapter Minutes 1879–1900.

JOHN PILKINGTON NORRIS 1823–1891

Norris was born at Chester on 10 June 1823, the son of a local physician, Thomas Norris. He was educated at Rugby during the period of the great headmaster Thomas Arnold, and gained an open scholarship to Trinity College, Cambridge. A distinguished scholar, he graduated B.A. in 1846 and M.A. in 1849. In 1848 he became a Fellow of Trinity. He was ordained deacon in 1849 and priest in 1850. Much of his early career was devoted to the promotion of education in Church elementary schools. He became an inspector of Church schools in Staffordshire, Shropshire and Cheshire in 1849, and entered upon his duties with enormous enthusiasm. In 1863 he moved to supervise Church schools in Kent and Surrey.

In 1864 he was appointed to a canonry in Bristol cathedral and was installed on 9th July 1865. He remained as a canon of Bristol until his death in 1891, but combined this with a succession of other church appointments. Throughout his life he was also a prolific author. His publications included classical, theological and educational works, as well as handbooks on biblical subjects, lectures and histories of the cathedral and St Mary Redcliffe. He was also examining chaplain to the Bishop of Manchester, an Inspector of Church Training Colleges and a member of the Church Convocation.[14]

Norris became vicar of St George's, Brandon Hill in Bristol in 1870, and was a popular, energetic parish priest. The church had been built in 1823 and its interior design laid much emphasis on preaching. This hardly fitted with the High Anglican tradition adopted by Canon Norris, and within a year of his appointment he had secured a faculty to install a new raised altar and to reconstruct the chancel area.[15]

He threw himself zealously into diocesan work especially education, and in 1876 became rural dean of Bristol. A year later he was appointed vicar of St Mary Redcliffe. His interest in his magnificent church and its history led to a scholarly article in the *Transactions of the Bristol and Gloucestershire Archaeological Society in 1878* and to considerable conservation work on the building. Finally in 1881 Norris was appointed Archdeacon of Bristol.[16]

In 1858 Norris married Edith Grace Lushington, and the marriage produced four sons, two of whom followed their father into the Church. One son became vicar of St Bartholomew's, Reading, while another became a missionary in China.[17]

No sooner had Norris been appointed to a Bristol canonry than the construction of a new road along the north side of the cathedral revealed part of the foundations of the medieval nave. This had been started by Abbot Newland in the late-fifteenth century, but the work had been abandoned at the Reformation. The discovery fired Norris's imagination and his desire to see a new nave built for the cathedral. Although he had so recently joined the Cathedral Chapter, he immediately obtained an interview with the Mayor and councillors of Bristol, persuading them to alter the line of the road so that in the future it would be possible for a new nave to be built

[14] *Dictionary of National Biography.*
[15] B.R.O. P/StG B /Chw/c-d, Faculties for St George's, Brandon Hill, 1871 and 2873.
[16] M.Q. Smith, *St Mary Redcliffe*, 1995; BRO EP/J/6/2/65, Faculties for St Mary Redcliffe 1845–1961.
[17] *DNB.*

along the line of the medieval foundations. Without his far-sighted action, the nave as it now exists could not have been built. Thereafter, Norris was to be the most energetic supporter of the campaign for a new nave and its most successful fund-raiser. Unfortunately his involvement in this project led to a succession of disagree-ments with Dean Elliot. The Dean and other members of the Chapter remained lukewarm in their response to the campaign for a new nave. They doubted whether the huge sums which were necessary could be raised, and suggested that at most a small extension should be built. For several crucial years the Chapter were far from wholehearted in their support for the enterprise, and the relationship between the Dean and Canon Norris, although always correct, was at best strictly formal and certainly never cordial. This relationship, which strained the Christian charity of both men, will be discussed in the next section.[18]

Canon Norris was also closely involved in other aspects of the life of the cathedral. His interest in its history and architecture led to the publication of a guide to the cathedral in 1882 and to a major article in the *Transactions of the Bristol and Gloucester-shire Archaeological Society* in 1890. He also sought out and purchased from antiquar-ian booksellers some of the cathedral manuscripts which had earlier been lost or which had been scattered by the Bristol rioters in 1831.[19]

In 1836 the diocese of Bristol was united with the diocese of Gloucester. The Dorset part of Bristol diocese was returned to Salisbury, while the north Wiltshire deaneries of Malmesbury, Chippenham and Cricklade, formerly in Salisbury diocese, became part of the new diocese of Gloucester and Bristol. The loss of separate diocesan status was deeply unpopular in Bristol, even though the city retained its cathedral. There were several proposals to reverse the arrangements, and in 1861 the citizens of Bristol petitioned the Queen in Council for a restoration of the Bristol diocese. Canon Norris became a leading figure in this cause. It was largely due to his work that the bishopric was finally restored in 1897. He accompanied the Mayor of Bristol and several councillors on a deputation to the Home Secretary in 1877 to solicit his help in securing the new bishopric. In 1883 he secured an interview with the Prime Minister, W.E. Gladstone, and obtained his active support for a parliamentary bill in 1883. This was passed by parliament in 1884 as the Bishopric of Bristol Act. It gave the Ecclesiastical Commissioners power to restore the bishopric of Bristol as soon as an income of £3000 per annum was provided. The proposed new diocese was to consist of the city of Bristol and its environs, together with the deaneries of Malmesbury, Chippenham and Cricklade. There-after, Canon Norris devoted himself, with boundless energy and enthusiasm, to rais-ing money for the new bishopric. A Bristol Bishoprick Fund was established in 1884 with Norris as secretary. He rapidly obtained an impressive list of supporters, includ-ing many leading dignitaries in Bristol, local gentry, the Merchant Venturers and influential national figures. As secretary, Norris arranged public meetings, wrote innumerable articles, letters to the press and to private individuals pleading for

---

[18] For a fuller account of all events leading to the reconstruction of the cathedral nave see J.H. Bettey, *Bristol Cathedral: The Rebuilding of the Nave*, Bristol Historical Association, 1993.

[19] BRO DC/E/1/1b-c. Volumes of leases of cathedral properties. A note at the front of the first volume records that the papers "loose and crumbling" were purchased from Kerslake, bookseller, in Park Street by Canon J.P. Norris, who had them bound.

funds. Gladstone sent a donation of £50, partly because of his admiration for the theological works of a previous bishop of Bristol, Joseph Butler, whom he described as one of the greatest theologians of the Church of England. Norris himself contributed £1,500 to the fund, and as a result of his efforts large sums of money were raised. By the time Norris died in 1891 some £50,000 had been contributed to the project, most of it as a result of his efforts. After his death, a collection in his memory raised the remarkable sum of £11,500 which was devoted to the cause. The bishopric was finally re-established in 1897. The fact that such large sums were subscribed for the bishopric in Bristol at the same time that the Church was also raising money for the cathedral nave and for the building of new churches in the expanding new suburbs makes Norris's success even more remarkable. Norris's enthusiasm and successful fund-raising were in marked contrast to Dean Elliot's attitude. The Dean took little part in the campaign, and remained largely indifferent to it.[20]

Norris was also concerned with church provision in the rapidly-growing suburbs of Bristol. This led to his appointment by the bishop as chairman of a Commission of Enquiry into the subject in 1881, and to the building of six new churches and several new mission churches. For although Canon Norris gave the initial impression of a stern, withdrawn and scholarly figure, his infectious enthusiasm for the projects he espoused made him an exceptionally good and successful fund-raiser. The money which was raised in Bristol to his memory is a measure of the respect and regard which he was accorded in the city.[21]

His concern for the poor in Bristol was demonstrated soon after his arrival in the city. In the cholera epidemic of 1865–66 he established with the dedicated help of his wife a "Sanitary Mission" to assist the poor with hygiene, disinfecting their houses and with general health care. The Mission sent helpers and advisors into all the worst-afflicted areas of Bristol in a movement which foreshadowed the modern health visitors. It was to play a significant part in containing the disease in the summer of 1866 and ensuring that it did not again become widespread thereafter.[22]

As one of the most vigorous, active and popular clergymen in Bristol, and by far the most eminent of the cathedral canons, Norris seemed to many people the obvious successor to Gilbert Elliot as Dean of Bristol. Unfortunately, when Elliot died on 11 August 1891 Norris himself was seriously ill with bronchitis. It must have been with great sadness that he learned that Francis Pigou, Dean of Chichester, had been appointed as the new Dean of Bristol. Thereafter Norris's condition deteriorated rapidly, and he died on 29 December 1891. Shortly before his death he learned that he had been chosen as Dean of Chichester to replace Pigou.

In marked contrast to the obituaries written for Dean Elliot, the local newspapers were fulsome in their praise for Norris, and for the work which he had done in Bristol. *The Bristol Times and Mirror*, for example, praised his work on the cathedral nave, for the restoration of the diocese, on education and on the numerous other

[20] B.R.O. 12153/1 Norris MSS.

[21] Elizabeth Ralph & Peter Cobb, *New Anglican Churches in Nineteenth-Century Bristol*, Bristol Historical Association, 1991, 15–16.

[22] D. Large, *The Municipal Government of Bristol 1851–1901*, Bristol Record Society, 50, 1999, 130.

good causes, deplored the fact that he had not been appointed as Dean of Bristol, and concluded that for years he was "the constantly resident and only really active member of the Chapter of Bristol". The obituary also declared that "He may be said with literal truth to have called into existence the scheme for the establishment of a separate See for Bristol. . . . To him also we owe nearly all that has been done in the matter of Cathedral restoration." The minutes of the Cathedral Chapter which are merely formal about Elliot's death include a record of "the deep sense of grievous loss . . . by the removal of one whose friendship and wise counsel have been so helpful to them for so many years", and the fact that members of Chapter send their "sympathy to Mrs Norris and her sons in the heavy bereavement which it has pleased God to send upon them".[23]

CONFLICT AND CONTROVERSY

It was perhaps inevitable that the strong-minded and staunchly low-church Dean would not for long work in harmony with the energetic high-anglican canon. Certainly the totally different characters and churchmanship of the two men led to disagreement between them soon after Norris arrived in Bristol and continued until both men died in 1891. The record of their disagreements can be traced in the Chapter minutes and other cathedral records, as well as in the copious notes which Canon Norris himself made of Chapter business.[24]

Hardly had Canon Norris taken up his post at Bristol than the Cathedral Chapter found itself in negotiation with the city over the sale of the Deanery which closed off the south-west corner of College Square. The Bristol Improvement Committee wished to purchase the Deanery and demolish it to make way for a new road to be built along the southern edge of College Green. This was later to be called Deanery Road. The Chapter did not object to the road and were willing to sell the Deanery, but the Dean also proposed throwing open to the public the space at the west end of the cathedral, on the site of the former nave, that is effectively to make the area part of College Green which was at that time shaded with large trees and was a popular place for walks and public recreation. Such a move might have prevented or hindered any future proposal to rebuild the cathedral nave. Norris strongly objected to this plan, both because the former nave was consecrated ground and also in order to keep the land free for a possible rebuilding of the nave. After meeting with the Mayor (William Naish) and Council during the summer of 1865, Norris got his way, and a clause was inserted into the agreement over the Deanery and the road which allowed for a rebuilt nave at some time in the future.[25]

No sooner had work started on construction of the new road than the workmen uncovered the foundations of the former north porch and part of the medieval nave wall. Norris immediately sought a further meeting with the Mayor and the Council

---

[23] B.R.O. DC/A/8/8 Chapter Minutes 1879–1900; *Bristol Times & Mirror* 30 December 1891.

[24] B.R.O. DC/A/8/16, Canon Norris's *Memoranda of Chapter Meetings 1865–1891*; BRO DC/A/8/7 Chapter Minutes 1858–1879; DC/A/8/8 Chapter Minutes 1879–1900.

[25] B.R.O. DC/A/8/16; J. Latimer, *Annals of Bristol in the Nineteenth Century*, 1887, 429–30.

and persuaded them to move the line of their road a short distance to the north, so that the nave could be rebuilt on its medieval foundation.

As mentioned earlier, the discovery of the medieval foundations fired Norris with enthusiasm for replacing the nave, whereas Elliot and other members of Chapter remained diffident towards the proposal and doubted if sufficient funds could be raised. During discussions in Chapter an agreement was eventually reached that an appeal for funds should be launched, but it was stipulated that any new nave should be in the same style of architecture as the chancel, and Elliot was strongly of the opinion that three or four bays of a new nave was all that should be built and that the work should proceed bay by bay as money was raised rather than planning the whole work from the beginning. He certainly felt that it would be impossible to raise the necessary money for any larger or longer nave. For some time Elliot continued to remain aloof from the project, taking no part in the appointment of an architect, nor in the massive fund-raising campaign.

In marked contrast to the Dean's lack of enthusiasm and doubts about the project for re-building the cathedral nave, Canon Norris was tireless in his promotion of the scheme. In July 1866 on his own initiative Norris issued an appeal for funds to the citizens of Bristol and called a meeting in the Colston Hall to discuss the possibilities. The scheme caught the imagination of Bristolians who were eager to have a cathedral worthy of the size, wealth and importance of their city. A committee of eminent citizens was formed with Henry Cruger William Miles of Kingsweston House as its chairman, William Killigrew Wait of Clifton as its secretary and Canon Norris as its energetic treasurer. Thereafter the project developed with remarkable speed. Canon Norris was hugely successful in obtaining contributions, and by December 1866 more than £11,000 had been raised and the eminent architect George Edmund Street had been appointed to design the new nave. Faced with this massive enthusiasm, the Dean and other members of the Chapter gave their support to the scheme, but remained detached from it, taking little part in the details or in the continuing work of fund-raising.

Nonetheless contributions continued to pour in. Street's design for the new nave was approved, although his previous work on several well-known Tractarian churches cannot have endeared him to Dean Elliot. The foundation stone of the new nave was laid in April 1868, and work continued steadily during the next few years. As Treasurer of the Committee, Canon Norris continued to devote much time and energy to fund-raising, and there can be no doubt that without his work the project would not have been started, nor would it have reached such a rapid and successful conclusion. By 1877 the new nave was virtually complete and could be used for public worship although the western towers still had to be built. The opening service was held on 23 October 1877. So far, some £48,000 had been raised.[26]

Meanwhile, there were other causes of disagreement between the two men. In 1869 Norris proposed in Chapter that weekday Communion services should be held in the cathedral. The three other canons supported this proposal, but Elliot as Dean, firmly refused to allow such services to take place. The matter was raised again in 1871 with the same result. In his notes of the Chapter meeting held on 4 July 1871

---

[26] For fuller details see J.H. Bettey, *Bristol Cathedral: The Rebuilding of the Nave*, 1993.

Norris wrote that the proposal for a weekly communion service at Noon was "Pressed on the Dean by all four [canons]. The Dean refuses".[27]

Also in 1871 there was a fierce dispute in Chapter concerning the allocation of houses in the cathedral precinct, in particular as to whether the Archdeacon of Bristol, James Randall, should be allowed to occupy the abbey gatehouse. This was proposed by the Dean but objected to by Norris, who was supported by the other canons. On this issue the Dean was forced to give way. In 1872 Norris put forward a scheme for the establishment of a Diocesan Training Centre attached to the cathedral. This failed to get support from the Dean, and the scheme was eventually abandoned. With his life-long interest in education, Canon Norris longed to see the cathedral as a centre of scholarship, training clergy for work in the Church and teachers for the Church schools. He devoted much effort to various schemes and proposals, including a theological seminary and a teacher training college in the cathedral precinct, offering to give up his own house to provide accommodation for these institutions. All his plans for such establishments failed to attract the support of the Dean or of the other canons. Canon Norris did, however, play an active part as governor of Bristol Cathedral School.[28]

Another disagreement in Chapter during the 1870s concerned major repairs to the central tower. As work proceeded on the new nave, the architect, G.E. Street, was more and more concerned about the state of the tower and its buttresses. He urged immediate action, and was wholeheartedly supported by Norris, but the Dean constantly delayed any decision by the Chapter, so that it was 1876 before the necessary major work was commenced. The Dean decided that because of the extensive work on the tower, it was necessary to close the cathedral during summer 1877, and this also led to a disagreement between the Dean and Canon Norris. The closure was announced by the Dean without any prior consultation with the Chapter. At the next Chapter meeting which was on 2 October 1877, Norris moved a resolution deploring that the cathedral had been closed and that no provision had been made for the continuance of the daily services. The Dean refused to accept the resolution on the grounds that no previous notice of it had been given to the Chapter Clerk. Undeterred, Norris raised it again at the December Chapter meeting and it was agreed that such a complete closure should not be permitted in future.[29]

In June 1882 Norris wrote to the Dean requesting that, as Archdeacon, he might use the Cathedral Chapter House for clerical visitations. The Dean refused, saying that he objected to diocesan clergy being summoned to the cathedral.[30]

The year 1876 saw by far the most bitter and serious of the disputes between the Dean and Canon Norris. As with other disagreements, much of it was conducted by correspondence, all of it icily correct and formal, and without any reference to personal well-being, or any expressions of goodwill or cordiality. After the fashion of the time, each addressed the other as "My Dear Elliot" or "My Dear Norris". After Norris became Archdeacon in 1881, the Dean always addressed him as "My Dear

[27] B.R.O. DC/A/8/16.
[28] *Ibid.*
[29] *Ibid.*
[30] *Ibid.*

Archdeacon". The dispute concerned the installation around the recently-completed porch of the new nave of four statues of saints.

Work on the nave had proceeded so rapidly and well that it was now possible to build the north porch which was to be the principal entrance to the building. The enthusiastic Secretary of the Nave Restoration Committee, William Killigrew Wait, a wealthy corn merchant who was a Bristol City Councillor and also M.P. for Gloucester, generously provided the money to build the porch and thus complete the main part of the new nave. The design by the architect, G.E. Street, incorporated niches for statues around the entrance to the porch, in the traditional medieval style. For these niches figures of saints were carved by the well-known sculptor, James Frank Redfern (1838–76), who had worked with Street for many years. The choice of subjects to be represented by the statues was left to the carver. When the statues were placed in position during the early spring of 1876, there was an outcry of protest in Bristol. As well as the Virgin and Christ Child, the carver had produced the figures of the four doctors of the medieval church, St Gregory, St Ambrose, St Jerome and St Augustine of Hippo. Each was distinguished by the traditional attributes, a papal tiara, a scourge, a cardinal's hat and a burning heart. All the forces of mid-Victorian protestantism and anti-Catholicism immediately sprang to life. The local papers were filled with letters expressing Protestant outrage, and on 3 April 1876 a crowded meeting of protest was held in the Colston Hall at which violent passions were roused and fighting broke out among the assembled company. Chairs were thrown and blows exchanged. A resolution was passed by a large majority demanding that the statues be removed immediately.[31]

The Dean had been on holiday with his wife in Italy, but returned in time to face all the furious protests. A meeting of the Chapter was held on 4 April, at which petitions and resolutions demanding the removal of the statues were presented from various Protestant organisations. Horrified by the strength of feeling that the statues had aroused, and in spite of the protests of Canon Norris and his plea for delay, Chapter resolved that the Dean should take action to remove the statues.

In vain did Canon Norris urge compromise and suggest that they should endeavour by way of friendly conference to close the difference which had arisen. He reported that the donor, Henry Killigrew Wait, was willing to pay for alterations to the statues so as to remove those features regarded by the critics as "Popish". He also strongly advised that the Nave Restoration Committee should be consulted before any action was taken, since the Committee felt that they were being unjustly charged with bad faith in the matter. Notwithstanding these objections, the other members of Chapter were willing to leave matters to the Dean, whose evangelical views were certainly not in sympathy with the attributes of the statues.[32]

Two days later, early on the morning of 6 April 1876, the Dean arranged for a gang of workmen to remove the statues from their niches. Using ropes, they tore down the offending figures, damaging some of them in the process. A local newspaper reported that "a more rough and open exhibition of iconoclasm has not been seen in Bristol since the days of Oliver Cromwell." Later, the niches were to be filled with innocuous statues of the evangelists.[33]

---

[31] *Bristol Times & Mirror*, 4 April 1876.
[32] BRO DC/A/8/7; DC/A/8/16.
[33] *Bristol Times & Mirror*, 4 April 1876.

The Dean's precipitate action provoked a vigorous protest from the cathedral's architect, G.E. Street, who complained that hitherto the Dean had taken no interest in the nave or any of its details.

"But you will excuse my saying that, seeing with what singular care you avoided discussing anything connected with the new works with me, I should have thought it a grave impertinence to ask your opinion of any of the details. I gathered from your manner you did not much like the work being undertaken, nor cared to make yourself in any way responsible for the character of any portion of it. You left all the responsibility, both for the cost and execution of my designs, to the Committee. . .".

Street went on to point out that "The designs of the figures were not mine, but those of the sculptor, Mr Redfern, who executed them." Street stated that he was abroad when the figures were put up, and that he felt that "Mr Redfern, the sculptor, was injudicious in making so much of some of the insignia of the four doctors." But the details, and in particular the cardinal's hat and the papal tiara could easily have been altered, "and these alterations could be made now if the statues have not been damaged (as I am informed they have been) by the careless and hasty way in which your removal of them was effected".

A tragic victim of the controversy was the sculptor, James Redfern, who was devastated by the uproar. Although only thirty-eight years of age, he fell seriously ill and died later the same year. James Frank Redfern (1838–76) was a gifted and well-known sculptor who had frequently been employed by Street. He had provided numerous statues of saints for many churches, including the cathedrals at Salisbury, Ely and Gloucester and at Westminster Abbey. His work had also been exhibited at the Royal Academy. He was devastated by the passionate controversy which his artistic work had created at Bristol, and deeply upset by the way in which his statues had been treated.[34]

The members of the Nave Restoration Committee who had worked so tirelessly and successfully to raise money to rebuild the nave felt gravely insulted by the Dean's action, and by the lack of any consultation with them. In particular they felt that the hasty removal of the statues was an unwarranted affront to their Secretary, W. K. Wait, who had so generously given the money for the porch. All the members of the Committee therefore resigned, writing to the Chapter to express their indignation that the Dean who had hitherto been indifferent to the work "expresses no regret for the outrage which has been committed or for the discourtesy offered as well to the donor of the porch as to the eminent architect who has been engaged in the work". The Committee declared that they would take no further part in the completion of the nave.[35]

The next meeting of Chapter was on 9 May 1876. A long memorandum was presented by Canon Norris, complaining of the Dean's actions and his refusal to compromise or to meet with the Nave Restoration Committee. The Dean made an

---

[34] A.E. Street, *Memoir of George Edmund Street*, 1888, 180–1. Redfern's statues were later rescued by Street and used to adorn the tower of East Heslerton church in the East Riding of Yorkshire.

[35] B.R.O. DC/A/8/7 Chapter Minutes 1858–79.

equally spirited reply, in which he strongly criticised the way in which Norris had acted against the wishes of the Chapter. Canon Norris was deeply upset by this controversy and by the Dean's censure, and seriously considered resigning as a canon of the cathedral. Finally, he wrote a long letter of protest to the Dean setting out his "strong feelings of indignation". The Dean, however, was unrepentant.

In his reply, written on 15 May 1876, he wrote that

> "My remarks at the last Chapter were intended to convey a warning rather than censure or rebuke. I thought then, and I still think, that your anxiety and zeal for the work which you had done so much to promote were leading you into unfair comment on the proceedings of the Chapter, and into a course of such hostile action towards it as to render necessary the interpolation of the warning and counsel which the duties of my office appeared to exact from me, when I may deem the conduct of any of the Canons is working injuriously in the interests of the Cathedral".[36]

Meanwhile, the Dean was left with no alternative but to supervise the completion of the work himself. A "Cathedral Completion Fund" was opened with the Dean as Treasurer. and donations were sought in order to finish the work. Here again, conflict with Canon Norris could not be avoided, for Norris had remained as Treasurer of a separate committee whose purpose was to raise money to build the north-west tower of the new nave as a memorial to Bishop Butler, the eminent theologian who had been bishop of Bristol from 1738–1750. The popularity and enthusiasm of Canon Norris meant that he was much more successful at fund raising than the Dean, and more money was collected for the tower than for the completion of the nave. In January 1877, therefore, the Dean had to request that Norris stopped collecting money for the tower in Bristol since he claimed that this would "revive jealousies, rivalries, misrepresentation and antagonisms which have already done much mischief and ought to be discouraged, not encouraged".[37]

Finally on 23 October 1877 the opening service for the new nave was held before a great gathering of clergy and civic dignitaries. Sadly, the members of the Nave Restoration Committee whose efforts had ensured the successful completion of the work did not attend. Canon Norris, however, continued his work for the cathedral. His contribution was finally recognised in June 1888 when Mrs Norris was invited to lay the cap stone of the north-western tower and when an elaborate service attended by 3,000 people was held in the cathedral to celebrate the final completion of the nave.[38]

During 1877 Canon Norris became vicar of St Mary Redcliffe, although he remained as a canon of the cathedral, and controversy with the Dean did not cease. One source of continuing disagreement concerned the manner in which the Holy Communion service was conducted in the cathedral. Norris maintained that the Bread and Wine for the Communion should not be placed upon the altar until just before the prayer for the Church Militant, as the rubric in the Book of Common

---

[36] B.R.O. DC/A/8/16.

[37] B.R.O. DC/F/3/1a-b Minute Book of the Committee for the North-West Tower 1875–77.

[38] *Bristol Times & Mirror*, 24 October 1877; 9 June 1888.

Prayer directs. He suggested that until that point in the service the Bread and Wine should be placed on an adjacent table, ledge or aumbry. The Dean was adamant that the long-established custom at the cathedral was to place these elements on the altar or Holy Table at the beginning of the service, and that this practice should be continued. In this the Dean was supported by the Bishop. Canon Norris appealed to the Bishop, C.J. Ellicott, who supported the Dean and confirmed that the custom followed in the cathedral was the general practice throughout the diocese. Eventually after long correspondence, the Dean agreed that when Canon Norris celebrated Holy Communion in the cathedral he might follow the rubric as he wished. The long argument over the matter now seems remarkably petty, but it is another indication of the strained relations between the two men.[39]

The conflicting churchmanship of the two men is also revealed in a dispute which occurred in 1883. Norris had for long urged that there should be more frequent Communion services in the Cathedral, but the Dean had refused all requests. In the Chapter meeting of 1 October 1883 Norris tried again. In his notes of the meeting he recorded "JPN (i.e. himself) begged for Holy Communion on Saints' Days. The Dean refused". Norris went on to ask for special services in the cathedral on other important festivals, but noted sadly "The Dean *vetoes* any continuance of special services beyond Advent and Lent".

A final, major disagreement arose in response to the Royal Commission on the Condition of Cathedral Churches in 1883. The Commissioners issued a detailed questionnaire to every cathedral. This asked for information on all aspects of the life of each cathedral, its fabric, services, clergy, staff, statutes, educational provision, finances and relations with the bishop and the diocese. At Bristol Dean Elliot submitted long and detailed replies to the Commissioners' enquiries. Again he laid stress on the powers of the Dean to govern the cathedral, control its functions, supervise all aspects of its life and admonish, regulate and reprove the canons as necessary. He again maintained that the power of the diocesan bishop within the cathedral and over its administration was strictly limited, and that the responsibility of each canon was confined to the duty of residing and officiating at the service and preaching for three months in each year. Above all, he laid further stress on the powers of the Dean to direct the character of worship within the cathedral, ". . . the regulation of the cathedral services is altogether with the dean".[40]

Not surprisingly Canon Norris objected to many features of the Dean's replies to the Commissioners. He therefore wrote to the Commissioners, stating his own views. In addition, however, he trumped the Dean's interpretation of the cathedral's constitution by a masterly stroke of his own. The Statutes provided for Bristol cathedral at its foundation by Henry VIII in 1542 had never been translated from the original Latin. Using his classical education, Norris provided a complete and elegant translation of the Statutes. They showed clearly that the cathedral was intended to be a community of priests headed by a dean, similar to the Augustinian community which it replaced. They laid emphasis on communal life, and on worship, preaching and teaching. The canons were to be supported by a staff of laymen,

---

[39] B.R.O. DC/A/8/16.
[40] Report of the Royal Commission on the Condition of Cathedral Churches, and Evidence presented to the Commissioners, C3823, Vol. XXI, 1883–84.

including a teacher for a boys' school, an organist and a master of choristers. Clearly much stress was to be laid on the quality and beauty of the daily round of services, and on regular preaching by the canons. The over-riding power and control claimed by Dean Elliot were not envisaged at the foundation of the cathedral. Canon Norris's translation of the Statutes was printed by the Commissioners as an Appendix to their Report, together with two lengthy letters from Canon Norris in which he set out his own views of how the cathedral should be organised and the functions which it should fulfil. In his letters Norris allowed himself to express all the pent-up frustrations about the cathedral which had accumulated since his appointment as a canon in 1864. His major concerns were delivered under four headings and can be summarised as follows:

MAINTENANCE OF WORSHIP

"Here Bristol Cathedral seems to me sadly in arrear. Our service is far less helpful to my devotion than that of many other cathedrals that I visit. I may instance the fact that we are only allowed to have the Holy Communion at the high service twice a month (though for eight consecutive years all the four canons were unanimous in desiring that it might be weekly). ... Holy Communion on saints' days is not permitted. Nor are we allowed to have any choral accompaniment of this our highest act of worship even on the great festivals".

THE PREACHING OF GOD'S WORD

"Here again I have to confess to much disappointment. Two sermons on Sunday, with one additional week-day sermon during Advent and Lent, seems hardly to fulfil the requirement of our Statutes that we should 'be instant in season and out of season in preaching God's word' ".

EDUCATION

"The cathedral school has, I rejoice to say, been very greatly improved; but we were clearly intended by Archbishop Cranmer to be a seminary for the training of students, 'whom the bishop might transplant as out of a nursery into all parts of his diocese' I long to see the cathedral itself becoming a theological college. And I should rejoice to see such students gradually displacing the salaried singing men, whom we hire from all parts of the town to do what members of the cathedral church were intended to do. Our worship would gain immensely in reverence, and need not lose in musical proficiency by such a change".

ASSISTANCE TO BE RENDERED TO THE BISHOP

"Under this head nothing is done here; ordinations are not held in this cathedral, and as to our assisting the bishop as his council, it is simply out of the question until the cathedral Chapter does more to win the sympathy and confidence of the diocese".

Canon Norris went on to discuss the unsatisfactory status of honorary canons, the disadvantages of residential canons being present in Bristol for only three months each year, the urgent necessity of more and better services and of more frequent preaching if the cathedral was to fulfil the aspirations of its founders and become "the mother church of the diocese".

Perhaps aware that his outspoken criticism of the situation at Bristol would cause offence to the Dean when his letter was printed by the Commissioners, Canon Norris wrote again a few months later to clarify and extend some of his suggestions for change and to disclaim any intention of personal attack on the Dean. With a restraint which was typical of all the correspondence which had passed between them over the years, Norris wrote as follows:

> ". . .I hope and trust the Commissioners will not construe anything I said as imply-
> ing personal grievance. From the head of our chapter, in common with every
> member of the chapter, I have met with uniform courtesy and kindness, and
> where there was a difference of view the most patient forbearance. That our views
> do somewhat differ as to what is desirable in the services of a cathedral is to me
> a matter of sincere regret. I feel sure the Dean will pardon my having stated my
> own views so plainly in reply to the Commissioners' invitation".[41]

Although during the final years of his life Dean Elliot seldom came to the cathedral from his residence in Clifton, nonetheless he continued to maintain a strict control over its government and over the character of its services. The pleas for change which Canon Norris made to the Commission in 1883 had no effect during his lifetime. Norris outlived the Dean by only a few months; consequently he did not live to see many of the changes which he had so earnestly desired introduced by Elliot's successor, Francis Pigou. Nor did he live to see the restoration of the Bristol diocese in 1897, a development which he so heartily desired and which he had done so much to promote. It was the misfortune of Canon Norris's career, and a constant source of frustration, that his twenty-seven years as a canon of Bristol cathedral coincided with the absolute and austere rule of a Dean from whom he differed so much in character, churchmanship and aspirations for the cathedral.

---

[41] *Ibid.* ; B.R.O. DC/A/7/6/4–5.

XIII

Officers of the Society 1941–2000

DAVID SMITH

WHEN Miss Ralph joined the Society in 1941 she found a situation unique in its history. By resolution taken on 16 October 1939 meetings of Council had been suspended and the Society's business was managed by a nominated executive committee. (This resolution was rescinded at the AGM for 1943). The leading light of the Society was Roland Austin, elected President for the duration of the war, who in 1941 also held the offices of Treasurer, Librarian and Editor of the *Transactions*.

Miss Ralph's organisational ability was quickly recognised and in 1943 she became Secretary for Bristol. The then General Secretary, the Rev. F W Potto Hicks, did not command universal support and in 1948 Miss Ralph was elected to succeed him. 40 years later she recalled with amusement an incident which preceded her first council meeting as Secretary. Unnoticed, she followed two very senior members—Roland Austin being one—into the meeting and overheard one of them say "Humph! We've got a woman Secretary now. The Society really is going downhill!"

The information in the following lists has been extracted from the *Transactions*. By a happy coincidence Roland Austin published lists of officers of the Society for 1876–1940 in the *General Index* to volumes 51–60 of the *Transactions*. So these lists bring the story up-to-date as well as coinciding with the period of Miss Ralph's membership.

Officers were elected at the AGM which until 1953 usually took place in July. So the presidential year ran from July to July in contrast to the Society's membership year which runs from January to December. The date given in the lists below is the year of election to office. Honours and distinctions are as recorded in the *Transactions* at the time of election.

PRESIDENT

1938–45	Roland Austin MA FSA
1945	E W W Veale LLD FSA
1946	T Overbury FRIBA FSA
1947	Wilfrid Leighton FSA
1948	Lt Col A B Lloyd-Baker DL DSO TD
1949	Mrs E M Clifford FSA FRAI FSAScot
1950	Lady Apsley
1951	Sir Lionel G Taylor MA

1952–53	W I Croome MA FSA
1954	Mrs D P Dobson-Hinton LittD FSA
1955	H Stratton-Davis MC FSA FRIBA
1956	Prof David Douglas MA FBA
1957	H F Trew FRIBA MTPI
1958	Prof I A Richmond CBE LittD LLD FBA FSA
1959	F S Wallis BSc PhD FGS FMA
1960	The Very Rev Seiriol Evans MA FSA
1961	Miss Joan Evans DLittD LLD FSA HonARIBA
1962	Glyn E Daniel MA FSA LittD
1963	The Very Rev D Harrison MA
1964	Prof J M Cook MA FSA
1965	Prof A H Smith OBE PhD DLitt FSA
1966	L E W O Fullbrook-Leggatt MC BA
1967	I E Gray MBE MA FSA
1968	P V McGrath MA
1969	Capt H S Gracie CB MA FSA
1970–71	T H B Burrough TD RWA FRIBA
1972	D C W Verey MA FSA ARIBA
1973	Mrs Margaret Sharp MA PhD
1974–Dec 1975	Canon J E Gethyn-Jones MBE MA FSA
1976	Miss Elizabeth Ralph MA FSA
1977	C R Hudleston MA FSA
1978	The Very Rev Gilbert Thurlow MA FSA FRHistS
1979	Bryan Little MA
1980	B J Ashwell MC FSA FRIBA
1981	D Large MA BLitt
1982	G Webster OBE MA PhD FSA
1983	Prof B W Cunliffe MA PhD FBA FSA
1984	C R Elrington MA FSA
1985	N Thomas MA FSA FMA
1986	Brian S Smith MA FSA
1987	Basil Cottle MA PhD FSA
1988	George C Boon BA FSA FRHistS FRNS
1989	Brian C Frith
1990	Canon D G Walker DPhil FSA FRHistS
1991	C Bishop MA ARIBA
1992	D G Vaisey MA FSA
1993	Prof Keith Branigan BA PhD FSA
1994	Canon B G Carne Bcom FSA
1995	Bernard Rawes FSA
1996	J H Bettey PhD MA FSA
1997	E G Price JP FSA
1998	P L Dickinson
1999	Warwick J Rodwell DLitt DLC FSA FRHistS
2000	Professor P M Warren MA PhD FSA

NOTES

1. In 1953 the date of the AGM was moved from July to March. Mr Croome was asked to continue in office so that his successor could serve for a full twelve months.
2. Canon Gethyn-Jones was asked to continue in office in order that Miss Ralph could serve as President for the whole of the Society's Centenary year.
3. Mr Rawes died in office so did not serve a full year.

GENERAL SECRETARY

1938–48	The Rev F W Potto Hicks
1948–86	Miss Elizabeth Ralph
1986–	D J H Smith MA FSA

CHAIRMAN OF COUNCIL

The Chairman of Council is elected annually at the AGM. The term of office is limited to three years.

1939–42	C E Boucher BSc
1942–45	T Overbury FRIBA FSA
1945–48	Sir Lionel G Taylor MA
1948–51	H F Trew FRIBA
1951–54	F S Wallis PhD DSc
1954–57	Lt Col A B Lloyd-Baker DL DSO TD
1957–60	Miss Joan Evans DLitt LittD FSA
1960–63	Capt A A Scott TD
1963–66	The Hon W R S Bathurst TD MA FSA FGS
1966–69	Capt H S Gracie CB MA FSA
1969–72	J A Cannon MA PhD
1972–75	G T StJ Sanders
1975–78	D Large MA
1978–81	The Very Rev Gilbert Thurlow MA FSA FRHistS
1981–84	Prof P M Warren MA PhD FSA
1984–85	Sir Folliott Sandford KBE CMG
1985–89	M J H Liversidge MA FSA
1989–92	K M Tomlinson JP MB BS
1992–95	Sir George White FSA
1995–97	Miss E M Bliss JP BA FSA
1997–2000	J H Bettey PhD MA FSA

NOTES

1. Due to illness Sir Folliott Sandford resigned during 1985. The Vice-Chairman, Michael Liversidge, served as Chairman for the remainder of the year.

TREASURER

1938–44	Roland Austin MA FSA

1944–47	I V Hall MA
1947–50	Capt A A Scott TD
1950–70	The Hon W R S Bathurst TD MA FSA FGS
1970–	H G M Leighton MA FSA

NOTE
1. The Honourable W R S Bathurst died in office; Mr Leighton was appointed acting treasurer until elected at the next AGM.

LIBRARIAN

1914–51	Roland Austin MA FSA
1951–54	P W Bennett
1954–73	A J I Parrot FLA
1973–76	V A Woodman
1976–89	G A Hiatt BA ALA
1989–91	Mrs J Voyce ALA
1991–99	G Baker MSc ALA
1999–	S Bailey BA MA

EDITOR

1923–49	Roland Austin MA FSA
1949–59	Miss Joan Evans Dlitt FSA
1959–70	Capt H S Gracie CB MA FSA RN
1971–72	Capt H S Gracie jointly with Brian S Smith MA
1972–78	Brian S Smith MA FSA
1979–80	Brian S Smith jointly with N M Herbert BA PhD
1981–83	N M Herbert BA PhD
1983–87	S T Blake BA PhD AMA and A Saville BA FSA MIFA
1988–91	S T Blake and G C Boon BA FSA FRHistS FRNS
1992–94	G C Boon BA FSA FRHistS FRNS
1994–	A R J Jurica BA PhD

RECORDS PUBLICATIONS

Up to 1950 the Society had only published occasional monographs. Following the generous bequest of A Bruce Robinson a Records Section was established, resulting in the publication of 13 volumes in the period 1952–85. The General Editor for the first year was Wilfrid Leighton; between 1952 and 1980 Professor P V McGrath discharged that office with great distinction. No successor was formally appointed.

Following a special general meeting held on 2 October 1987 the Society established a Gloucestershire Record Series to publish annually a volume of original sources for the history of Gloucestershire. The first General Editor was Peter Ripley

MA who died in March 1988 before a volume could be published. The first volume was seen through the press jointly by D J H Smith and Dr K M Tomlinson.

RECORD SERIES GENERAL EDITOR

1988–95	D J H Smith MA FSA
1995–	Prof C R Elrington MA FSA

Index